Achieving
BROAD-BASED
SUSTAINABLE
DEVELOPMENT

ACHIEVING BROAD-BASED SUSTAINABLE DEVELOPMENT

GOVERNANCE, ENVIRONMENT, AND GROWTH WITH EQUITY

JAMES H. WEAVER
MICHAEL T. ROCK
KENNETH KUSTERER

Kumarian Press

TO PAULA CRUZ
IN MEMORY

Achieving Broad-Based Sustainable Development: Governance, Environment, and Growth with Equity.

Published 1997 in the United States of America by Kumarian Press, Inc., 14 Oakwood Avenue, West Hartford, Connecticut 06119-2127 USA.

Parts of chapter 2 appeared previously in the *International Journal of Comparative Sociology.* Permission to reprint this material is gratefully acknowledged.

Production supervised by Jenna Dixon
Copyedited by Linda Lotz   *Typeset by Sarah Albert*
Text design by Jenna Dixon   *Proofread by Beth Richards*
Index by Barbara J. DeGennaro

Printed in the United States of America on recycled acid-free paper by Thomson-Shore, Inc. Text printed with soy-based ink.

Library of Congress Cataloging-in-Publication Data
Weaver, James H., 1933– .
    Achieving broad-based sustainable development : governance, environment, and growth with equity / James H. Weaver, Michael T. Rock, Kenneth Kusterer.
    p.   cm. — (Kumarian Press books on international development)
    Includes bibliographical references and index.
    ISBN 1-56549-059-2 (alk. paper) — ISBN 1-56549-058-4 (pbk. : alk. paper)
    1. Sustainable development. 2. Democracy. 3. Economic development—Environmental aspects. 4. Economic policy. 5. Social policy. I. Rock, Michael T. II. Kusterer, Kenneth C. III. Title. IV. Series.
HC79.E5W43   1996
363.7—dc20
                                                    96-4728

06 05 04 03 02 01 00 99 98 97   10 9 8 7 6 5 4 3 2 1   1st Printing 1997

Contents

Illustrations

Acknowledgments

We owe many debts of gratitude to those who contributed to this book, which was made possible through support provided by the Biden Pell Program in the Office of Private and Voluntary Cooperation of the Bureau of Humanitarian Response, U.S. Agency for International Development (USAID), under the terms of Grant No. OTR 0230-A-00-817300. The opinions expressed herein are those of the authors and do not necessarily reflect the views of USAID.

The people in the Development Education Program of USAID, Beth Hogan and David Watson, were extraordinarily helpful and gave us complete freedom to write the book without any review. They also facilitated our testing it in workshops with development educators across the country, and those groups gave us valuable feedback.

Our students at the American University and Bennington College and the participants in the Development Studies Program sponsored by USAID read, listened to, criticized, and forced us to improve our presentation of the concepts in this book. They are in a real sense coauthors.

Our research assistants, editors, sometimes fellow authors, reviewers, and critics rendered extraordinary service but, of course, bear no responsibility for the final product: David Brat, Veronica Graham, Dileni Gunewardena, Kenneth Jameson, Kevin O'Keefe, Douglas Lehman, Charles Wilber, and the participants in the International Political Economy Task Force of the Churches Center for Theology and Public Policy.

Finally and most importantly, we are indebted to our original coauthor, Paula Cruz, who died of cancer early in the writing process. She was there when we first began to develop the concept of broad-based sustainable development, and she helped create the first proposal for this book. Much has changed and grown since those first efforts, but the book clearly bears her imprint. We hope it honors her memory.

Introduction

WHY DID WE WRITE THIS BOOK, and why should you read it? One reason is to convince you that the goal of broad-based sustainable development (BBSD), which is equitable, participatory, and environmentally sustainable, must replace the narrower goal of economic growth, which has been pursued by rich and poor countries alike since World War II. Growth is indeed a part of BBSD, but it must be a special kind of growth.

Unfortunately, most Americans, as well as most other people in the world, are still convinced that economic growth itself will solve many of our problems. But this emphasis on development, narrowly defined as economic growth, has produced pernicious results, despite its many successes. Economic development often ignores *people*. This was wonderfully expressed by a president of Brazil, who said in the 1970s that the Brazilian economy was doing fine, but the people weren't faring so well. This was not unique to Brazil. It is not true, as President Kennedy said in the 1960s, that "a rising tide lifts all boats." As efficient as the market economy is in generating growth, it leaves many people out. It is necessary to undertake specific policies to change this.

Government policies are also necessary to protect inalienable rights, to promote good governance and democracy, to provide opportunities for all people to participate, and to protect the environment. When these things don't happen, BBSD does not occur. All too often, governments pursue economic policies that benefit those in government at the expense of the people, as in the Philippines, Zaire, and Brazil. Such policies not only concentrate the benefits of growth in a few hands but in many cases actually retard overall economic growth. Other governments, such as those in China, Indonesia, Korea, and Taiwan, that are committed to economic growth have run roughshod over human rights and excluded people from participating in decision making, all in the name of economic growth. All countries, including the United States, have acted as if there were no ecological limits to growth.

We find the results of these policies morally repugnant and unaccept-able. When governments fail to adopt economic growth–oriented poli-cies, as they have in much of South Asia and sub-Saharan Africa, poverty and misery result. If they pursue growth by trampling fundamental human rights, as has happened in the communist world, Africa, Asia, and Latin America, they diminish the human spirit. When growth is pursued at the expense of equity, it dooms large numbers of people to misery. When growth destroys the environment, endangers our health, and threatens our descendants' ability to live on this planet, it is difficult to see this as either sustainable or desirable.

So, we need a new goal. And we need to identify what governments must do to attain that goal. We are not convinced by the economic phi-losophy of laissez-faire that prevails in the United States at the end of the twentieth century. We profoundly disagree with this approach to solving our problems. Markets are wonderful institutions and can function with great efficiency, but unregulated markets do not lead to social justice, environmental sustainability, a good society, or BBSD. No doubt, the slave market functioned efficiently in the United States, and free-market economists of the day probably wrote about how the market equilibrated prices for slaves so that the supply equaled the demand. Slavery was not ended by market forces but by progressive, radical people who believed the system to be evil and unjust and were willing to give their lives to the struggle to end it. For this reason, much of the emphasis in this book is on what governments can and must do if BBSD is to be achieved.

What Is Broad-Based Sustainable Development?

Broad-based sustainable development has four components. The first is a healthy, growing economy that constantly transforms itself to maintain and enhance the standard of living. Second, the benefits of economic growth are equitably shared; women, minorities, immigrants, the poor, and the handicapped get a fair deal from economic growth. The third component includes respect for human rights, good governance, a healthy civil society of nongovernmental organizations (NGOs), and an increas-ingly democratic society. The fourth is sustainability, which means that in the process of economic growth, we don't destroy the environment—foul the air, poison the water, pollute soils, mine the resource base, or destroy places of natural beauty—so that our descendants can enjoy the same or a higher standard of living.

What is a broad-based sustainable world? Are we approaching it, or moving away from it? The answer to the first question is easy. A broad-based sustainable world is a world at peace, where healthy, growing economies are undergoing structural transformation, the benefits of economic growth are widely shared, there is respect for human rights, all governments are democratic, and the world's natural environment is being conserved.

A healthy, growing global economy is one that produces rising living standards; jobs for those who are willing, able, and seeking to work; stable prices; balance of payments; and equilibrium among nations. Global structural transformation means increasing the productivity of low-technology and low-productivity countries so that their citizens can share in the benefits of modern life. If the benefits of this growth were widely shared, income inequalities and the incidence of poverty across and within countries would decline and measures of human development—life expectancy, literacy, and infant mortality—would improve. A broad-based sustainable international political system would require a federation of democratic nations. This voluntary organization of governments would protect human rights and would ensure the peace through a United Nations–controlled police force.

Defining a broad-based sustainable world is easy. Figuring out how to get there is much harder. How close are we to BBSD? It depends on whether you see the glass as half full or half empty. There is little doubt that much progress has been made since the end of World War II. To begin with, we have not experienced a third world war, nor has atomic war occurred. By itself, this is an enormous achievement. World peace and the Bretton Woods order[1] ushered in dramatic economic growth on every continent. This is one of the striking accomplishments of humankind. Per capita incomes increased dramatically, prices were relatively stable, and balance-of-payment deficits were manageable. Real structural transformation took place. The share of gross domestic product (GDP) and employment in low-productivity agriculture declined, and the GDP in higher-productivity industry and services rose. Capital was redirected from capital-surplus regions, countries with more savings than can be invested at home, to capital-scarce regions, countries where savings are scarce relative to investment opportunities. New technology was introduced and increased productivity.

The benefits of this rapid economic growth have been widely shared, and the global incidence of poverty has fallen. One of the poorest and most populated regions in the developing world in 1960, East Asia (including China), has increased its share of world income dramatically. It has also experienced a rapid decline in the incidence of poverty.

There have also been dramatic improvements in human development. Between 1950 and 1990, combined life expectancy for men and women in developing countries increased from forty years to sixty-three years, the under-five mortality rate dropped from 280 per thousand to 100 per thousand, and the literacy rate increased from 46 percent in 1970 to 69 percent in 1992. Nothing like this has ever happened before!

We have achieved greater respect for human rights and for human freedom and democracy. National and international human rights organizations now operate in most countries and report regularly on human rights abuses. There is some evidence that this reporting can reduce and even stop gross abuses of human rights. During the 1970s, concern for human rights came to be an accepted part of the foreign policy of some of the industrialized countries, including the United States. With the end of the Cold War, some countries have been denied foreign aid on the basis of violations of human rights. The United Nations has sometimes imposed effective sanctions on nations judged guilty of egregious violations of human rights, such as South Africa. There has been progress in increasing governments' respect for human rights.

The world is much more democratic than it has ever been. Between 1974 and 1990, thirty countries underwent democratic transitions. Almost all the countries in Latin America and the Caribbean are democratic. Countries in Africa are experiencing a move to democracy, and most of the former communist countries are more democratic.

We have made the least progress in developing an international political and economic order that is consistent with conserving the environment. But even here, some progress has been made. The United Nations Conference on the Environment and Development (UNCED) in Rio in 1992 was a step in the evolution of a global consensus to take the environment seriously. Even though no enforcement mechanism was established, a principle was established that no nation has the right to pollute another nation's environment.

Evidence of Failure

Important problems remain. The global economy has become more unstable, and its growth has slowed dramatically. The two oil price shocks of the 1970s and the debt crises and recessions of the 1980s and 1990s have had brutal impacts on the developing world. In the mid-1990s, poor countries owed debts of $1.4 trillion to rich countries. The rich countries insisted that these debts be serviced, no matter how much privation and suffering it caused. In two regions of the developing world, Latin America and sub-Saharan Africa, the 1980s was a decade of declining living standards.

The United Nations Conference on Social Development, held in Copenhagen in 1995, painted a grim picture of life in the poor countries. There are more poor and hungry people in the world than at any time in history. More than a billion people live in conditions of absolute poverty, which means that they cannot satisfy their most basic needs: work, food, clothing, shelter, medical care, education, and culture. Seventy percent of these are women. They don't even have access to safe drinking water, much less a minimally adequate diet. Approximately 700 million people go to bed hungry each night. Malnutrition in the young creates permanent, irreversible brain damage so that malnourished children grow up to be less than fully human. This occurs at a time when the world produces enough food for everyone, and the problem facing many countries is food surpluses.

Two million children die each year from infectious diseases, which could be prevented at very little cost. Eighty million children do not attend primary school and thus will grow up illiterate and unable to function in a literate world.

Many governments around the world—in Somalia, Sudan, Rwanda, Liberia, Lebanon, Yugoslavia, parts of the former Soviet Union, and Cambodia—have collapsed. This makes development impossible. In the decade of the 1980s, virtually the only developing countries that did well were in East Asia. The problems associated with reforming the economies of the former communist countries seem particularly intractable.

There are also serious economic troubles in the industrialized countries. Economic insecurity in the United States increased in the last part of the twentieth century. In the post–World War II period, blue- and white-collar workers came to expect that they would get good jobs upon finishing school, keep those jobs the rest of their lives, and experience a rising standard of living. They expected to own their own homes, have health insurance, own cars, and be able to take annual vacations. Beginning in the 1970s, these expectations failed to be realized. Real hourly earnings in private nonagricultural industries began falling in 1974. Real median family money income (the midpoint at which half the families are below the median and half above) fell from 1979 to 1993.[2] This decline occurred despite the fact that two family members were in the labor force rather than one as had generally been the case in the 1950s and 1960s. So in the 1990s, two income earners working a total of eighty hours a week generated less income than one income earner had been able to earn in forty hours in an earlier period. The percentage of persons living below the poverty level in the United States rose from 11.7 percent in 1979 to 15.1 percent in 1993.[3]

Corporations began downsizing and permanently laying off both blue-collar and white-collar workers in great numbers. Many formerly prosperous industrial cities became economically depressed as plants closed and industry relocated. Workers in the United States could no longer count on keeping good jobs throughout their lives.

Income inequality in the United States also grew in the 1980s and 1990s. In 1980, the poorest 20 percent of the people received 5 percent of income, whereas in 1991, their share had fallen to 3.8 percent. The richest 20 percent received 41.5 percent of income in 1980, and this had grown to 46.5 percent in 1991.[4] There was some evidence that income inequality was also increasing in other industrialized countries.

In the last few years of the twentieth century, the world economy seems to be moving back to an international political and economic order like that created after World War I. We are in danger of recreating the disastrous circumstances of the period between the two world wars. In fact, the present can be seen as another interwar period. We have to look at the changes that are necessary to preserve peace and prevent World War III.

The parallels to the period between World War I and World War II are frightening. Rich countries are insisting that poor countries repay all their debts, just as the United States and the Allies imposed onerous war-debt repayments on Germany and just as the United States imposed impossible repayments on its allies after World War I. The United States and its allies refused to buy the exports of these countries in order to protect their own domestic industries. This whole system had disastrous consequences.

There is strong support for trading blocs and protectionism—governments using tariffs and quotas to protect infant industries, regions, and people from the instability accompanying free trade—just as there was after World War I. The United States is no longer able to serve as the hegemonic or dominant power in the international economy after the end of the Cold War, just as Britain was no longer able to play that role after World War I.

There is an all too close similarity between what is happening in Russia today and what happened in Weimar Germany in the 1920s. Russia has lost a war (the Cold War), has lost much of its territory, has seen the military disgraced, has lost faith in the dominant ideology, and has seen the middle class destroyed by runaway inflation. The Russian economy is in shambles, there is widespread decadence, crime is rampant, organized crime controls large sectors of the economy, weak leadership is trying to establish democracy in a country that has been authoritarian for centuries, and Russia is receiving little help from the West. This is similar to what happened to Germany after World War I. Will this lead to an outburst of national socialism in Russia, similar to that which occurred in Germany?

These circumstances led to the Great Depression, the spread of fascism, and World War II. Unless we learn from history, we may be damned to repeat it. These circumstances have also led to cynicism and defeat about the prospects for global development. One of our purposes in writing this book is to hold out a hopeful vision of a better future for all humanity. We present evidence of the progress that has already been made and introduce the policies that need to be followed if broad-based sustainable development is to be achieved. Our policy recommendations are based on what we have learned over the last generation of development work and research.

Because we have worked in and done research on sub-Saharan Africa, Asia, Latin America, and the states of the former Soviet Union, and because none of us has worked in or researched the countries of North Africa or the Middle East, we felt more comfortable using examples only from the regions we are familiar with. We apologize in advance for this shortcoming.

The book is written from an interdisciplinary perspective, with the assumption that the reader does not have prior training in economics, political science, sociology, or ecology. All the terms that may be unfamiliar are defined the first time they are used in the chapters.

Notes

1. The Bretton Woods conference of July 1944, attended by representatives of forty-four nations, resulted in the creation of the International Monetary Fund and the International Bank for Reconstruction and Development.
2. *Economic Report of the President*, 1995, 310.
3. *Economic Report of the President*, 1995, 310.
4. Bread for the World Institute, *Hunger 1994* (Silver Spring, Md.: Bread for the World Institute, 1994), 170.

Part I

Approaching Broad-Based Sustainable Development

Introduction to Part I

*T*HIS BOOK IS STRUCTURED TO HELP you answer three simple questions: (1) What is broad-based sustainable development (BBSD) and why should the world adopt it as the goal of development (Chapter 1)? (2) What are the strengths and weaknesses of past development strategies and experiences (Chapters 2 and 3)? (3) What government policies are needed to promote BBSD (Chapters 4–17)?

This first part of the book (Chapters 1–3) explains why we felt it necessary to write this book at this point in history. We argued in the introduction that much has been accomplished in development since 1950 but that recent developments—the slowing of the world engine of economic growth, increased instability in the world economy, the failure of development to be equitably shared, the lack of human freedom, the spread of environmental degradation, and the economic and political difficulties faced by countries of the former Soviet Union—have spread fear, cynicism, and defeatism about the prospects for global development. They have also spread cynicism about the role that governments play in promoting and retarding development. This has led some to argue for a return to laissez-faire.

By drawing on what we have learned over the last generation, we argue that there is reason to have hope and to believe in a vision of a better future for all humanity. There is also reason to argue that governments must play an active role in this process. In short, we argue that there is much that governments can and must do. Most of the chapters of this book define in precise terms the positive role that government must play if we are to achieve that better future.

We define that better future with the simple phrase *broad-based sustainable development*. In Chapter 1, we rigorously define BBSD, present various ways to measure it, and introduce the data sources used to measure it. All subsequent chapters in the book can and should be evaluated from the perspective of BBSD.

The concept of BBSD introduced in Chapter 1 emerged from the last forty-five years of development experience. Because of this, Chapters 2 and 3 provide an overview of development experience and its relationship to BBSD. We begin by examining development performance in the developing world between 1950 and 1990. Chapter 2 demonstrates that those forty years saw the most rapid improvement in the human condition in all of recorded history. During this period, there were unprecedented improvements in living standards, life expectancy, and literacy. But the chapter also shows that performance was quite variable: Countries in Asia, particularly East Asia, did markedly better than those in Latin America and the Caribbean. In turn, those countries did better on average than countries in sub-Saharan Africa.

Chapter 3 relates development performance to alternative development strategies. We review the debates among development economists over development strategy and the role of government, identify the four dominant capitalist development strategies followed by developing countries, examine the experience of China and Russia with a socialist development strategy, and relate each of the strategies to BBSD. Although the chapter has a strong focus on development strategy or development policy, it also points out that differences in initial conditions—in domestic politics, landholding patterns, and the spread (or lack) of basic literacy—contribute to the many differences in performance observed in Chapter 2.

1

The Concept of Broad-Based Sustainable Development

*T*HE OVERRIDING GOAL OF DEVELOPMENT is to improve human well-being and to enable human beings to achieve their potential. Many leaders of developing and industrialized countries, nongovernmental organizations (NGOs), development professionals, and the international aid agencies have come to agree that in order to achieve this broad goal, four subgoals must be pursued. They are (1) a healthy, growing economy undergoing **structural transformation**; (2) an economy in which the benefits are widely distributed; (3) a political system that provides for human rights and freedoms, **effective governance**, and (4) a political economy that is consistent with preservation of the environment. This multidimensional perspective on development is a new way of looking at development that has emerged from forty years of experience.

■ **structural transformation**
the process of moving resources from lower to higher productivity so that the economy can sustain a higher standard of living for the population

■ **effective governance**
competence, accountability, rule of law, and accessibility of information

The first goal of development in the 1940s and 1950s was **economic growth**. Later, this was broadened to specify that the economy also had to be undergoing a structural transformation. A second component was added in the 1970s and can be summarized as growth with equity. A third aspect was added in the 1970s and 1980s and started with a concern for human rights. Later, this was broadened to include enhancements of civil society, effective governance, and democracy. The 1980s and 1990s brought a last component, which was concern that economic growth be consistent with the preservation of the environment.

■ **economic growth**
growth of real(inflation-adjusted) per capita income

A Healthy, Growing Economy Undergoing Structural Transformation

In the early post–World War II period, development clearly meant economic growth. The way to tell whether countries were developed or underdeveloped was to look at their per capita income. Countries that were developing were ones in which per capita income was growing rapidly. It was assumed that the other aspects of modernization, such as respect for human rights and democracy, would accompany or soon follow rapid economic growth.

The World Bank in its annual *World Development Report* lists countries in ascending order, from the country with the lowest to the highest per capita **gross national product** (GNP). Table 1.1 shows that Mozambique and Tanzania had the distinction of having the lowest per capita GNPs in 1993 (equivalent to US$90). In the same year, Japan had the highest per capita GNP with US$31,490.[1] Countries that are not classified as high-income countries are considered less developed, and those with high income are considered developed.

■ **gross national product (GNP)** *market value of all goods and services produced anywhere by citizens of a country in a given year*

When it came to measuring development success, the criterion was simple. How fast did per capita income grow each year? We see from Table 1.1 that, according to the criterion of average annual growth rate of real per capita GNP, the successful countries between 1980 and 1993 were Korea (8.2 percent), China (8.2 percent), Botswana (6.2 percent), and Hong Kong (5.4 percent). The clear failures were Côte d'Ivoire (−4.6 percent), and Saudi Arabia (−3.6 percent).

In the 1950s, Simon Kuznets added the concept of structural transformation to the definition of development.[2] We describe the economic component of development in terms of two critical requirements: (1) a healthy, growing economy, which involves per capita income growth, relatively full employment of labor and **capital**, relatively stable prices, and external equilibrium or a sustainable **balance of payments**; and (2) that the economy be undergoing a structural transformation.

■ **capital** *money invested in production, also goods used to produce other goods*
■ **balance of payments** *measure of the economic transactions a country has with the rest of the world*

Per Capita Income Growth

Despite the recognition that other aspects of development matter, the most common measurement of national economic performance is still the growth rate of **real per capita income**.[3] Using **nominal income** would tend to give the illusion of growth. The problem with comparing per capita incomes among countries is that each country has

■ **real per capita income** *income adjusted for inflation*
■ **nominal income** *income measured at current prices*

Table 1.1   Per Capita GNP and Annual Average per Capita GNP
Growth and Inflation Rates

Country	Per Capita GNP, 1993 (US$)	Average Annual per Capita GNP Growth Rate, 1980–93 (%)	Average Annual Rate of Inflation, 1980–93 (%)
Low-Income Economies			
Mozambique	90	–1.5	42.3
Tanzania	90	0.1	24.3
Kenya	270	0.3	9.9
India	300	3.0	8.7
Nigeria	300	–0.1	20.6
Ghana	430	0.1	37.0
Pakistan	430	3.1	7.4
China	490	8.2	7.0
Sri Lanka	600	2.7	11.1
Côte d'Ivoire	630	–4.6	1.5
Egypt	660	2.8	13.6
Lower-Middle-Income Economies			
Indonesia	740	4.2	8.5
Bolivia	760	–0.7	187.1
Philippines	850	–0.6	13.6
Guatemala	1,100	–1.2	16.8
Jamaica	1,440	–0.3	22.4
Peru	1,490	–2.7	316.1
Algeria	1,780	–0.8	13.2
Costa Rica	2,150	1.1	22.1
Russian Federation	2,340	–1.0	35.4
Botswana	2,790	6.2	12.3
Turkey	2,970	2.4	53.5
Upper-Middle-Income Economies			
Brazil	2,930	0.3	423.4
South Africa	2,980	–0.2	14.7
Malaysia	3,140	3.5	2.2
Chile	3,170	3.6	20.1
Mexico	3,610	–0.5	57.9
Gabon	4,960	–1.6	1.5
Argentina	7,220	–0.5	374.3
Republic of Korea	7,660	8.2	6.3
Saudi Arabia	7,550	–3.6	–2.1
High-Income Economies			
Hong Kong	18,060	5.4	7.9
France	22,490	1.6	5.1
Germany	23,560	2.1	2.8
Sweden	24,740	1.3	6.9
United States	24,740	1.7	3.8
Japan	31,490	3.4	1.5

Source: World Bank, *World STARS (Socio-economic Time-series Access and Retrieval System) Data Diskette* (Washington, D.C.: World Bank Publications, 1995).

its own currency and expresses its income in terms of that currency. How can we tell whether an Indian with an income of 20,000 rupees is better or worse off than a Mexican with an income of 20,000 pesos or an American with an income of 20,000 dollars?

In the years following World War II until 1971, the world economy operated on the basis of **fixed exchange rates**. During this period, the convention developed of expressing all countries' incomes in dollars so that international comparisons could be made. After 1971, when the United States abandoned the fixed rate of the dollar with respect to gold, many countries of the world moved to **floating or flexible exchange rates**. It became increasingly difficult to make sensible international comparisons of incomes based on conversion to the dollar. A partial solution to this problem is the convention of using three-year moving averages of exchange rates in an effort to eliminate wild fluctuations in the value of currencies with respect to the dollar. (This is how the data presented in Table 1.1 were arrived at.)

- **fixed exchange rates** *all currencies expressed in comparison to the U.S. dollar, and the value of the U.S. dollar expressed in relation to gold valued at $35 an ounce*
- **floating (flexible) exchange rates** *the value of each country's currency fluctuates, based on supply and demand*

A second problem with converting incomes to dollars through the foreign exchange rate is that the value of the foreign exchange rate is determined by the demand and supply for goods and services that are traded internationally. **Nontraded goods** do not enter into the determination of the foreign exchange rate. This tends to understate the value of a developing country's income, because the prices of many nontraded goods and services are much lower in developing countries than they are in the United States. This is because wages in developing countries are much lower. For example, in 1992, the exchange rate was approximately 30 Indian rupees to the U.S. dollar. One could get a haircut in India for 10 rupees, or the equivalent of 33 cents. In the United States at the time, haircuts cost many times that amount. Clearly, 30 Indian rupees would buy many more services in India than a dollar would buy in the United States.

- **nontraded goods** *goods and services that are not traded internationally*

To deal with this problem, the United Nations (UN) and international economic organizations established the International Comparison Project (ICP) and developed the concept of **purchasing power parity (PPP)**. According to Table 1.2, the per capita income in India based on the foreign exchange rate was $300 in 1993. It was $1,220 in PPP dollars. This tells us that in 1993, the typical Indian lived the way an American would live in the United States on $1,220. He would eat cheap

- **purchasing power parity (PPP)** *conversion factor to translate other countries' incomes into U.S. dollars of comparable value*

Table 1.2   Comparison of per Capita GNP and PPP Estimates of per Capita GNP

Country	Per Capita GNP, 1993 (US$)	PPP Estimates of per Capita GNP, 1993 (Current International Dollars)
Low-Income Economies		
Mozambique	90	550
Tanzania	90	580
Kenya	270	1,290
India	300	1,220
Nigeria	300	1,400
Ghana	430	1,970
Pakistan	430	2,170
China	490	2,330
Sri Lanka	600	2,990
Côte d'Ivoire	630	1,400
Egypt	660	3,780
Lower-Middle-Income Economies		
Indonesia	740	3,150
Bolivia	760	2,420
Philippines	850	2,670
Guatemala	1,100	3,350
Jamaica	1,440	3,000
Peru	1,490	3,220
Algeria	1,780	5,380
Costa Rica	2,150	5,520
Russian Federation	2,340	5,050
Botswana	2,790	5,160
Turkey	2,970	3,920
Upper-Middle-Income Economies		
Brazil	2,930	5,370
South Africa	2,980	–
Malaysia	3,140	7,930
Chile	3,170	8,400
Mexico	3,610	6,810
Gabon	4,960	–
Argentina	7,220	8,250
Republic of Korea	7,660	9,630
Saudi Arabia	7,550[a]	11,170[a]
High-Income Economies		
Hong Kong	18,060	21,560
France	22,490	19,000
Germany	23,560	16,850
Sweden	24,740	17,200
United States	24,740	24,740
Japan	31,490	20,850

[a] 1992 values.

Source: World Bank, *World STARS (Socio-economic Time-series Access and Retrieval System) Data Diskette* (Washington, D.C.: World Bank Publications, 1995).

carbohydrates (beans and rice), wear secondhand clothes and rags, live in a homemade shelter of discarded wood and cardboard or sleep on the street, and probably not have access to medical care or education. This is the way the typical Indian lived in 1993 and still lives today.

For some countries, using PPP dollars makes an enormous difference in measures of the standard of living. China is a striking case. Using foreign exchange rate conversions, China had a per capita income of $490 in 1993. However, in PPP dollars, the per capita income in China was $2,330—over four times greater. This reflects the low prices of many services provided by the Chinese government that cost much more in industrialized countries.

Increasing use is being made of estimates of per capita income expressed in PPP dollars.[4] Such estimates for many countries are available in the World Bank's annual *World Development Report*.

Relatively Full Employment

In addition to rapid growth of income, a healthy economy has relatively full employment of labor and capital. The transition from a feudal and agrarian society and economy is an extremely painful one. Peasants are forced to leave the land and farming and move to cities to sell their labor in labor markets. Whether there is a demand for their labor is one of the real tests of successful development. So measures of unemployment are important in judging the success and the humaneness with which the transition is taking place.

Unfortunately, there are few reliable indicators of employment and unemployment in developing countries. Estimates are particularly hard to make and interpret in essentially agriculture-based economies. The estimates that do exist are often for urban areas only. A further complication in measuring employment arises when we add the concept of **underemployment**. There are still fewer reliable estimates of the utilization rate of capital in developing countries, in spite of the fact that this is an important indicator of the **efficiency** of the economy.

■ **underemployment** *the phenomenon of people working only part time or at jobs below their skill levels when they would prefer to work full time at more highly skilled jobs for which they are qualified*

■ **efficiency** *production of goods and services in such a way as to minimize the use of resources*

The International Labor Organization (ILO) collects and publishes data on these variables in its annual report.

Governments in high-income countries regularly collect and publish data on the percentage of the labor force that is employed and unemployed.

They also collect and publish data on industrial capacity utilization rates, which indicate the degree to which capital is idle.

Relatively Stable Prices

A further component of a healthy economy is relatively stable prices or low levels of **inflation**. Rapid rates of inflation tend to make planning for the future difficult and discourage **investment**. Data on price levels in developing countries are generally published in the World Bank's annual *World Development Report* and *World Tables*, but the reliability of the data is mixed. It is difficult to analyze price data. In some cases, governments make this more difficult because inflation performance is politically sensitive.

> ■ **inflation** *overall increase in the prices of an economy's goods and services*
> ■ **investment** *money used to purchase goods which will be used to produce more goods*

There are three ways of measuring price changes: the **consumer price index**, the **wholesale price index**, and the **GDP deflator**. We use the GDP deflator index throughout this book, because it is the broadest measure of how well a country is doing in ensuring price stability. It is found in the International Monetary Fund's (IMF's) annual *International Financial Statistics* and the World Bank's *World Development Report*.

> ■ **consumer price index** *measure of changes in the prices of goods that consumers buy (e.g., food, clothing, housing, health services)*
> ■ **wholesale price index** *measure of the prices of goods that businesses buy (e.g., steel, cement, trucks, factories)*
> ■ **GDP deflator** *measure of changes in the prices of all goods produced in the economy and purchased by consumers, producers, government, and foreigners*

Table 1.1 presents data for average annual inflation rates (using the GDP deflator) for a sample of countries for the period 1980 to 1993. The range of inflation rates is enormous, from Brazil's 423 percent per year to Saudi Arabia's –2.1 percent per year. The relationship between rates of inflation and rates of economic growth is not clear. The predictability of inflation is also important. People have adjusted to rather high rates of inflation in some Latin American countries and continued to save and invest. However, once inflation passes a certain point, it is no longer predictable. In such situations, it can easily move into **hyperinflation**, as it did in Bolivia in the mid-1980s. The currency becomes essentially worthless, and people are reduced to bartering goods for goods. Several countries in the former Soviet Union and in Eastern Europe experienced hyperinflation in the early 1990s.

> ■ **hyperinflation** *price increases of 10 percent or more per day*

External Equilibrium

Finally, a healthy economy requires external equilibrium or a sustainable balance of payments. There are three components of a nation's balance of payments: the **current account**, the **capital account**, and the **overall account**. As is common practice, we use the current account balance as a percentage share of **gross domestic product** (**GDP**) to measure how successful a country is at balancing its dealings with the rest of the world. This measure can be found in the IMF's *International Financial Statistics*.

■ **current account** *measure of the flow of goods and services and the payment of interest and dividends between a country and the rest of the world*

■ **capital account** *measure of the flow of investment funds between a country and the rest of the world*

■ **overall account** *the stock and changes in the stock of gold reserves, deposits with the IMF, and hard or convertible currencies*

■ **gross domestic product** (**GDP**) *market value of all goods produced within a nation and purchased by consumers, producers, government, and foreigners*

The current account balance is important because it tells us whether a country is living within its means. Countries must export in order to import. They can run current account deficits only if they can get someone to loan them money. They cannot do this forever.

Table 1.3 presents data on the current account balance as a percentage of GDP for the last three years for which data are available. A general rule of thumb is that a current account deficit of 3 to 5 percent can probably be financed. The table reveals that Jamaica has been running a current account deficit equal to 7 percent of its GDP. This is obviously unsustainable. So are the current account deficits of Costa Rica and Kenya. These countries will have to stabilize their economies—reduce expenditures abroad and/or export more.

Structural Transformation

Although a growing economy is important, it is not enough to have just rapid economic growth. The structure of the economy must be transformed in such a way that it is able to sustain a higher standard of living for the population now and in the future. Countries that had rapid growth of per capita income from oil revenue but did not transform the structure of the economy, such as Gabon, did not develop.

Structural transformation requires a great increase in agricultural productivity and a shift from an agriculture-based economy to an economy based on industry and services, from an economy characterized by uneducated and low-productivity workers to one with educated and

Table 1.3   Current Account Balance as a Percentage of GDP
(1989–91)

Country	Current Account Balance (% of GDP)
Low-Income Economies	
India	−2.4
Kenya	−5.2
Pakistan	−4.1
Ghana	−3.7
China	2.4
Sri Lanka	−4.2
Egypt	−1.3
Lower-Middle-Income Economies	
Bolivia	−4.2
Philippines	−1.9
Jamaica	−7.1
Costa Rica	−6.6
Turkey	−2.4
Upper-Middle-Income Economies	
Brazil	−0.3
Botswana	4.2
Mexico	−3.1
Gabon	−1.3
Republic of Korea	−1.5
High-Income Economies	
Germany	−1.5
United States	−1.0
Japan	3.2

Source: International Monetary Fund, *International Financial Statistics Yearbook 1993* (Washington, D.C.: International Monetary Fund, 1993), 140–41.

high-productivity workers, from a reliance on human labor to greater use of machines, from an economy with relatively few crops and products to a diversified economy with many different crops and products, from a relatively closed economy with few exports and imports to an open economy with a large share of imports and exports in the GDP, from a reliance on **primary goods** for export to an increasing share of manufactured goods and services in exports, and from an economy characterized by low saving and **investment rates** to one with high saving and investment rates and increasing urbanization.

■ **primary goods** *nonprocessed goods (e.g., agricultural products and raw materials)*

■ **investment rate** *the share of GDP invested*

Structural transformation can be measured using **time-series data** on the percentage of the labor force engaged in agriculture as opposed to industry and services; the percentage of GDP originating in agriculture, industry, and services; the percentage of GDP saved and invested; the percentage of GDP exported; and the percentage of exports of primary goods as compared with manufactured goods. Estimates for many of these measures can be found in the World Bank's annual *World Tables*.

■ **time-series data** *data for a number of years*

Table 1.4 presents a summary of the degree to which structural transformation took place in selected countries between 1970 and 1993. Korea is one country that has undergone a structural transformation during this period. The share of GDP originating in agriculture fell from 25 percent to 7 percent, and the share of manufacturing rose from 21 percent to 29 percent—comparable to the share in Germany. Korea became an industrialized country in twenty-three years—just one generation.

Any number of other countries represented in the table could be cited as failures in the effort to undergo structural transformation: Kenya and Ghana, where the share of manufacturing actually fell; and India, with a very small change in the share of manufacturing. Gabon, with its income from oil, is a classic case of a country with a high per capita income that did not undergo a structural transformation.

In order to undergo structural transformation, industrialized countries must give up their low-wage manufacturing industries, such as textiles, to low-wage countries and move into high-wage, high-skill manufacturing industries and into services. There is a reluctance to do this on the part of workers and **capitalists** in these low-wage industries. Therefore, policies must be designed so that winners, who can buy cheap products abroad, can compensate the losers. Table 1.4 reflects the structural transformation that took place in Germany between 1970 and 1993. The share of manufacturing in GDP fell from 38 percent to 27 percent and the share of services increased from 47 percent to 61 percent.

■ **capitalists** *owners of capital*

Table 1.5 reflects the change in exports as a percentage of GDP between 1970 and 1993. Change in export share is a good measure of countries' effectiveness in opening their economies to the rest of the world and achieving international competitiveness. Clearly, it is crucial for small countries such as Costa Rica, Jamaica, and Kenya to export, because they must import. There is no way that such countries can produce all the goods and services they need at home. It is less clear that exports are crucial for such large countries as the United States, India,

Table 1.4   Sector Shares of GDP for Agriculture, Manufacturing, and Services (1970 and 1993)

Country	Agriculture (% of GDP) 1970	1993	Manufacturing (% of GDP) 1970	1993	Services (% of GDP) 1970	1993
Low-Income Economies						
Mozambique	–	33	–	–	–	55
Tanzania	41	56	10	5	42	30
Kenya	33	29	12	10	47	54
India	45	31	15	17	33	41
Nigeria	41	34	4	7	45	24
Ghana	47	48	11	8	35	36
Pakistan	37	25	16	17	41	50
China	34	19	30	38	28	33
Sri Lanka	28	25	17	15	48	50
Côte d'Ivoire	40	37	13	–	36	39
Egypt	29	18	–	16	42	60
Lower-Middle-Income Economies						
Indonesia	45	19	10	22	36	42
Bolivia	20	–	13	–	48	–
Philippines	30	22	25	24	39	45
Guatemala	–	25	–	–	–	55
Jamaica	7	8	16	18	51	51
Peru	19	11	20	21	50	46
Algeria	11	13	15	11	48	43
Costa Rica	23	15	–	19	53	59
Russian Federation	–	9	–	–	–	39
Botswana	33	6	6	4	39	47
Turkey	30	15	17	19	43	55
Upper-Middle-Income Economies						
Brazil	12	11	29	20	49	52
South Africa	8	5	24	23	52	56
Malaysia	29	–	12	–	46	–
Chile	7	–	25	–	53	–
Mexico	12	8	28	22	59	63
Gabon	19	8	7	12	34	47
Argentina	10	6	32	20	47	63
Republic of Korea	25	7	21	29	46	50
Saudi Arabia	4	–	9	–	26	–
High-Income Economies						
Hong Kong	2	0	29	13	62	79
France	–	3	–	22	–	69
Germany	3	1	38	27	47	61
Sweden	–	2	–	26	–	67
United States	3	–	34	–	63	–
Japan	6	2	36	24	47	57

Table excludes nonmanufacturing industry (e.g., petroleum, mining).
Source: World Bank, *World STARS (Socio-economic Time-series Access and Retrieval System) Data Diskette* (Washington, D.C.: World Bank Publications, 1995).

and China, which have large domestic markets and such varied resource bases that they can be much more self-sufficient.

Yet study after study has found a positive relationship between the growth of the export share of GDP and the growth rate of GDP. The type of export matters, however. The really successful exporting countries are those that have managed to change their exports from primary goods to manufactured goods.[5] Manufactured exports provide increased employment and increased income, particularly for women in developing countries. Thus, the share of exports in GDP has come to be an important indicator of success in equitable development.

Table 1.5 reveals that in twenty-three years, Indonesia was able to increase its export share from 13 percent to 28 percent of GDP and to increase its share of manufactures in exports from 1 to 53 percent. India, in contrast, only increased its share of exports from 4 percent to 11 percent of GDP. Although the share of manufactures in exports was 74 percent in 1993, this reflected virtually no change since 1970. Some countries actually saw their share of exports fall, such as Saudi Arabia and Bolivia.

Distributing the Benefits of Growth

Life Expectancy, Mortality, Literacy

How well are the benefits of economic growth distributed among the population? This can be measured in part by life expectancy. Longevity is a good measure of a country's capacity to provide a high quality of life for its citizens. A second aspect closely related to life expectancy is the mortality rate, measured by infant mortality rates or mortality rates for children under age five years. Literacy rates for both men and women indicate how well a country prepares its people to cope in a modern, literate world. The rate of literacy for women is a particularly good index of whether women have equal access to the education necessary to function successfully in the economy. Life expectancy, infant mortality, and literacy are all measures of human development. Access to safe water, sanitation, and health care are further measures of a society's commitment to including all people in the development process.

Table 1.6 presents data on under-five mortality rates, life expectancy, and illiteracy rates. One of the striking things revealed in this table is the great range of performance among the low-income countries. China and

Table 1.5 Export Shares of GDP (1970 and 1993)

Country	Exports of Goods and Nonfactor Services (% of GDP)		Manufactures as Percentage Share of Merchandise Exports	
	1970	1993	1970	1993
Low-Income Economies				
Mozambique	–	21	8	21
Tanzania	26	31	13	–
Kenya	30	42	12	–
India	4	11	75	74
Nigeria	8	36	1	2
Ghana	21	20	1	23
Pakistan	8	16	57	85
China	3	24	–	81
Sri Lanka	25	33	1	73
Côte d'Ivoire	36	34	6	17
Egypt	14	25	27	33
Lower-Middle-Income Economies				
Indonesia	13	28	1	53
Bolivia	27	22	3	19
Philippines	22	32	8	77
Guatemala	19	18	28	30
Jamaica	33	60	46	65
Peru	18	10	1	17
Algeria	22	22	7	3
Costa Rica	28	40	20	33
Russian Federation	–	39	–	–
Botswana	23	61	–	–
Turkey	6	14	9	72
Upper-Middle-Income Economies				
Brazil	7	8	15	60
South Africa	22	23	41	74
Malaysia	42	80	8	65
Chile	15	28	5	19
Mexico	6	13	33	52
Gabon	50	47	9	3
Argentina	7	6	14	32
Republic of Korea	14	29	76	94
Saudi Arabia	66	43	0	9
High-Income Economies				
Hong Kong	92	143[a]	96	93
France	16	23	75	78
Germany	21	22	90	90
Sweden	24	33	75	86
United States	6	10	70	82
Japan	11	9	94	97

[a] Higher than 100 percent because of re-exports of imported goods and services (to and from China).

Source: World Bank, *World STARS (Socio-economic Time-series Access and Retrieval System) Data Diskette* (Washington, D.C.: World Bank Publications, 1995).

Sri Lanka, with relatively low incomes, have achieved remarkably low child mortality and high life expectancy. They performed better, in fact, than countries with many times their per capita incomes. Other countries, such as Gabon, despite having a high per capita income, have very poor human development indicators. Hong Kong, with less than half the per capita income of the United States, has a better under-five mortality rate than does the United States. Illiteracy rates for women are high in several of the countries listed in Table 1.6. In Mozambique, India, Nigeria, Pakistan, Côte d'Ivoire, Egypt, Guatemala, Algeria, Gabon, and Saudi Arabia, more than half the women are illiterate.

Income Distribution

■ absolute poverty line
*measure of the minimum
income necessary to
meet basic human needs*

The distribution of income, particularly the share of income going to the poorest 20 percent of the population, and the poverty ratio, the percentage of the population living below the **absolute poverty line,** are good measures of whether a society shares the benefits of its economic growth widely or concentrates the benefits in the hands of a wealthy and powerful elite. Table 1.7 presents the data available on income distribution. The issue of income distribution is very sensitive politically, and many developing countries do not collect and publish such data.

Comparing the data on income distribution in Table 1.7 with the levels of income in Table 1.1 shows that high-income countries have more equal income distribution than countries with lower per capita incomes. Of the countries for which data are available, it is clear that Japan has the most equal income distribution. The poorest 20 percent of the population receives 9 percent, and the richest 20 percent receives 38 percent of the national income. This is the most equal distribution recorded in any capitalist country. Income distribution in the United States is considerably more unequal than in either Germany or Japan.

At the other extreme, Brazil holds the record for the most unequal income distribution. The top 20 percent of the population in Brazil receives 68 percent of the income, and the top 10 percent receives almost half the national income. The top 10 percent in Brazil has a philosophy of "share and share alike." They take half the national income and leave the other half for the other 90 percent of the people.

Since 1990, the United Nations Development Program (UNDP) has published an annual *Human Development Report*, which contains much of the data described above. The UNDP has also constructed a human

Table 1.6 Mortality Rates, Life Expectancy, and Illiteracy Rates

Country	Under-Five Mortality (per 1,000 Live Births), 1992 Female	Male	Life Expectancy at Birth (Years), 1993 Female	Male	Adult Illiteracy Rates (%), 1990 Female	Male
Low-Income Economies						
Mozambique	269	283	48	45	79	67
Tanzania	139	158	53	50	–	–
Kenya	95	110	60	57	42	31
India	108	104	61	61	66	52
Nigeria	174	192	52	49	61	49
Ghana	120	138	58	55	49	40
Pakistan	129	142	63	61	79	65
China	32	43	71	68	38	27
Sri Lanka	19	24	74	70	17	12
Côte d'Ivoire	121	18	2	49	60	46
Egypt	80	93	65	63	66	52
Lower-Middle-Income Economies						
Indonesia	82	98	65	61	32	23
Bolivia	106	115	61	58	29	23
Philippines	44	56	69	65	11	10
Guatemala	76	84	68	63	53	45
Jamaica	15	19	76	72	1	2
Peru	61	75	68	64	21	15
Algeria	66	80	69	66	55	43
Costa Rica	15	19	79	74	7	7
Russian Federation	20	28	74	62	–	–
Botswana	37	49	67	63	35	26
Turkey	66	72	69	65	29	19
Upper-Middle-Income Economies						
Brazil	70	76	69	64	20	19
South Africa	63	77	66	60	–	–
Malaysia	14	20	73	69	30	22
Chile	18	24	78	71	7	7
Mexico	37	49	74	68	15	13
Gabon	143	162	56	52	52	39
Argentina	33	38	76	69	5	5
Republic of Korea	13	18	75	68	7	4
Saudi Arabia	29	38	72	69	52	38
High-Income Economies						
Hong Kong	7	9	82	76	–	–
France	8	11	81	73	<5[a]	<5[a]
Germany	7	9	79	73	<5[a]	<5[a]
Sweden	6	8	81	76	<5[a]	<5[a]
United States	9	12	79	73	<5[a]	<5[a]
Japan	5	7	83	76	<5[a]	<5[a]

[a] According to the United Nations Educational, Scientific, and Cultural Organization.
Source: World Bank, *World STARS (Socio-economic Time-series Access and Retrieval System) Data Diskette* (Washington, D.C.: World Bank Publications, 1995).

Table 1.7   Income Distribution

| Country | Year | Percentage Share of Income and Consumption | |
		Lowest 20 percent	Highest 20 percent
Low-Income Economies			
Tanzania	1991[a]	2.4	62.7
India	1989–90[a]	8.8	41.3
Kenya	1992[a]	3.4	61.8
Pakistan	1991[a]	8.4	39.7
Ghana	1988–89[a]	7.0	44.1
China	1990[b]	6.4	41.8
Sri Lanka	1990[a]	8.9	39.3
Indonesia	1990[a]	8.7	42.3
Lower-Middle-Income Economies			
Côte d'Ivoire	1988[a]	7.3	42.2
Bolivia	1990–91[a]	5.6	48.2
Philippines	1988[a]	6.5	47.8
Peru	1985–86[a]	4.9	51.4
Guatemala	1989[b]	2.1	63.0
Morocco	1990–91[a]	6.6	46.3
Jamaica	1990[a]	6.0	48.4
Algeria	1988[a]	6.9	46.5
Costa Rica	1989[b]	4.0	50.8
Chile	1989[b]	3.7	62.9
Upper-Middle-Income Economies			
Brazil	1989[b]	2.1	67.5
Botswana	1985–86[c]	3.6	58.9
Malaysia	1989[b]	4.6	53.7
Mexico	1984[b]	4.1	55.9
Republic of Korea	1988[d]	7.4	42.2
High-Income Economies			
Hong Kong	1980[d]	5.4	47.0
France	1989[d]	5.6	41.9
Germany	1988[d]	7.0	40.3
United States	1985[d]	4.7	41.9
Sweden	1981[d]	8.0	36.9
Japan	1979[d]	8.7	37.5

[a] Data refer to expenditure shares by fractiles of persons and are ranked by per capita expenditure.
[b] Data refer to income shares by fractiles of persons and are ranked by per capita income.
[c] Data refer to expenditure shares by fractiles of households and are ranked by household expenditure.
[d] Data refer to income shares by fractiles of households and are ranked by household income.
Source: World Bank, World STARS (Socio-economic Time-series Access and Retrieval System) Data Diskette (Washington, D.C.: World Bank Publications, 1995).

development index (HDI), which combines the three variables of life expectancy, literacy, and per capita income measured in PPP dollars. This index is an attempt to move beyond the narrow concept of per capita income as the measure of whether a country is experiencing development.

Increasing Freedom, Effective Governance, and Democracy

Experts have long agreed that development has a political component, but they have never agreed on exactly what that means. The main controversy has been between those who understand the development of human rights, freedom, and democracy as goals in and of themselves and those who understand the development of effective political systems of governance as a part of economic development.

The first group argues that human rights, freedom, and democracy are key elements of human progress, that they must be included in any definition of development, and that any measurement of a society's development must therefore include measures of its degree of human rights, freedom, and democracy. They recognize that there might not be any correlation between rapid economic growth and freedom or democracy, as was the case in the fast-growing countries of China, Taiwan, and Korea during the 1960s, 1970s, and 1980s. Their position, and ours, has been to insist that freedom and democracy must be accorded a priority equal to economic growth in any definition of the goals of development. This was the position of the UNDP in its recent attempts to create a human freedom index (HFI) or a political freedom index (PFI) as a separate but equal measure to complement its human development index.

The World Bank, in contrast, has emphasized the need for growth of effective systems of governance or development management. Effective governance is considered an indispensable component of economic growth, since without it, neither the private sector nor the government can carry out its development functions. This second group sees freedom and democracy either as cultural values that are not shared by all developing peoples or as later goals to be contemplated only after economic growth has enabled people to satisfy more **basic human needs** (BHNs). In sum, this group sees effective governance as essential to development, but freedom and democracy are optional.

■ **basic human needs (BHNs)** *food, clothing, shelter, basic health care, and education*

Clearer definitions are needed of the concepts under debate: human rights, freedom, governance, democracy. Freedom and human rights are related ideas. In the classic tradition of political thought, freedom has been specified in terms of a list of inalienable human rights, including the right to life, to due process, to assemble, to speak, to organize, to practice religion, to travel, and to work or to practice an occupation. In the past hundred years, other rights to basic human needs have been added, including the right to work, food, shelter, health care, and access to education. These rights (except education) are more controversial, especially in the United States, where popular culture continues to regard these as personal responsibilities of individuals rather than as societal obligations. However, they are accepted in almost all other industrialized countries and in the documents and treaties of the UN.

The human rights perspective on freedom thus calls an individual free if she is secure in her ability to pursue any and all of these rights without fear or intimidation. Societies are referred to as free if the population of that society is free. Societies distribute freedom differentially among their populations. Majority ethnic groups may be free, minorities less so; men may be free, women less so; the affluent may be free, the indigent less so; citizens may be free, immigrants less so. The issue of how free a society is, therefore, involves two dimensions: first, how many rights the most free sectors of the population enjoy; second, what proportion of the total population belongs to the most free sectors and enjoys those rights.

Freedom is measured by Freedom House's annual ratings of civil liberties.[6] It has also been measured by the Humana index, the basis for the UNDP's first effort to create an HFI.[7] Charles Humana listed forty rights guaranteed by UN charters and international treaties and then ranked countries according to how many of those rights were available to its citizens. Freedom is also measured by the UNDP's 1992 PFI, particularly its components of personal security, rule of law, and freedom of expression.[8]

International human rights monitors usually agree that some human rights are more basic than others—especially the right to life (literally the right not to be arbitrarily executed), the right not to be tortured, and the right not to be imprisoned without due process of law. International human rights monitoring organizations, such as Amnesty International, concentrate on trying to force governments to respect these most basic human rights, even in societies where no other freedoms are allowed. Basic human rights conditions for all countries are described in the annual editions of the *Amnesty International Report*.

Effective governance has been defined by the World Bank as consisting of four related dimensions: (1) technical and managerial competence in public administration, (2) accountability of public officials for their actions, (3) predictability and the rule of law, and (4) adequate and accessible information systems.[9] Two of these dimensions, accountability and the rule of law, are closely related to issues of **democracy** and freedom.

■ **democracy** *political system based on competitively selected leaders, public decision making, and popular participation*

Accountability is increased when public officials are elected, when their deliberations and decisions are open to the public, when financial records and audits of their performance are accessible to the media and the public, when there are competitive private alternatives to government agencies and facilities, and when professional groups or civic associations serve as independent monitors of government practices. For all practical purposes, this amounts to saying that governments are more accountable when their political systems are more democratic.

An **effective rule of law** has five elements: (1) a set of rules known in advance; (2) rules that are actually applied; (3) a means of ensuring that the rules are enforced; (4) an independent judicial system able to make binding decisions about how rules are to be interpreted; and (5) established and predictable procedures for changing the rules. Once an effective rule of law is in place, individuals and organizations can assess risks, make rational decisions, make investments, and start new programs. The energies and initiatives of all parts of the

■ **effective rule of law** *predetermined rules for which there are established means of application, enforcement, interpretation, and change*

private sector—individuals, corporations, nonprofit service agencies—can be unleashed. Absent an effective rule of law, all this activity, if it exists at all, will be driven underground into the informal economy. In a sense, an effective rule of law "frees" the private sector to start up lawful activities without fear of corrupt or arbitrary government repression. The only existing measure of a country's effective rule of law is the rule of law component of the UNDP's PFI.

Most modern political scientists define democracy as a political system characterized by (1) leadership selected on the basis of a competition for public support, (2) decision-making processes that are both publicly known and open to public influence, and (3) institutions that both provide channels for public participation and secure the safety of those who choose to participate.

Table 1.8 contains the ratings for political rights and civil liberties assigned by Freedom House to thirty-six countries in 1995. Political rights measure the degree to which residents of a country enjoy access to democratic government, as defined above. Civil liberties measure the degree to

Table 1.8   Comparative Measures of Freedom (1995)

Country	Political Rights	Civil Liberties
Low-Income Economies		
Mozambique	3	5
Tanzania	6	6
Kenya	6	6
India	4	4
Nigeria	7	6
Ghana	5	4
Pakistan	3	5
China	7	7
Sri Lanka	4	5
Côte d'Ivoire	6	5
Egypt	6	6
Lower-Middle-Income Economies		
Indonesia	7	6
Bolivia	2	3
Philippines	3	4
Guatemala	4	5
Jamaica	2	3
Peru	5	4
Algeria	7	7
Costa Rica	1	2
Russian Federation	3	4
Botswana	2	3
Turkey	5	5
Upper-Middle-Income Economies		
Brazil	2	4
South Africa	2	3
Malaysia	4	5
Chile	2	2
Mexico	4	4
Gabon	5	4
Argentina	2	3
Republic of Korea	2	2
Saudi Arabia	7	7
High-Income Economies		
Hong Kong	5	2
France	1	2
Germany	1	2
Sweden	1	1
United States	1	1
Japan	2	2

1 = most freedom; 7 = least freedom.
Source: Freedom House Survey Team, *Freedom in the World: The Annual Survey of Political Rights and Civil Liberties, 1994–95* (New York: Freedom House, 1995).

which they enjoy human rights or freedom. The scale is from 1 (most free) to 7 (least free). Predictably, residents of the United States and Sweden scored 1 in both categories. However, the residents of Japan were not judged to be as free and received ratings of 2.

The developing countries we think of as moving toward democracy, such as Sri Lanka, score relatively well (4) on political rights but less well on civil liberties, because of the high degree of communal violence and the attendant governmental repression. Korea has made major gains in its scores as it has moved toward greater guarantees of freedom and a functioning democracy.

Protecting the Environment

The final component of BBSD is environmental preservation. Except for the work of Thomas Robert Malthus—who argued that population growth would be greater than the growth of the capacity to produce food and that mass famine was inevitable— thinking about development since the industrial revolution has been predicated on an assumption that there are no limits to global growth. Virtually all models of development were either restricted to a national level or, if they were global, assumed that the scale of global economic activity was small relative to the **source** or the **sink**. When rapid economic growth was limited to small populations, this assumption may have been warranted.

■ **source** *natural resource availability in the ecosystem*

■ **sink** *capacity of the ecosystem to absorb the waste from human productive activity*

Increasing evidence now suggests that such an assumption is false. The last four decades have extended economic growth from about one-quarter to virtually all of humankind. This extension has increased living standards, raised life expectancy, reduced infant mortality, and significantly improved the quality of life for billions of people. But this expansion of economic activity has also been associated with global climate change, deteriorating air and water quality, rapid rates of deforestation, and significant losses of species and biodiversity. The World Bank estimates that world output could increase by a factor of three by 2030. Unless ways are found to break the link between economic growth and pollution, the World Bank argues, tens of millions of people could get sick or die each year from industrial pollution.[10]

Table 1.9 presents the World Bank's estimates of energy consumption and carbon dioxide emissions, the largest contributor to global warming, for some developing and industrialized countries on a per capita basis. The range of such emissions is striking. The United States, with per capita income lower than that in Japan, emits more than nineteen tons of carbon per person, approximately twice the level emitted in Japan. This is largely because the United States keeps the cost of energy low.

Table 1.9 makes the same point that the developing countries made effectively at the United Nations Conference on the Environment and Development (UNCED) in Rio in 1992: the United States has per capita emissions of carbon dioxide that are many times higher than those in developing countries. If we are really serious about cleaning up the global environment, the people in the rich countries will have to change.

Because past economic growth has been associated with severe degradation of the environment, it is all too easy to assume that there is an unresolvable conflict between meeting people's needs—the central goal of development—and protecting the environment. Such an assumption is unwarranted on four grounds. First, environmental quality is part of the improvement in welfare that development brings. Second, environmental damage such as degraded soils and polluted water and air will undermine future productivity and thus must be overcome as part of the development process. Third, a growing body of evidence suggests that the link between economic growth and environmental degradation may not be as definite or as permanent as was once believed. Finally, poverty itself has been shown to be an important contributor to environmental degradation in poor countries; thus, alleviation of poverty may reduce some pressures on the environment.

■ **environmentally sustainable development** *development that meets present needs without threatening future generations' ability to do the same*

The challenge facing us is to find ways to promote **environmentally sustainable development.** Although there is no clear agreement on how to define sustainable development, most agree with the Brundtland Commission that environmentally sustainable development is "development that meets the needs of the present without compromising the ability of future generations to meet their own needs."[11]

Assessing whether development is sustainable or unsustainable is not easy. Environmental baseline data are scarce, and time-series data that permit the identification of trends are even more rare. However, both data collection and analysis are getting better. The World Resources Institute,[12] the United Nations Environment Program's Global Environmental Monitoring System (GEMS),[13] and the World Bank[14] are

Table 1.9　Global Carbon Dioxide Emissions and Energy Consumption

Country	Carbon Dioxide Emissions: Tons of Carbon per Capita, 1991	Energy Consumption: Kg. Oil Equivalents per $100 per Capita GDP 1965	1991
Low-Income Economies			
Mozambique	.07	–	–
Tanzania	.07	48	42
Kenya	.18	140	36
India	.81	169	132
Nigeria	.15	30	455
Ghana	.22	54	31
Pakistan	.55	129	70
China	2.20	195	187
Sri Lanka	.26	59	37
Côte d'Ivoire	.51	–	–
Egypt	1.54	224	105
Lower-Middle-Income Economies			
Indonesia	.92	241	43
Bolivia	.81	76	37
Philippines	.70	87	31
Guatemala	.44	39	16
Jamaica	1.91	131	59
Peru	.88	62	20
Algeria	2.16	–	154
Costa Rica	1.06	65	32
Russian Federation	12.31[a]	–	–
Botswana	1.69	162	15
Turkey	2.49	103	48
Upper-Middle-Income Economies			
Brazil	1.43	123	33
South Africa	7.18	311	97
Malaysia	3.33	96	41
Chile	2.42	85	38
Mexico	3.92	113	41
Gabon	5.02	33	28
Argentina	3.55	107	50
Republic of Korea	6.05	197	30
Saudi Arabia	13.96	276	69
High-Income Economies			
Hong Kong	–	51	12
France	6.56	122	18
Germany	12.13	176	18
Sweden	6.23	176	15
United States	19.53	173	35
Japan	8.79	145	13

[a] U.S.S.R.

Source: World Bank, *World STARS (Socio-economic Time-series Access and Retrieval System) Data Diskette* (Washington, D.C.: World Bank Publications, 1995).

developing impressive point-in-time estimates and time-series data for a large number of environmental indicators. Microlevel or small-scale models of resource extraction in renewable and nonrenewable resources make it possible to estimate **sustainable yields**. Empirical work on the links between air and water quality and human health and productivity makes it possible to set appropriate environmental standards.

■ **sustainable yields** *achieved when the depletion rate of a resource does not exceed its replacement rate*

At the macroeconomic level, the United Nations System of National Accounts (SNA), which estimates GDP, is being revised to reflect environmental degradation and the depletion of the resource base.

Data Sources

We have indicated the most appropriate sources of data for each of the components of BBSD. We must caution that the data in developing countries are of varying quality. Some countries, such as Korea and India, have outstanding data. In many other countries, the available data leave much to be desired.

We often refer readers to data published by the IMF and the World Bank. These international economic organizations have impressive staffs of economists and statisticians gathering, analyzing, and publishing data on all the member countries. If the people in these organizations think that information is not valid, they simply do not publish it. Thus, we rely on the data they produce.

It is clear that information on the performance of the economy is far better than that on equity, the political component, or the environment. Economic data have been gathered in industrial countries since the 1930s and in developing countries since the 1950s, whereas efforts to collect data on equity came later and are politically charged—particularly in the case of distribution of income within a country. It was only in the 1970s and 1980s that serious efforts to gather data on political performance were initiated. Only one time series for this variable exists and is collected by a private organization, Freedom House. Information on the environment has been systematically collected only since the 1980s, and very few indicators are available for most countries. Environmental data are also collected and published by a private organization, World Resources Institute.

Despite the weakness of the data, we make use of them throughout the book, because we are convinced that some data are better than none.

They at least indicate the rough orders of magnitude of these variables. It is also clear that until there is a demand for such data to make international comparisons of performance in achieving BBSD, such data will not be collected and improved.

Critiques of the Goal of BBSD

How realistic is the goal of broad-based sustainable development? Many in developing countries argue that it is not possible for their countries to experience rapid economic growth and a structural transformation of the economy while distributing the benefits of this growth widely throughout the population. It is argued that all growth is inequitable. Income inequality is a necessary condition so that those with high incomes can save and make the necessary investments to trigger the structural transformation. Early research by Simon Kuznets demonstrated that income inequality in the industrialized countries increased during the first several decades of development.[15] Only after a certain level of per capita income was achieved did income inequality begin to decrease.

Critics also correctly argue that the industrialized countries did not respect human rights or allow unions and were not democracies during their developmental phase. The United States practiced genocide toward the indigenous population, used human slaves to produce the cotton that was used as a principal export to pay for the importation of the capital goods necessary to bring about industrialization, produced its first industrial goods in factories staffed by women and children with no protection from the grossest forms of exploitation, and did not allow non-landowners, women, and minorities the right to vote. It is argued that to expect today's developing countries to meet the same criteria for political performance that are now applied in the industrial countries is to doom them to failure on both the economic and the political front.

It is also argued that economic development cannot be accomplished while applying environmentalists' criteria for preservation of the environment. The United States cut down most of its forests during its development phase and now argues that developing countries should conserve their forests. It is argued that such a policy will doom countries to failure.

These are tough issues and ones that will be discussed fully in the chapters that follow. We agree that achieving BBSD is extraordinarily difficult, but we will argue that it is possible and is, in fact, the only option if humanity is to survive. One of the reasons we support BBSD is that it is an equally appropriate goal for both industrialized and developing countries. No country has achieved it, and there is much for all of us to do.

Notes

1. World Bank, *World Development Report 1994* (New York: Oxford University Press, 1994).
2. Simon Kuznets, "Economic Growth and Income Inequality," *American Economic Review* 45 (March 1955): 1–28.
3. The two measures of per capita income used are per capita GNP and GDP.
4. For a fuller discussion of the methodology for computing ICP income estimates, see Robert S. Summers and Alan H. Heston, "The Penn World Table (Mark 5): An Expanded Set of International Comparisons, 1950–1988," *The Quarterly Journal of Economics* 106 (May 1991): 327–68.
5. Ronald V. A. Sprout and James H. Weaver, *The Global Distribution of Income and Human Development*, working paper (Washington, D.C.: American University, 1993).
6. Freedom House, *Freedom in the World: Political Rights and Civil Liberties, 1985–1986*, Freedom House Book Series (New York: Greenwood Press, 1986).
7. United Nations Development Program (UNDP), *Human Development Report 1992* (New York: UNDP, 1992).
8. UNDP, *Human Development Report 1992*.
9. World Bank, *Managing Development: The Governance Dimension* (Washington, D. C.: World Bank, 1991).
10. World Bank, *World Development Report 1992* (New York: Oxford University Press, 1992), 9.
11. World Commission on Environment and Development (the Bruntland Commission), *Our Common Future* (New York: Oxford University Press, 1987).
12. World Resources Institute, *World Resources 1992* (New York: Oxford University Press, 1992).
13. United Nations Environment Programme (GEMS), *Assessment of Urban Air Quality* (Geneva: UNEP, 1988).
14. World Bank, *World Development Report 1992*.
15. Kuznets, "Economic Growth and Income Inequality," 4–6.

2

Forty Years of Economic Development: 1950–90

THERE IS A TENDENCY TO EMPHASIZE the enormous poverty that still exists after forty years of economic development effort. Although the problems of poverty, malnutrition, and human suffering in the developing world are real, it is also important to emphasize how much progress has been made since 1950. The purposes of this chapter are to review that progress and to assess what we know about what has distinguished the more successful developing countries and regions from the less successful. To start with, we provide a broad overview of development performance of the developing countries during the stable and prosperous 1950–75 period, followed by an overview of the 1975–90 period, during which the global economy was in turmoil. After reviewing overall achievements, we examine the growing disparities among the world's regions and reach some conclusions about how to achieve better development performance in the years ahead.

Twenty-Five Years of Development, 1950–75

Our assessment of this early period is limited to three dimensions of performance: growth, poverty reduction, and meeting basic human needs. The major points to be made about the period from 1950 to 1975 are:

1. The developing countries averaged a real gross domestic product (GDP) per capita growth rate of 3.4 percent between 1950 and 1975. This was faster than that of either the developed or the developing countries in any comparable period prior to 1950.[1]

2. The improvements in human welfare were spectacular. Life expectancy in the developing countries rose as much in the two decades after 1950 as it did in the 100 years of industrialization of the current developed nations.

Infant mortality declined significantly, smallpox and plague were virtually eliminated, and despite a doubling of the global population, malaria
and cholera killed fewer people in 1975 than they did in 1950. The number
of pupils in primary school tripled, those enrolled in secondary and tertiary schools increased sixfold, and the proportion of the adult population
that was literate increased from 33 percent in 1950 to 50 percent in 1975.

3. The high average growth rate in the developing world masked a
wide divergence. At one extreme, a group of countries in East Asia and
the Middle East grew at more than 4.2 percent per capita annually,
whereas a large number of countries in South Asia and sub-Saharan
Africa grew at less than 2 percent annually. Thus, we see the beginning of
fragmentation of the developing world along the lines of clear winners
and losers. This fragmentation appears to occur along regional lines, with
East Asia outperforming Latin America and the Caribbean, which in turn
outperformed sub-Saharan Africa and South Asia.

4. There was no clear relationship between the rate of growth and
either the degree of income inequality at any point in time or the trend in
inequality over time. Fast growers included both highly equal and highly
unequal societies; the same is true for slow growers.

5. Many of the countries that achieved rapid growth and high equity
began the development process with relatively equal income distributions; many of those that experienced rapid inequitable growth started
with sharply unequal distributions. Initial distribution of income seems
to be an important determinant of a country's trend in inequality.

6. Countries in which some people became worse off between 1950 and
1975 included at least as many slow growers as fast growers. This suggests
that growth probably cannot be blamed for increases in absolute poverty.

7. There appears to have been more than one route to equitable growth
and development. Some countries succeeded via a market and outward-
oriented strategy; others, like China, followed a socialist and inward path.

8. Historical experience suggests that political stability, whatever the
form of government, and stability of the economic rules of the game are
important and underrated sources of economic growth.

Development Performance Since 1975

How well do these findings apply to performance in the more turbulent
post-1975 period? Several obvious differences stand out. Most importantly,

the world engine of growth has slowed. The real gross domestic product (GDP) per capita growth rate for developing countries was 3.9 percent between 1965 and 1973.[2] Growth declined to 2.9 percent between 1973 and 1980 and to 1.2 percent between 1980 and 1989. This slowdown in growth in the developing world paralleled a similar decline in the industrialized world, where the corresponding figures were 4.1, 2.6, and 2.2 percent. This slowing of the engine of growth reduced the real GDP per capita growth rate for all developing countries to 2 percent per year between 1975 and 1989. This is nearly 60 percent lower than the rate in the 1950–75 period and is more in line with the longer-run historical experience of industrialized and developing countries prior to 1950.

The slowing of growth fell unevenly across the developing world. Two groups of countries—the forty countries classified by the World Bank as low-income economies and the East Asian economies—grew faster after 1980 than they had grown before; two other groups—those in Latin America and the Caribbean and those in sub-Saharan Africa—did markedly worse, as noted in Table 2.1. This regional pattern made it even more obvious that the developing world was fragmenting along the lines of clear winners and losers.[3] This has attracted an enormous amount of attention and has spawned a rich literature that studies individual country cases.

In 1975, data on poverty and income distribution and an understanding of how each varied with growth were quite limited. More recent research on the later period confirms the observations of the 1950–75 period:[4]

1. There was no systematic relationship between growth and inequality. Inequality increased in about as many growth situations as it decreased. Fast growers included both highly equal and highly unequal societies. The same was true for slow growers.

2. Poverty tended to decrease with economic growth in most, but not all, cases.

3. There was no clear relationship between the rate of growth and either the degree of inequality at any point in time or the trend in inequality over time.

As a result of this research, we now have a clearer understanding of how initial conditions and policies affect the relationship among growth, equity, and poverty. Improvements in both poverty and human welfare are related to the rate and kind of growth. The kind of growth that leads to the fastest reductions in poverty is that which is based on relatively

Table 2.1   Real GDP per Capita Growth Rates (% per annum)

Region	1965–80	1980–90
Low-income group	2.6	4.1
East Asia	5.1	6.2
Sub-Saharan Africa	1.5	−1.0
Latin America and Caribbean	3.5	−0.5

Source: World Bank, *World STARS (Socio-economic Time-series Access and Retrieval System) Data Diskette* (Washington, D.C.: World Bank Publications, 1995).

equal distributions in education and the ownership of land and a growth strategy that increases the demand for these broadly owned income-producing assets. Moreover, as Fields states, the initial distribution of income does indeed exert an influence on the trend in inequality: if you start out relatively equal, you are likely to end up relatively equal; if you start out relatively unequal, you are likely to end up there as well.[5]

Growing Regional Disparities

Although it is important to recognize that differences among countries in one region can often be greater than differences among regions, it is clear that a new regional hierarchy among developing countries has emerged. Countries in Asia, including the poor countries of South Asia, have on average outperformed those in Latin America, and those in Latin America have on average outperformed those in sub-Saharan Africa. Explaining the differences in performance among regions has become a booming academic field. Some analysts focus on the successes in Asia, especially East Asia; others focus on the failure of development in sub-Saharan Africa; still others try to explain the lost promise of Latin America.[6] What insights does this literature provide?

Development Failure in Sub-Saharan Africa

Despite the enormous differences among countries in sub-Saharan Africa, a clear picture emerges from development there. Of the thirty-six poorest countries in the world, twenty-two (61 percent) are in sub-Saharan Africa.[7] Measured real income per capita in the region is about what it was in

1960. This is the only low-income region in the world that has not experienced a substantial increase in income per capita (see Table 2.1).

It is also the only developing region that has not participated in the rapid growth in world trade—which expanded 2.4 times in real terms between 1961 and 1990 but essentially stagnated for countries in sub-Saharan Africa. As a result, Africa's share of developing country exports fell from 12 percent in 1961 to 5.8 percent in 1990. Sub-Saharan Africa also experienced very little change in the composition of its exports. It began its first development phase a decade after independence (1960–69) as an exporter of primary products, and despite efforts to break the links with its colonial past, the region remains an exporter of primary commodities. In 1992, 76 percent of its export earnings still came from primary goods (see Table 2.2).

This region is also the only one that has failed to experience a decline in population growth rates (see Figure 2.1). Population growth rates in sub-Saharan Africa continue to rise, having averaged 2.1 percent per annum in the 1960s, 2.8 percent in the 1970s, and 3.1 percent in the 1980s.

These high population growth rates are combined with poor performance in agriculture. For the most part, there has been no green revolution in African agriculture. Cereal yields in the region are about half those in Asia and Latin America (see Figure 2.2). Fertilizer application rates are less than 5 percent of those in East Asia and less than 20 percent of those in Latin America.[8] Stagnant and declining yields in the face of rising population growth rates have led to a long-run decline (about 1 percent per year) in food production per capita (see Figure 2.3). As a result, about 20 percent of the region's population is undernourished, and food imports have been rising at about 7 percent per year.[9]

Performance in the manufacturing sector has not been much better than that in agriculture. Growth rates in manufacturing started out strong but have been rapidly declining.[10] The contribution of manufacturing to GDP has been virtually unchanged. Only a minuscule percentage of the labor force is employed in manufacturing, and manufacturing exports remain a small percentage of total exports. Declining rates of return on investment suggest that much of the investment in manufacturing is highly inefficient.

Although there have been important gains in meeting basic human needs (BHNs) in the region, sub-Saharan Africa's BHNs performance lags considerably behind that of other low-income countries. Despite a regional GNP per capita that is roughly equal to that of China and India, the region's life expectancy is 20 percent less, the under-five male mortality

Table 2.2   Composition of Exports (% Primary Commodities)

Region	1970	1992
Sub-Saharan Africa	83	76
Latin America and Caribbean	88	62
South Asia	53	27
East Asia and Pacific	67	26

Source: World Bank, *World STARS (Socio-economic Time-series Access and Retrieval System) Data Diskette* (Washington, D.C.: World Bank Publications, 1995).

rate is nearly 2.5 times higher, and the **gross primary enrollment rate** is only 58 percent of that of the region comprising China and India (see Table 2.3).

■ **gross primary enrollment rate** *percentage of an age group enrolled in primary education*

■ **terms of trade** *prices received for exports compared with prices paid for imports*

The 1980s and 1990s were particularly difficult years for countries in this region. Between 1980 and 1990, income per capita declined by about 1 percent per year.[11] Declining imports and declines in the **terms of trade** contributed to a massive deterioration in the balance of payments.[12] The failure to respond early to the two oil price shocks in 1973 and 1979 contributed to a massive buildup of foreign debt (from $6 billion in 1970 to nearly $160 billion in 1990).[13]

To sum up, this is the only region of the world that did not experience a significant increase in income per capita, experienced rising population growth rates, and failed to achieve green revolution technology breakthroughs in agriculture. Its industrial performance is weak and declining, its BHNs performance is low relative to that of other low-income countries, and it was hard hit by the external shocks of the 1970s and early 1980s.

Why have countries in this region fared so poorly compared with other low-income countries? To start with, there is universal acknowledgment that the region began the period in the worst condition of any developing area. Africa started on its path from colonial exploitation a generation later than other former colonies in Asia and the Middle East and many generations later than those in Latin America. At the end of colonialism, when the period we are studying began, Africa was uniquely disadvantaged in terms of lack of infrastructure, development institutions, and educated people.

It also suffered a particularly pernicious form of imperialism that included massive deportation of its people as slaves. The Belgians were incredibly brutal in Zaire, as were the Portuguese, and both countries resisted leaving. The Portuguese did not leave Mozambique and Angola

Figure 2.1   Regional Population Growth Rates (1961–89)

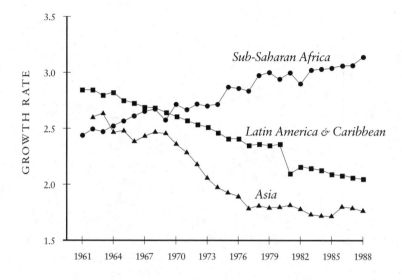

Source: F. Urban et al., "World Agricultural Trends and Indicators," data set (diskette) (Washington, D.C.: Department of Agriculture, Economic Research Service, 1990).

until the 1970s; the colonizers did not give up in Zimbabwe until 1980 and in South Africa until 1994. This has obviously hampered development efforts.

Several additional arguments have been developed to explain why performance has continued to deteriorate. The first emphasizes the link between fragile and weak economies at independence and the international economic environment. Recurrent drought, a poor natural resource base, and a high dependence on primary exports interacted with an increasingly hostile international economic environment to push the region's fragile economies over the edge.[14]

The argument that sub-Saharan Africa's problems can be explained by declining terms of trade is not without merit, but it is not entirely consistent with all the facts. Two examples make this clear. Between 1972 and 1987, Nigeria, a major oil exporter, experienced a 219 percent improvement in its terms of trade.[15] Despite this enormous windfall, real per capita GDP growth averaged -0.9 percent, inflation averaged 17.6 percent, the balance of payments deteriorated, and investment as a share of GDP declined from an average of 23 percent between 1972 and 1980 to about 12 percent between 1981 and 1987. Over this same period,

Figure 2.2   Regional Cereal Yields (1961–89)

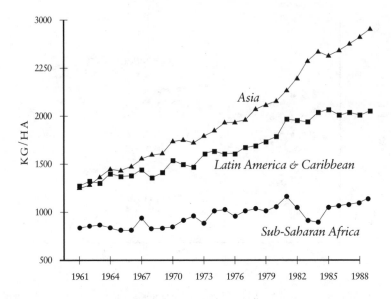

Source: F. Urban et al., "World Agricultural Trends and Indicators," data set (diskette) (Washington, D.C.: Department of Agriculture, Economic Research Service, 1990).

Kenya experienced a 49 percent deterioration in its terms of trade.[16] Despite this, Kenya's economy performed reasonably well. Real per capita GDP increased at about 1.5 percent per year, the investment-to-GDP ratio remained stable at about 24 percent of GDP, the inflation rate averaged a little under 10 percent, and the balance of payments deficit was brought under control. These differing responses to shifts in the terms of trade cast serious doubt on explanations of failure that rest on this factor. The question that needs to be asked is why some countries in the region managed to respond to external shocks better than others.

One obvious answer to this question rests with the weak governance capacity of central governments in the region.[17] Good development performance is uniquely dependent on the capacity of national governments to govern—that is, to decide on, implement, and enforce policies. Unless these things are done and done well—by technically competent bureaucracies that are organizationally effective and accountable—development does not occur. One of the fundamental problems in most countries in the region is that the colonial legacy made it difficult to build effective and efficient nation-states that could govern well. In this region, national

Figure 2.3   Index of Food Production per Capita (1961–89)

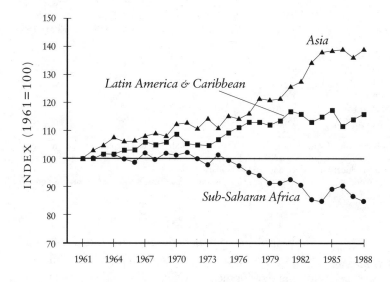

Source: F. Urban et al., "World Agricultural Trends and Indicators," data set (diskette) (Washington, D.C.: Department of Agriculture, Economic Research Service, 1990).

boundaries were drawn arbitrarily by colonial powers, and national politics are characterized by small or nonexistent middle classes, tremendous ethnic and linguistic diversity, weak state institutions, and a late start in education. In such contexts, the first generation of national leaders focused attention on building a nation-state, a government apparatus, and a sense of national identity. To do this, they built centralized national systems of political power based on their personal charisma and reputations as leaders of the independence struggle, the use of force, and **patronage**.

■ **patronage** *practice of giving government benefits to supporters to buy their loyalty*

The resulting patron-client politics relied on several institutions left over from the colonial era. The most prominent of these were publicly owned marketing boards, which bought and sold export crops and inputs for their production. These boards paid low prices to farmers for their crops and sold the crops for higher prices on the world market. The governments used the revenue gained to support a large government workforce and to invest in inefficient state-owned industries in pursuit of **import-substitution industrialization (ISI)**.

■ **import-substitution industrialization (ISI)** *an attempt to industrialize by producing products at home that were previously imported*

Table 2.3   Basic Human Needs Performance

Region	Per Capita GNP (1991 $)	Life Expectancy (years), 1991	Under-Five Male Mortality Rate (per 1,000), 1991	Gross Primary Enrollment Rate,[a] 1990
China and India	350	66	80	119
Other low-income countries	350	55	148	79
Sub-Saharan Africa	350	51	186	68

[a] This is the ratio of school enrollments to school-age children. It can surpass 100 when repeaters and older children still in primary school push enrollment rates higher than the age cohort. This is common when education first becomes widely available.

Source: World Bank, *World STARS (Socio-economic Time-series Access and Retrieval System) Data Diskette* (Washington, D.C.: World Bank Publications, 1995).

■ **economic rents**
unearned income that results from government restrictions shielding the rent seekers from normal competition

The policies pursued by governments following ISI created large **economic rents** for urban elites while undermining development.[18] Once the world engine of growth started to slow, it was no longer possible to sustain even modest growth rates, and the cumulative consequences of weak governance and poor policies began to take their toll.

But this outcome should not lead us to conclude that there is little hope for development in sub-Saharan Africa. It now appears that many of the first-generation leaders were successful at the nation-building task. This provides an opportunity to shift the focus from nation building to managing development.

The economic crisis of the 1980s and the exit of the subcontinent's first generation of leaders have provided an opportunity for this shift to occur. A new generation of leaders is emerging, and some are turning attention to managing development. A similar process occurred in Asia, particularly in East Asia during the 1960s. As in Africa, the first-generation leaders, the nation builders (whether in Indonesia, Korea, or China), were not particularly good at managing the economy for development. Following economic and political crises, these leaders were replaced by others who were more capable of managing economic development.

Lost Promise: Latin America versus Asia

Unlike other regions in the developing world, Latin America started out with several advantages that promised strong development performance.

Because independence came early (in the nineteenth century) for most countries in the region, state building and effective governance should have been completed earlier, enabling governments to focus on developmental tasks. This advantage was complemented by several others. This region has a rich natural resource base. By 1960, many of the countries in the region also had highly developed industrial bases, highly developed human resources, and highly developed institutional structures. Despite these initial advantages, development in Latin America has been disappointing.

Growth in Latin America, compared with that in Asia, has been anemic, erratic, and unequal. Between 1965 and 1989, Latin America's real per capita GDP growth rate was approximately 45 percent of Asia's. During the 1980s, growth of per capita income accelerated in Asia (5.1 percent per year) and turned negative in Latin America (-0.5 percent per year).[19] The long-run consequences of these differences in growth rates are startling. In 1970, real per capita income in South Korea was 83 percent of that in Brazil; by 1990, it was 221 percent of that in Brazil. In 1970, Thailand's real per capita income was about 40 percent of Peru's; by 1990, it was 125 percent of Peru's.

Latin America's inflation experience compares even less favorably. The average annual inflation rate in the region between 1961 and 1989 was 74.9 percent, more than twelve times that in Asia. During the 1980s, inflation accelerated across Latin America, averaging 192.1 percent per year, while inflation in Asia declined to under 8 percent per year.[20]

Latin America also fares poorly in comparison with Asia on income inequality. Three successive World Bank studies of income distribution show that the share going to the bottom quintile declined only in Latin America.[21] Of the sixteen countries in Latin America, fifteen in Africa, and twenty-two in Asia for which there are income distribution data, income inequality is most pronounced in Latin America (see Table 2.4). At the country level, the poorest 20 percent of the people in South Korea get 5.7 percent of national income, whereas the lowest quintile in Brazil receives only 2.4 percent. The richest 20 percent of the people in Brazil receive 63 percent of national income, whereas the same group in Korea receives only 45 percent.

The differences in the incidence of poverty are equally striking. In Brazil, with a per capita income of $2,160 in 1988, 24 percent of the people lived below the poverty line. In Indonesia, with a per capita income of only $440, only 17 percent of the population lived below the poverty line.[22] If the poorest 20 percent in Brazil (with 2.4 percent of income) had the same share of income as the poorest 20 percent in Indonesia (8.8 percent of income), poverty in Brazil would be virtually eliminated.

Despite Latin America's substantial early manufacturing base, the growth and export performance of Latin American industry lags significantly behind that of Asia. Between 1960 and 1990, manufacturing production in East Asia grew almost two times faster than that in Latin America (see Table 2.5). Poor manufacturing growth led to weak growth of manufacturing exports. Manufactures constituted less than 6 percent of Latin America's exports in 1962, compared with nearly 26 percent of East Asia's. Although Latin America's exports of manufactures grew to 32 percent of exports by 1990, this fell far short of the experience in Asia.[23] This poor export performance has been accompanied by recurrent foreign exchange crises and a debt crisis.[24]

Of the most severely indebted countries in the developing world in 1989, twelve of the top twenty, seven of the top ten, and four of the top five were in Latin America.[25] For most of these heavily indebted countries, **debt service** consumed 30 percent or more of export earnings. Few countries in Asia have such debt problems. Only one of the top seventeen debtors, the Philippines, is Asian, and debt service in Asia rarely exceeds 20 percent of export earnings.

■ debt service *principal and interest for the repayment of debt*

To sum up, development performance in Latin America has been characterized by slow and erratic growth, massive poverty and inequality in the face of substantial wealth, high and rising inflation rates, an anemic industrial sector, recurrent balance of payment crises, a massive buildup of foreign debt, and a virtual collapse of the economies during the 1980s.

Why has a region with such enormous initial advantages done so poorly? Possible answers include differences in initial conditions—in resource endowments, in landholding patterns, in attitudes about trade, and in how these interacted with cultural, linguistic, and ethnic differences within populations—which contributed to significant differences in development policies. For the most part, these initial conditions were combined in pernicious ways in Latin America.

The countries in Latin America are relatively resource rich compared with their counterparts in East Asia.[26] As a result, exports of primary products, especially minerals, have been the engine of growth. Resource-based exports proved to be an easy source of foreign exchange earnings, but the cost was often the exploitation of ethnically and linguistically distinct indigenous populations by small groups of politically powerful, landed elites of European extraction. In those places where economic policies took advantage of the region's resource base, the result was export enclaves, skewed income distribution in favor of land and mineral resource owners, and authoritarian, antidemocratic politics.[27] In several countries,

Table 2.4   Intraregional Distribution of Income

Population	South Asia	East Asia	Africa	Latin America
Poorest quintile	8.1	6.6	6.0	3.3
2nd quintile	12.2	11.4	8.2	7.2
3rd quintile	16.1	16.6	11.5	11.9
4th quintile	21.8	24.9	18.4	19.8
Richest quintile	42.0	40.4	55.9	57.9

Data are the most recent estimates, usually from the mid to late 1980s.
Source: J. Weaver and R. Sprout, "The Income of Nations and How It Changed," unpublished manuscript, Department of Economics, American University, Washington, D.C., December 1992.

this process created deep class divisions along racial, ethnic, and regional lines. When this occurred, the state-building process and, hence, a focus on development proved to be almost impossible.[28] Where the resource base was less rich and ethnic tensions less problematic (for example, Costa Rica), state building and development have been much easier.

The countries in Asia, especially East Asia, faced a very different dynamic. Virtually everywhere in East Asia—in Japan during the late nineteenth century, in Taiwan and Korea in the early twentieth century, and in China in the late 1940s—the power of landed elites was broken. In each instance, the heavy investments in agricultural modernization that followed the development of smallholder agriculture proved to be politically stabilizing.[29] East Asia is also more culturally, linguistically, and ethnically homogeneous, which made state building and a focus on development easier in East Asia. Because the East Asian resource base was less rich, countries there (except for China) never experienced the politically, socially, and economically distorting effects of resource-based export-oriented policies in the presence of highly unequal distributions of ownership of land and natural resources. As a result, attitudes toward trade and markets were very different. Instead of fearing trade, countries in the region (especially resource-poor Japan, South Korea, and Taiwan) erected a state-dominated neo-mercantilist incentive structure that promoted first-stage ISI.[30] But when returns to that strategy slowed, those countries—along with China in the 1980s—shifted to an incentive structure that promoted the export of labor-intensive manufactures.

The Latin American experience with primary exports made such a shift in policies more difficult. The unequal ownership of land and natural resources in the region caused the technocratic and intellectual elites to be skeptical of increased foreign trade, because such trade would further enrich the owners of the resources. Those committed to open and

Table 2.5   Annual Rate of Growth of Manufacturing Production

Region	1960–65	1970–80	1980–91	1960–90
Latin America	5.2	8.0	1.3	5.4
Africa	8.3	3.5	n/a	5.6
East Asia	5.1	10.5	10.6	9.9
South Asia	8.7	4.6	6.7	5.9

n/a, not available.

Source: Data for 1960–65 are from J. Sheahan, *Patterns of Development in Latin America* (Princeton, N.J.: Princeton University Press, 1987), 85. All other years are from International Bank of Reconstruction and Development, *World Development Report 1993* (New York: Oxford University Press, 1993), 240–41.

democratic politics favored ISI policies and feared export-oriented poli-cies because of their impact on domestic politics. Because the region's ISI policies went hand in hand with policies—such as the promotion of organized labor, labor-based political parties, and a social welfare state—that were inconsistent with the region's potential **comparative advantage** in manufac-tured exports, a shift to export-led industrialization would have required wage repression and a rolling back of social welfare. This proved to be politically difficult. But even if it were politically feasible, proponents of ISI policies doubted that export-led growth would work.[31] They viewed Western markets as highly protected, saw world trade substantially slow-ing, and rejected arguments about the necessity of investing in agricul-tural modernization.

■ **comparative advantage** *premise that a country should produce for export those goods that it produces best and import those goods that it doesn't produce as efficiently*

Populist governments in the region neglected agriculture, imposed high **tariffs** and **quotas** on imports, and **overvalued exchange rates**. Because populist governments lacked the political capacity to tax both old and new elites, all too often they resorted to inflationary finance. The consequences of populist poli-cies are well known: low growth, high inflation, recurrent balance of payment crises, and low political stability. When populist governments were replaced by authoritar-ian governments—as occurred in Brazil in 1964 and in Argentina, Uruguay, and Chile in the 1970s—economic policies tended to become more export oriented, and macroeconomic stability was reasserted. Although the policies of author-itarian governments resulted in a significant expansion of manufactured exports, those policies also reinforced existing inequalities.

■ **tariffs** *taxes on imported goods*
■ **quotas** *limits on the quantity of goods imported*
■ **overvalued exchange rate** *result of a government giving its currency a higher value than it would have in a free market*

A number of important insights emerge from this review of the last forty years of development.

First, despite the substantial poverty and human suffering that remains in the developing world, there have been substantial achievements. Real growth in per capita GDP between 1950 and 1990 was higher than in any other period in recorded history. There has also been remarkable progress in human development. For the most part, improvements in human development indicators continued despite the slowing down of the world engine of growth after 1975.

Second, we now have a clearer understanding of the relationships among growth, poverty, and equity. The relationship between poverty and growth and between inequality and growth in any one country appears to be the result of both the initial distribution of income-earning assets and government policies. Growth will be more equitable and will tend to reduce poverty not only when the initial distribution of assets is more equitable but also when governments invest in creating ■ **human capital** **human capital** and when the growth strategy increases *an educated and* the demand for those income-earning assets that are *skilled population* more broadly owned—primarily labor, but also land when it is relatively equitably distributed among smallholders.

Third, we now see that initial conditions exert a substantial influence on development policies and outcomes. Latin America's nineteenth century experience with the export of primary products, the unequal distribution in the ownership of land, and the unresolved conflict between landed elites and urban commercial elites interacted to make pro-growth policies very difficult. Sub-Saharan Africa's colonial legacy, its ethnic, cultural, and linguistic diversity within arbitrary national boundaries, and little colonial investment in education go a long way toward explaining the region's policy choices and corresponding development failures. By contrast, East Asia's greater cultural, linguistic, and racial homogeneity, its smallholder agriculture, its strong sense of national identity, and a shared security threat from the communists have made state building easier and provided opportunities for a national focus on development.

Fourth, we now understand the importance of stable economic rules of the game and stable governments, of whatever form, for development performance. We also know that the economic rules of the game are more likely to be stable if there is political stability. We have gained an understanding of how difficult, if not impossible, this is to achieve in countries where the nation-building process is not very far along. If governments are trying to knit together a nation from disparate ethnic, linguistic, or cultural groups, as in sub-Saharan Africa, or if they are trying to restructure political power, as in Latin America, basic political stability will often be lacking, and efforts to provide stable economic rules of the game will be hampered.

We cannot minimize the role that violence and the threat of violence had on the rapidly industrializing countries in East Asia. In East Asia, the development miracles took place in a period of political stability that depended on breaking the political power of landed elites. This was accomplished in large part because of fear of the internal or external communist threat. Korea faced North Korea, and Hong Kong and Taiwan faced China. Malaysia, Thailand, and Indonesia had powerful internal communist movements threatening the elite.

The Philippines faced an internal threat, but it did not have the effect of bringing reform there. Some argue that development in the Philippines was blocked by the United States' role. The independence treaty in 1946 was unequal. It gave the United States unlimited access to markets in the Philippines but gave the United States the right to limit exports from the Philippines to the United States. The U. S. government strongly supported a series of reactionary and corrupt governments, including that of Ferdinand Marcos.

There is no clearer case of the threat of communism as an incentive for radical reform than Taiwan. Chiang Kai-shek had lost mainland China to the communists as a result of his inability to bring about land reform and end the rampant corruption. When he arrived in Taiwan, with heavy military protection and massive aid from the United States, he launched sweeping land reform and reduced government corruption. Of course, it was easier to reform the land belonging to the native Formosans than to reform the land of the rich landlords in China. Authoritarian developmental states were accepted by the people as legitimate in order to deal with internal and external threats.

We also know that how governments go about the nation-building process has a significant impact on whether a country adopts sound development policies. If patronage is used to hold power, as in sub-Saharan Africa, the cumulative effect is likely to undermine long-run development prospects. Development policies are not likely to be much better if legitimacy and national identification are based on building new political coalitions in the face of a dominant landed oligarchy. This is what occurred in Latin America, resulting in too much patronage and inefficiency in the modern industrial sector, which stymied the transition to export-led industrial policies.

Finally, it has become clear that shifting policies away from patronage and toward development is not easy in the absence of crisis. Political and governing elites in both sub-Saharan Africa and Latin America clung to failed policies for far too long. This was partly because of prevailing development orthodoxy, which stressed limited gains from trade, the failure of markets to work, and the importance of state planning and investment. But even if development theory had not overemphasized the state sector of the economy, it would have been politically difficult for elites in these regions to turn against their newly won bases of support. Crises played an important role in the shifts in development policy in East Asia. There, existing or new authoritarian governments used crises to consolidate political power, reform public-sector bureaucracies, and build a collaborative relationship between government and business around the export of manufactures, while excluding labor and landlords from economic and political decision making.

Many of the positive initial conditions mentioned above in East Asia were missing in Latin America, sub-Saharan Africa, and South Asia, particularly India. Thus, it is not surprising that countries there have not done as well as those in East Asia.

These findings are a salutary answer to simple arguments about getting economic policies right. They should not be used, however, to undermine arguments about the importance of policy in development performance. Experience has demonstrated that policies matter. Nor is there an intention to imply that past history wholly determines future outcomes. The world is too complex for such simple conclusions.

Notes

This chapter is based in part on an article by Michael T. Rock entitled "Twenty-Five Years of Economic Development Revisited," *World Development* 21 (1993): 1787–1801. That material is used here with kind permission from Elsevier Science Ltd., The Boulevard, Langford Lane, Kidlington, OX5 1GB, UK.

1. David Morawetz, *Twenty-Five Years of Economic Development* (Baltimore: Johns Hopkins University Press, 1977). In their long period of economic growth, developed countries managed to increase per capita income at about 2 percent per annum.
2. Unless otherwise indicated, all real GDP growth rates quoted in the text are from International Monetary Fund (IMF), *International Financial Statistics Yearbook, 1991* (Washington, D.C.: IMF, 1991), 160–63, and all population

growth rates quoted in the text are from F. Urban et al., "World Agricultural Trends and Indicators," data set (diskette) (Washington, D.C.: U.S. Department of Agriculture, Economic Research Service, 1990).

3. Of the fast growers, seven were in Asia, two were in Africa, and one was in the Middle East. Of the slow growers, none was in Asia, five were in Africa, two were in Latin America–Caribbean, and three were in the Middle East.

4. G. Fields, "Growth and Income Distribution," in *Essays on Poverty, Equity, and Growth,* ed. G. Psacharopolous (New York: Pergamon Press, 1991), 1–52, and World Bank, *World Development Report 1990* (New York: Oxford University Press, 1990), 3, 40.

5. Of the twenty-two countries reported in Fields, "Growth and Income Distribution," 16–21, there is remarkable stability in rank ordering by income inequality. Eight of the ten countries that started with the lowest inequality ended there as well. Nine of the ten that started with the highest inequality ended there.

6. Representative examples include J. Sheahan, *Patterns of Development in Latin America* (Princeton, N.J.: Princeton University Press, 1987); World Bank, *Sub-Saharan Africa: From Crisis to Sustainable Growth* (Washington, D.C.: World Bank, 1989); and S. Haggard, *Pathways from the Periphery* (Ithaca, N.Y.: Cornell University Press, 1990).

7. World Bank, *World Development Report 1992* (New York: Oxford University Press, 1992), 218.

8. World Bank, *World Development Report 1992,* 225.

9. World Bank, *Sub-Saharan Africa,* 89.

10. Between 1965 and 1973, manufacturing grew at 10.1 percent per annum; this declined to 8.2 percent per year between 1973 and 1980 and to 3.1 percent per year between 1980 and 1990. World Bank, *World Development Report 1992,* 221.

11. IMF, *International Financial Statistics Yearbook,* 118–19, 121, 125.

12. Sub-Saharan Africa's terms of trade declined by about 10 percent between 1980 and 1987. World Bank, *Sub-Saharan Africa,* 24.

13. World Bank, *Sub-Saharan Africa,* and World Bank, *World Debt Tables 1990–91* (Washington, D.C.: World Bank, 1992).

14. D. K. Fieldhouse, *Black Africa: 1945–1980* (London: Allen and Unwin, 1986), chaps. 2, 4.

15. Terms of trade data are from World Bank, *World Debt Tables,* 458–59.

16. IMF, *International Financial Statistics Yearbook,* 136–37.

17. R. Jackson and C. Rosberg, "Why Africa's Weak States Persist: The Empirical and Juridical in Statehood," in *The State and Development in the Third World,* ed. A. Kholi (Princeton, N.J.: Princeton University Press, 1986), and R. Sandbrook, "The State and Economic Stagnation in Tropical Africa," *World Development* 14 (1986): 319–32.

18. For a discussion of the similarities in this policy across countries in the region, see R. Gulhati and S. Yalamanchili, "Contempory Policy Responses to Economic Decline, in *The Crisis and Challenge of African Development,* ed. H. Glickman (New York: Greenwood Press, 1988), 86–116.

19. Calculated from GDP growth data in IMF, *International Financial Statistics Yearbook,* and population growth data in Urban et al., "World Agricultural Trends."
20. World Bank, *World Development Report 1992,* 218–19.
21. Sheahan, *Patterns of Development,* 23.
22. World Bank, *World Development Report 1990,* 43, 178, 179.
23. Manufactured exports constituted 69 percent of East Asia's exports and 70 percent of South Asia's exports by 1990. World Bank, *World Development Report 1992,* 249.
24. Sheahan, *Patterns of Development,* 87.
25. World Bank, *World Debt Tables 1990–91,* 19.
26. Fuel, mineral, and metals exports were about 45 percent of Latin America's exports in 1965, whereas they were only 20 percent of East Asia's exports. (World Bank, *World Development Report 1992,* 249).
27. This led some to ask whether market-oriented economic policies required political repression in Latin America. See J. Sheahan, "Market-Oriented Economic Policies and Political Repression in Latin America," *Economic Development and Culture Change* 28 (January 1980): 267–92.
28. For a generic discussion of the state-building process in Latin America, see L. Diamond et al., *Democracy in Developing Countries: Latin America* (Boulder, Colo.: Lynne Rienner, 1988), 5–9.
29. For a discussion of the politically stabilizing effects of land reform in East Asia, see R. Hofheinz and K. Calder, *The East Asia Edge* (New York: Basic Books, 1982), 89–94.
30. C. Johnson, "Political Institutions and Economic Performance: The Government Business Relationship in Japan, South Korea and Taiwan," in *The Political Economy of the New Asian Industrialism,* ed. F. Deyo (Ithaca, N.Y.: Cornell University Press, 1987), 136–65.
31. R. Prebisch, "Commercial Policy in the Underdeveloped Countries," *American Economic Review* 49 (May 1959): 251–73.

3

Development Strategies

BETWEEN THE END OF WORLD WAR II and the collapse of communism, two distinct models of development—one capitalist and the other socialist—vied for the attention of the developing world. Most countries adopted capitalist- or market-oriented approaches to development, but a significant number of countries followed a socialist alternative. The purposes of this chapter are to outline the three dominant capitalist models of development—a laissez-faire model, an import-substitution industrialization model, and a growth with equity model; to outline the two most important socialist models of development—the Russian and Chinese models; and to demonstrate how each affects broad-based sustainable development (BBSD).

Laissez-Faire

The first capitalist development strategy was **laissez-faire.** It was followed by Great Britain in the nineteenth century and to a lesser degree by the other capitalist economies of the West, including the United States. Since the end of World War II, only one developing country—Hong Kong, a

■ **laissez-faire** *doctrine of leaving the market alone and trusting that it will provide for all our needs*

colony of Great Britain—has followed something close to a laissez-faire model. Despite this, the ideas of laissez-faire have dominated much of the thinking and writing about economic development in the business and banking community, in international financial institutions such as the World Bank and the International Monetary Fund (IMF), and in official government development agencies such as the U.S. Agency for International Devel- opment (USAID). Moreover, they enjoyed a new popularity in the 1980s in the developing world. What is a laissez-faire approach to development? How does it affect BBSD?

The best example of it can be found in Adam Smith's *The Wealth of*

Nations, which was published in 1776. Smith argued that the goal of development is economic growth, so the goal of economic development theory is to provide insight into how growth might be accelerated. For Smith and modern neoclassical economists, the economic system best suited to achieve the goals of development is laissez-faire capitalism. In the capitalist economy, four institutions play important roles: private ownership of the **factors of production**, markets for the factors of production, the capitalist firm, and **commodities** markets.

■ **factors of production** *land, labor, and capital (machines)*

■ **commodities** *goods that are bought and sold*

Fitting these institutions together allows us to see how the system works. Individuals own land, labor, or capital. They take these into the factors market and sell them to capitalist firms. From the sale of these factors of production they get income. With their income they go into commodities markets to buy the goods and services they require from the capitalist firms. The firms then use the revenues obtained from selling commodities to buy or rent more capital, land, and labor and to produce more goods.

Individual firms decide what to produce and how to produce it. Firms choose what (and how much) to produce on the basis of what people want, what they are willing to pay, and what will be most profitable. They decide how to produce—what combination of workers, machines, and raw materials to use—on the basis of which **technology** is most profitable. These two decisions determine how many workers will be employed and how income will be distributed.

■ **technology** *the tools and techniques of production*

In this view of development, isolated, individual decisions by firms and consumers somehow work together without any master plan to guide the economy. This is because private ownership provides the incentives for people to work hard. They do so in the hope of acquiring great wealth and with the fear that if they do not work hard they will wind up in great poverty. The system provides the carrot of great wealth to motivate the donkey and the stick of poverty with which to beat it. As Smith stated, under the capitalist system, it is "not from the benevolence of the butcher, the brewer, or the baker, that we expect our dinner, but from their regard to their own interest."[1]

Because of this, the actions of private individuals bring about development, guided by the invisible hand of competition. Competition among firms results in efficient allocation of resources, innovation, and economic growth. Firms face the threat of being driven out of business if they do not continually innovate, invest, and reinvest. Thus, the economy grows.

Given such a system, the question remains: what should government do to encourage development? Adam Smith argued that successful development required government to do only a limited number of things. First and foremost, government must protect private property. Without protection of private property, no firm or individual would save or invest. A second proper function of government is to enforce private contracts or agreements between buyers and sellers. By enforcing private contracts, the government prevents force and fraud and ensures that markets do indeed function. In addition, the government must provide **public goods** and **quasi-public goods**. Finally, government must provide for a system of money and credit that brings **entrepreneurs** together with those who have money. Since entrepreneurial activity is central to development, government's proper role is to ensure that there is a money and banking system that allows entrepreneurs to obtain the needed funds. As part of this, government must provide for sound money, money that keeps its value over time. This can be done by keeping inflation low.

■ **public goods** *goods that, once produced, cannot be restricted to private owners (e.g., clean air, national defense)*
■ **quasi-public goods** *goods that can benefit private owners but also have spillover public benefits (e.g., roads, vaccinations, education)*
■ **entrepreneurs** *those who create new firms, new products, new ways of doing things*

Laissez-faire economists link these roles of government with assumptions about the stability of markets and the social harmony of competition. The emphasis is on providing a climate conducive to entrepreneurship. If government performs only those tasks necessary for markets to function effectively and leaves entrepreneurs alone, economic development will occur. In addition to the domestic strategy of laissez-faire, Smith and his followers advocated an international strategy called **laissez-passer**.

■ **laissez-passer** *doctrine of free international movement of goods, labor, and capital for investment*

Despite the positive results of laissez-faire strategies in the development of the West, over time, the negative costs became socially and politically unbearable. There were devastating business cycles with massive unemployment, culminating in the Great Depression of the 1930s. There was growth of monopolies, exploitation of women and children in mines and factories, extraordinary inequality in income distribution, dislocations of cities and regions, and environmental degradation. In short, laissez-faire generated high growth, but it also left many poor, contributed to income inequality, and degraded the environment. In many places, it appeared incapable of producing BBSD.

Import-Substitution Industrialization

In reaction to the failures of laissez-faire, labor movements, antimonopoly legislation, child labor laws, maximum-hour laws, restrictions on trade, state provision of health and welfare services, and environmental regulation became the norm in the industrialized capitalist countries. Given these developments in rich countries, it is not surprising that a laissez-faire approach to development gave way to a much more interventionist approach.

In fact, the post–World War II pioneers of development economics rejected the relevance of neoclassical economic theory and laissez-faire policies for developing countries. Their rejection of laissez-faire was based on its failures at home and the conviction that the institutions necessary for market economies to operate were not present in developing countries. Development economists held that markets for commodities, labor, land, capital, and finance were underdeveloped, nonexistent, or functioned badly in developing countries. Furthermore, the necessary institutions to make these markets work, such as clear property rights, were weak or nonexistent.

Early development economists emphasized a vicious circle of poverty in poor countries characterized by low income, little demand, a limited market, and little investment. They thought that the only way to break this circle was for government to plan a whole series of investments— a big push. Government would have to provide investment where the capital required was too large for private capitalists. Economists also emphasized the need for government to provide the infrastructure for industrialization: highways, ports, railroads, electrical generating stations, telecommunications, systems of education, and training to provide people with the necessary skills.

Several of the most influential development pioneers, such as Raoul Prebisch, argued that free trade would not lead to development in developing countries because of a tendency for the terms of trade to fall over time. Because of this, the early development economists argued against reliance on the export of primary products and advocated industrializing at home to produce those products that were previously imported.[2]

The general theme was clear: development equated with industrialization, and agricultural transformation was virtually ignored. Laissez-faire and free trade would not produce development. Instead, protection for domestic industry, minimal reliance on exports of primary goods, rejection of the market as the dominant instrument for resource allocation, and its replacement with central planning and government resource allocation were all promoted. The first development economists also called for government saving and investment and foreign assistance to make up for deficiencies in private saving and investment.

The capitalist development strategy that emerged was government-guided import-substitution industrialization (ISI). ISI emphasized industrialization as the key to development, with the government playing the key role in getting industry started. ISI began with the domestic production of consumer goods, such as textiles and clothing, that had previously been imported. This was followed by the production of **intermediate goods** and eventually capital goods.

■ **intermediate goods**
semiprocessed raw materials (e.g., cotton fiber, refined oil) used in the production of other goods

Many government interventions in markets were used to promote ISI industries. **Protectionism** was used to keep foreign goods out and to safeguard domestic "infant" industries. Exchange rates were deliberately overvalued,[3] and governments often established **multiple exchange rates** to encourage the importation of capital, intermediate goods, and raw materials. Governments used these multiple rates to control and allocate foreign exchange to crucial industries. Why did governments promoting ISI do this? It made imports cheap, particularly imports that were needed to support ISI production.

■ **protectionism**
government policy of using tariffs and quotas to protect local firms from international competition
■ **multiple exchange rates**
different rates imposed for different kinds of imports and exports

ISI governments often prohibited foreign investment entirely, or at least in certain industries. If foreign investment was allowed, it was seriously constrained, in that a majority of the stock had to be owned by local capitalists, and limits were placed on how much of the profits could be exchanged for a **convertible currency** to be repatriated to the investing country.

■ **convertible currency**
currency that can be easily exchanged for another currency (e.g., U.S. dollars and British pounds)

In addition to these trade and foreign exchange policies, governments replaced the market with a central planning agency to plan the economy, allocate resources, control prices, and administer foreign aid. Cheap credit and foreign aid for capital imports encouraged firms to import and adopt new technology. Credit was allocated to industries and firms favored by the government. Such firms were given subsidized interest rates, and special subsidies (tax holidays, free land, cheap electricity, and infrastructure projects) were established to encourage investment in certain industries. State-owned enterprises were established to initiate industrialization in those industries for which domestic capital could not produce the resources to establish firms large enough to achieve efficiency.

What were the consequences of these interventionist ISI development policies in the developing market economies? The countries following ISI began producing at home what had previously been imported. In some cases, such as Brazil, by the late 1960s, over 90 percent of most consumer goods were produced domestically. As a result of the ISI approach, many developing countries experienced rapid economic growth and industrialization. In the 1950s and 1960s, Korea, Taiwan, Brazil, Mexico, and Chile all had remarkable success following these policies. Each of these countries was able to use ISI policies to build substantial industrial bases, an emerging middle class, and an indigenous business class. By the 1960s, however, the viability of ISI was being subjected to close scrutiny and heavy criticism.

What were the fundamental problems associated with ISI? First, corruption in awarding protection to particular industries and firms was rife. Preferential access to foreign exchange, credit, and import quotas was usually granted on the basis of patronage rather than economic efficiency. When this happened, growth was slower and income inequality worsened. In many instances, such as in the Philippines, this promoted the development of crony capitalism. Second, state-owned enterprises turned out to be inefficient. In many countries, they produced shoddy goods at high prices, and instead of producing profits to be reinvested, they produced losses that had to be made up by the government. This contributed heavily to **fiscal deficits**.

■ **fiscal deficits** *gaps between government tax revenues and government spending*

Third, ISI policies that neglected investment in agriculture and taxed export agriculture heavily had two devastating effects. Low food prices discouraged the agricultural sector from modernizing and increasing output. The result was that countries following ISI strategies moved from being net food exporters to being net food importers. Export agriculture declined and stopped producing foreign exchange, which had been used to pay for imports. Food subsidies also contributed to fiscal deficits; they were financed by printing money and ultimately fueled inflation, which had a negative impact on investment and growth.

ISI policies also led to the creation of capital-intensive factories that generated too little employment. Thus, most people were left out of the modern industrial sector and had to eke out a livelihood in the **informal sector**, which was not favored or taxed by the state and where earnings were very low. Since the technology chosen tended to be more capital intensive, it

■ **informal sector** *small-scale enterprises that are not licensed or taxed by the government*

required more highly skilled engineers, accountants, and managers. This required that the educational system be designed to produce people with these skills. Since poor countries could not afford to provide both universal primary education and higher education for the elite, governments following ISI policies often chose to spend most of the education budget on higher education. The same was true of the health budget. Urban elites wanted modern hospitals and curative treatment; they were much less concerned about preventive care for the people in rural areas.

As a result, ISI strategies resulted in more income inequality. In many instances, it proved to be no better at achieving BBSD than laissez-faire. To make matters worse, high income inequality and a high incidence of poverty went hand in hand with an ultimate and inevitable slowdown in economic growth. In short, ISI policies reached a dead end on the road to BBSD.

Growth with Equity

By the early 1970s, development economists turned their attention to analyzing the impact of specific growth policies on equity and poverty. What they initially discovered proved to be quite distressing. Some studies—including an influential one on Brazil—found a growing inequity in income distribution in developing market economies.[4] In itself, this finding was not surprising. Kuznets had found that relative income distribution in Europe and the United States in the nineteenth century became less equal before it started to become more equal.[5] More troubling, however, was a controversial and influential study that found that absolute poverty was increasing; the poor were not only getting a smaller share, they were also getting absolutely poorer.[6] Moreover, another series of studies found that open unemployment was growing in developing countries and was growing fastest in those countries experiencing the most rapid growth.[7]

These studies convinced many that conventional development strategies, which focused on increasing economic growth, were not benefiting the poor. This led to a search for policies that promoted growth with equity. Virtually all the strategies that emerged recognized that equitable growth was not possible unless the productivity of the assets owned by the poor was increased.

Some argued that the slow growth of demand for labor in conventional growth strategies was responsible for both poverty and inequity. Different approaches were promoted to increase the demand for labor. The

International Labor Organization in Geneva, Switzerland, concluded that since the modern industrial sector produced too few jobs, the focus should be shifted to generating employment in the informal sector.[8] Others argued that employment in the more modern sector could be made more labor intensive if more appropriate technologies (that is, less capital-intensive technologies) were used. Another argument was that poverty, inequality, and unemployment were rising because the prices of capital and labor were wrong. In this view, capital subsidies and high minimum and social wages encouraged capitalists to demand too much capital and economize on the use of labor. If the prices of capital and labor were closer to market values, capitalist firms would demand less capital and more labor. This would cause employment and wages to rise, reducing poverty and income inequality. Finally, some neoclassical economists looked at the development experiences of Taiwan and Korea and argued that the key to their equitable growth had been their emphasis on labor-intensive exports. So a major effort was made to encourage countries to move into labor-intensive export industries.[9]

A second group argued that poverty and inequity could be reduced only if the return to agricultural land could be increased. The rationale was that most of the poor lived in rural areas and earned their living in agriculture. Because of this, Irma Adelman argued that equitable growth was not possible without equitable ownership of the basic productive asset in rural society—land. Therefore, she argued that land reform and smallholder agriculture were necessary.[10] John Mellor, among others, also emphasized the importance of developing agriculture first. This required investing in agriculture (in high-yielding seeds, irrigation, fertilizer, and agricultural research and extension) and paying farmers good (market) prices for the crops they produced.[11] These improvements would increase farm incomes and boost demand for labor-intensive agricultural and industrial goods, thereby generating employment.

Finally, a third group emphasized increasing productive investment in the assets of the poor or providing the poor with basic human needs. Some argued that investment in credit for small farmers and in the creation of human capital through education and training would increase the productivity of the poor and enable them to work their way out of poverty.[12] In an economy industrializing through labor- and skill-intensive exports, the basic productive asset was human capital. Therefore, education and training for all must be provided.[13] Still others, such as Paul Streeten and Mahbub ul Haq, argued that markets alone could not and would not provide the basic necessities to all, especially the poor.[14] The market does not provide for the old, the sick, children outside the family, and others unable to earn their keep in the free market. Their strategy called for governments to provide these necessities to those who were unable to provide for themselves.

Summary of Capitalist Development Strategies

What has the last fifty years of experience with capitalist development strategies taught us about the prospects of achieving broad-based development? Several things are now clear. First, not all growth is equitable and poverty reducing. If the initial distribution of income-producing assets (land, educated labor, and capital) is highly unequal, laissez-faire growth will result in high income inequality and a high incidence of poverty. Second, if governments intervene in the economy, as they did with ISI, how they intervene makes a big difference in growth, poverty, and inequality outcomes. If they stick to ISI policies after the first easy stage of ISI in light consumer goods, growth will come to an end. If ISI policies discriminate against smallholder agriculture, encourage capital-intensive industry, and economize on the use of labor, growth will be less equitable and less poverty reducing. Finally, governments can do a number of things to promote broad-based growth. It helps enormously if income-producing assets, particularly land and educated and healthy labor, are equitably distributed at the beginning of the development process. When land is not equitably distributed among smallholders, governments need to carry out land reform and increase the security of tenant farmers. In addition, governments must finance basic education and basic health care for all so that workers and farmers can take advantage of the opportunities provided by equitable growth.

But this is not enough. To be totally successful, an equitable growth strategy has to increase the demand for those income-producing assets—land and educated and healthy labor—that are most equitably distributed. Doing this requires heavy public-sector investments in rural infrastructure and agricultural research and extension; it requires favorable prices for small farmers for output and for inputs such as fertilizer and water. It also requires an industrial strategy that is labor intensive. Finally, governments must create a safety net to provide basic necessities for those who are bypassed by growth.

If these things are done, as they were in East Asia, capitalist market-oriented growth can be both more equitable and poverty reducing. Table 3.1 presents data on development performance in five Asian countries to illustrate the consequences of strategies in different countries in the same geographic region. Most of these countries were impacted by the colonial experience—Hong Kong, India, and Sri Lanka were all British colonies, and Korea was a colony of Japan. During the post–World War II period, all were subject to the same international economic rules of the game and the same rate of growth in the industrialized countries. Yet they have had radically different economic results. These differences are largely the result of different strategies (and hence policies) and differences in initial conditions. In some cases—particularly in East Asia—initial conditions and policies worked to produce high growth, low income inequality, and a rapid decline in the incidence of poverty. In other cases—such as in India—initial conditions and policies interacted to produce slow growth, higher inequality, and a high incidence of poverty.

It is important not to make the mistake of attributing all the differences in outcomes to differences in policies. Differences in initial conditions are responsible for some, maybe most, of the differences in outcomes.[15] Unfortunately, the focus on policy in each of the capitalist development strategies identified above tends to downplay the importance of initial conditions.

The focus on development strategies in this chapter also downplays the importance of domestic politics and of socioeconomic change. But it is clear from examining individual case histories that sociopolitical change is an important component of development performance. Differences in domestic politics can exert a strong influence on the choice of development strategy. Although domestic politics may not actually deny a country access to specific development strategies, it is important to recognize that sociopolitical change is an important part of the process of successful development.

Rejection of Capitalist Development Strategies

If capitalist, market-oriented, growth-with-equity development strategies are capable of producing broad-based growth, why did so many countries reject them in favor of a socialist road to development? And what do

Table 3.1   BBSD Indicators in Five Asian Countries

Indicators	China	Hong Kong	India	Korea	Sri Lanka
Population, 1992 (millions)	1,162.2	5.8	883.6	43.7	17.4
Population growth, 1970–80/1980–92 (%)	1.8/1.4	2.5/1.2	2.3/2.1	1.8/1.1	1.6/1.4
Per capita GNP, 1992 (US$)	470	15,360	310	6,790	540
Per capita GNP growth rate, 1980–92 (%)	7.6	5.5	3.1	8.5	2.6
Purchasing power parity estimate, 1992 (current international dollars)	1,910	20,050	1,210	8,950	2,810
Annual rate of inflation, 1980–92 (%)	6.5	7.8	8.5	5.9	11.0
Income share of highest 20%[a]	41.8	47.0	41.3	42.2	39.3
Income share of lowest 20%[a]	6.4	5.4	8.8	7.4	8.9
Agriculture as percent of GDP, 1970/1992	-/27	2/0	45/32	26/8	28/26
Manufacturing as percent of GDP, 1970/1992	-/-	29/16	15/17	21/26	17/15
Exports as percent of GDP, 1970/1992	-/-	92/144	4/10	14/-	25/32
Manufactures as percent of exports, 1970/1992	70/79	96/95	52/71	76/93	1/73
Female illiteracy, 1990	38	-	66	7	17
Adult illiteracy, 1990	27	-	52	4	12
Female life expectancy, 1970/1992 (years)	63/71	73/81	49/62	62/75	66/74
Infant mortality rate, 1970/1992 (per 1,000)	69/31	19/6	137/79	51/13	53/18
Political rights,[b] 1992	7	-	3	2	4
Civil rights,[b] 1992	7	-	4	3	5
CO_2 emissions (tons per million $ of GDP)	1,547	-	670	-	-
Rate of deforestation, 1981–85 (annual %)	-	-	0.3	-	3.5

[a] Data for India and Sri Lanka refer to expenditure shares by quintiles of persons ranked by per capita expenditure. For China, data refer to income shares by quintiles of persons ranked by per capita income. For Korea and Hong Kong, data refer to income shares by quintiles of households ranked by household income.
[b] On a scale of 1 to 7, with 1 being the best.

Sources: Freedom House, *Freedom in the World 1992–1993* (New York: Freedom House, 1993), 620–21; World Bank, *World Development Report 1994* (New York: Oxford University Press, 1994), 162–63, 166–67, 178–79, 190–91, 214–15, 220–21; World Bank, *World Development Report 1992* (New York: Oxford University Press, 1992), 204; and World Resources Institute, *World Resources 1992–1993* (New York: Oxford University Press, 1993), 266–67.

we know about the impact of socialist development policies on BBSD?

Rejection of capitalist models of development was based on three factors. First, the extraordinary development performance of the Soviet Union after the Russian Revolution suggested that there was an alternative to capitalism. Second, because most of the former colonies suffered greatly during the Great Depression, leaders of developing countries were all too aware of the instability of capitalism and its consequences for poor countries. Finally, many leaders and economists in developing countries blamed their poverty and lack of development on colonialism. As Andre Gunder Frank argued, relationships between rich and poor countries over the last three centuries fostered the development of underdevelopment in poor countries.[16] In this view, poor countries were poor and underdeveloped because the rich countries exploited them for their own benefit, denying them any chance of development.

What impact did capitalist imperialism have on the peoples of Asia, Africa, and Latin America? Critics argued that imperialism led to the extraction of wealth out of the colonies and that this prevented successful capitalist development and created dependency and underdevelopment. They believe that it continues to prevent successful capitalist development in developing countries today.

The starting point for the development of underdevelopment was the unequal nature of economic and political relationships between the first capitalist economies in Europe and North America and the emerging economies of Africa, Asia, and Latin America. During the long period of Western imperialism from the nineteenth century through World War II, imperial powers made two main types of investment in their dependent colonies.[17] First, much investment occurred in plantation agriculture. In the colonies, Europeans and North Americans produced goods—coffee, sugar, bananas, pineapples, tea, rubber—that could not be produced at home. Unfortunately, this investment did not transform the way work was done in traditional subsistence agriculture. The plantations used modern methods of production on a large scale, but traditional farmers continued growing their crops the way they had always done. This created a dual economy—one modern and highly productive, the other based on low-productivity subsistence agriculture.

The second type of investment was in extractive industries: gold, silver, bauxite, copper, tin, petroleum. This type of investment also failed to transform the colonial economies, and it reinforced dualism. The majority of skilled laborers and supervisors were imported; a few local laborers developed high-level skills and received high incomes. Small, rich enclaves grew around the mines. In the cases of both mining and agriculture, infrastructure development—such as the building of railroads to move the coffee, cocoa, copper, and petroleum to the seaports—reinforced the dual economy.

Although no great technological transformation occurred, social and economic changes did take place that had a negative impact on development. The colonizers seized the best land and drove the people off the farms into the mines or onto the plantations. This was accomplished through a variety of tactics, including slavery and indentured servitude. The economic gains from these new activities went to three different groups of people: to the Europeans and Americans who did the investing; to the expatriate elites who came from Europe and North America to manage the mines and plantations; and to the local elites, who served as managers, supervisors, and overseers.

These expatriates and local elites used their newfound incomes to establish and maintain political and security structures to ensure their continued political dominance. They also used their gains to import goods from Europe and North America that were being consumed by the elites there. The pattern of exports, imports, and consumption that followed linked the rich enclaves in these countries with economic and political power in the industrialized countries. As a result, no political or economic transformation occurred, and underdevelopment was reinforced.

A Socialist Alternative

If capitalist imperialism was the source of poverty and underdevelopment, withdrawing from the capitalist world economy and adopting a socialist model of development appeared to offer a real alternative.[18] In fact, when Russia established its system of state socialism in 1917, this was the first alternative to laissez-faire capitalism.

By state socialism, we mean an economic system in which the means of production are owned by the state rather than privately, and in which decisions about resource allocation are made by the government rather than through markets. Just as there are differences among capitalist development strategies, there are wide differences in socialist regimes. We have chosen to focus on the two most influential state socialist systems, those in Russia and China. Socialism operated quite differently in Poland and Hungary; in the market socialism practiced in Yugoslavia from the 1950s until the political breakup of that country; and in Tanzania, which attempted agrarian socialism based on Ujaama villages.

Prerevolutionary Russia and China were trapped in outdated feudal pasts. Although these countries were not formal colonies of the West, they were dependencies of the advanced capitalist countries to which they supplied food and raw materials. In both countries, revolutionary change finally swept away corrupt regimes and replaced them with anti-imperialist, antifeudal, and anticapitalist governments committed to rapid industrialization within the framework of Marxist-Leninist ideology. At the time of the Russian Revolution, no clear Marxist development model existed. The emergence of the model was strongly influenced by the nature of the Russian Revolution.

The model, although rooted in Karl Marx's economic philosophy, was dominated by the necessity of solving the problem of how to build socialism in a poor country. Russia's revolutionary Marxists were confronted with two questions. What kind of revolutionary transformation would be consistent with the philosophy of Karl Marx? And what were the implications for building socialism in a poor, economically backward peasant country surrounded by hostile, well-armed capitalist countries?

Russian Marxists answered the first question by arguing, as Marx had argued, that capitalists and laborers were in conflict within each country. Lenin, however, argued that in the new international capitalist system, imperialism would create a conflict among the capitalist countries and between rich and poor countries.[19] This gave rise to support for revolutionary movements in poor countries.

Marxists argued that the difficulties of building socialism in one poor, backward country that was militarily threatened by advanced capitalist countries required reliance on a vanguard party—the dictatorship of the proletariat.[20] This party of workers and peasants would ensure their safety from attack by both external and internal forces while they worked to build a modern industrial economy.

In both the Soviet Union and China, dictatorships of the proletariat assumed responsibility for building socialism. Politically, the totalitarian party-state protected the revolution from the reactionary forces of capitalism by outlawing multiparty competition for elective office, a free press, and autonomous organizations. Leninist political structures included a one-party state, party control over the mass media, party-state repression of human and civil rights, and state-created mass organizations and associations—which ensured that the transition would not be undermined by capitalist forces at home.

Economic strategy relied on nationalization of all foreign-owned assets, state ownership of land and industrial capital, and a central planning agency that determined prices and quantities and allocated inputs such as labor, capital, and raw materials. This system of central control was used to extract a surplus out of agriculture. The surplus was then used at the national level to finance rapid industrialization, especially the building of heavy industry.

Wilber describes the development strategy in the Soviet Union as embodying six aspects:

1. Industry was treated as the leading sector in the development program, and investment in agriculture was held to the minimum necessary to provide industry with a growing supply of agricultural products and labor.

2. A high investment (and savings) rate was maintained.

3. A large share of industrial investment was allocated to heavy industry.

4. A dual technology was adopted that employed the most advanced Western capital-intensive technology in basic production processes and labor-intensive technology in auxiliary operations. They used three shifts of workers to economize on capital and continued to use machinery long after it would have been discarded in the West.

5. Heavy emphasis was placed on vocational and technical training to build up an industrial labor force. The factories became schoolrooms after the day's work was done. Overstaffing was used to turn peasants into disciplined industrial workers.

6. An ISI policy was followed, which meant that prototypes and blueprints of factories and technicians were imported from the West and replicated in the Soviet Union until this imported capital could be used to construct factories that would replace the imports.[21]

Overall, the highly centralized Soviet system emphasized industry at the expense of agriculture, investment over consumption, heavy industry over light industry, the development of human resources, and insulation from other economies.

There were substantial differences between the Russian and Chinese development strategies, which grew out of the different experiences of taking power. In Russia, the revolution was predominantly an urban phenomenon, and the main participants were industrial workers, whereas in China it was peasant and rural based. This difference had an impact on the strategy chosen and the types of policies adopted.

Both regimes moved quickly to seize all foreign-owned assets in order to redistribute political and economic power. In the Soviet case, this took the form of centralized ownership, control of the means of production, and relatively rapid and complete expropriation of the landed estates and the industrial enterprises. In China, redistribution was somewhat less rapid. Peasants were encouraged to deal with landowners, many of whom were executed; others were incorporated into village units. Collectivization came about over a long period. Similarly, in the industrial sector, it was not uncommon for the former owner to continue working with the enterprise and receive some payment. But in both cases, the redistribution was profound.

The Chinese initially adopted a strategy of development imported from the Soviet Union. After the completion of the first five-year plan, however, they made an abrupt about-face. Whereas the Soviets' highest priority was rapid industrialization, the Chinese wanted to walk on two legs: industry and agriculture.

As the population was approximately 80 to 85 percent rural, the Chinese strategy emphasized development of the agricultural sector as well as light and heavy industry, and the pace of industrialization was slower. The prices received by farmers as compared with the prices paid by farmers were manipulated to favor the agricultural sector. Although the agricultural sector served to finance industrial development, the burden was not as extreme as that in the Soviet Union. Heavy industry received priority, but intermediate and light industry were not ignored.

Investment funds were limited, because the tax on the agricultural surplus was approximately 10 percent. As a result, the government encouraged the development of intermediate industries in rural areas. Because of the low tax and ideological biases against consumerism, more of the rural surplus was available to finance the simpler capital needs of agriculture, regional infrastructure and consumer goods industries. Encouragement of regional development harmonized with Chinese desires to create self-reliance and mass participation in production; it also checked migration from rural areas to urban centers by raising the standard of living in the countryside through increased employment and income. Urban wages were not allowed to rise.

The choice of technology played a crucial role in the Chinese strategy. Small and medium technology served the development goals of the Chinese to a greater extent than advanced Western technology could have. China relied on medium factories and labor-intensive techniques developed by the people. This technology allowed quick-yielding projects with high levels of employment.

State Socialism and BBSD

This basic Marxist-Leninist model became the pattern for most subsequent socialist development models.[22] Because the model justified the suppression of human rights in order to protect the regime, a limited social contract was created between the state and society to make this suppression more bearable.[23] In exchange for the lack of civil liberties and political power, the party-state guaranteed economic security in the form of jobs for everyone, and it promised significant increases in the standard of living and substantial benefits in health care and education.

This package of economic benefits was, in fact, the most conspicuous gain of Soviet and Chinese socialism. The Soviet Union experienced a long period of growth in which the country was transformed from a backward peasant economy to a highly industrialized one. Economic growth was truly impressive in the early years of state socialism, with a 5.5 percent average annual increase in per capita income between 1928 and 1937. This occurred alongside impressive gains in life expectancy, health status, and education (Table 3.2).

Russia experienced one of the most rapid industrializations of any country in the world. In 1913, prior to World War I, Russia was the sixth or seventh largest industrial power in the world, with an industrial output equal to approximately 12 to 13 percent that of the United States. Fifty years later, Russia was the second largest industrial power in the world, with an industrial output equal to approximately 48 percent that of the United States. This unprecedentedly rapid transformation was accomplished under very adverse circumstances.

Wilber compiled data comparing the results of development in the Soviet Union with those in Japan, which began the development process in 1868, and with Mexico, which had its revolution at approximately the same time as the Soviet Union.[24] Clearly, the Soviet Union did well in meeting the basic needs of its people—equal to or better than Japan or Mexico by 1962.

China experienced similar gains. Its long-run growth record was impressive, its basic human needs performance was remarkable, and its economic structure was radically transformed while achieving low income inequality.[25] Per capita income grew 4.2 percent per year between 1950 and 1975, prior to the market reforms. Of the ten largest developing countries, only Brazil, with 4.6 percent, had a faster rate of per capita income growth. Between 1980 and 1992, after the market reforms, per

Table 3.2 Development Performance in Russia

Period	Growth Rate of Real GNP (%)	Labor Force in Agriculture (%)[a]	Infant Mortality Rate (per 1,000)[a]	Life Expectancy (Years)[a]	Secondary Education (No. Enrolled per 1,000)[a]
1928–37	5.5[b]	–	182	47	108
1950–55	7.6[b]	–	81	–	–
1956–60	5.9[c]	41.2	35	69	361
1961–70	4.8[c]	29.3	25	70	483
1971–80	2.4[c]	23.5	27	–	638
1981–84	1.7[c]	22.5	26	68	686

Sources:
[a] B. P. Pockney, *Soviet Statistics since 1950* (New York: St. Martin's Press, 1991), 41, 67, 78, 81.
[b] A. Bergsen, *The Real National Income of Soviet Russia Since 1928* (Cambridge: Harvard University Press, 1961), 219.
[c] J. Millar, *The Soviet Experiment* (Chicago: University of Illinois Press, 1990), 187.

capita income growth was 7.6 percent per year.[26] Indicators of human development are equally impressive. Between 1958 and 1976, life expectancy increased from 41 to 67 years, and infant mortality dropped from 165 per 1,000 to 41 per 1,000 (Table 3.3).

In both countries, rapid growth ultimately gave way to slower growth, stagnating living standards, and recurrent shortages of consumer goods. The growth slowdown was partially a consequence of the high cost of maintaining an economic system that ignored economic efficiency. It was also related to diminishing returns of a growth strategy that depended on high and rising investment rates, increasing labor force participation, and increased exploitation of the resource base. Stagnating living standards and shortages of consumer goods followed directly from declining growth rates, high and rising investment rates, and the allocation of investment to heavy industry at the expense of consumer goods industries. Neither the Soviet Union nor China was able to invest and innovate in new technologies to produce new goods and services of which their people became aware.

The sociopolitical aspects of the Marxist-Leninist model also proved to be a fertile breeding ground for political opposition. In neither system was there respect for human rights, a rule of law, or accountable and transparent rule making. There was no democracy and no voluntary organizations that made up civil society. Ultimately, this absence of opportunity to protest and criticize the system and to suggest improvements was a critical problem.

The Chernobyl disaster in the Soviet Union revealed how incompetent the central government was and how little it cared about the health and welfare of the people. Environmental degradation and disregard for the safety of human beings were key in the revolutions against state socialism in Eastern Europe.

The human costs of socialist development in both the Soviet Union and China were high. No one knows how many died as a result of the forced collectivization of agriculture in the Soviet Union in the 1930s and from the purges and campaigns of terror. Total estimates range from 5 to 50 million unnatural deaths attributed to Stalin and his policies. Those who survived lived with the ever-present fear of a knock on the door one night from the secret police.

We are just now learning the costs of the strategy in China. Again, no one knows how many people died. Estimates of the number of people who starved as a result of the Great Leap Forward in 1958–61 range from 30 to 40 million. The total number of people who died of unnatural causes as a result of Mao's policies could be 40 to 80 million. This latter

Table 3.3   Development Performance in China

Period	Growth Rate of Real GNP (%)	Agriculture in Gross Value of Output[a] (%)	Infant Mortality Rate (per 1,000)	Life Expectancy (Years)	Gross Secondary School Enrollment (%)
1952–57	8.3[a]	64	–	–	–
1958–62	-1.5[b]	59	165[c]	41[c]	21[c]
1963–65	14.7[b]	42	90[d]	53[d]	24[d]
1966–75	7.3[b]	29	69[d]	62[d]	24[d]
1976–79	6.1[b]	26	41[d]	67[d]	46[d]

Sources:
[a] C. Risken, *China's Political Economy* (New York: Oxford University Press, 1988), 58, 270.
[b] International Monetary Fund, *International Financial Statistics, 1986* (Washington, D.C.: International Monetary Fund, 1986), 152–53.
[c] World Bank, *World Development Report 1983* (New York: Oxford University Press, 1983), 192, 196.
[d] World Bank, *World Tables, 1992* (Washington, D.C.: World Bank, 1992), 186–87.

figure, if true, would mean that 10 percent of the population died as a result of Mao's policies.

But we must remember that all development is a brutal, violent, wrenching process. U.S. development was based on a policy of genocide toward the Native Americans; the economy was built up on the basis of exporting cotton, an industry that employed one of the cruelest slave systems in history; and industry exploited women and children in mines and factories that were unfit places for human beings. In assessing the human costs of these social transformations and the costs of development, we must also remember that there are high costs of not developing. We are reminded of Mark Twain's comments in *A Connecticut Yankee in King Arthur's Court* on the Reign of Terror following the French Revolution, as quoted in Wilber:

> There were two "Reigns of Terror," if we would but remember it and consider it; the one brought murder in hot passion, the other in heartless cold blood; the one lasted mere months, the other lasted a thousand years; the one inflicted death upon 10,000 persons, the other upon a hundred millions; but our shudders are all for the "horrors" of the minor Terror; the momentary Terror, so to speak whereas, what is the horror of swift death by the axe, compared with life-long death from hunger, cold, insult, cruelty, and heart break?[27]

In any event, the argument that socialism is a viable development strategy or a way to achieve broad-based sustainable development is no longer tenable. In the 1980s and 1990s, both the Soviet Union and China attempted to reform their economies and polities in strikingly different ways. China became more market oriented, and the Soviet Union became more democratic. Chapter 6 analyzes these differences.

Notes

Many of the ideas in this chapter appeared in either James H. Weaver and Kenneth Jameson, *Development Economics: Competing Paradigms* (Lanham, Md.: University Press of America, 1981), or James H. Weaver and Kevin O'Keefe, "Whither Development Economics?" *SAIS Review* 12 (Summer 1991): 113–34.

1. Adam Smith, *An Inquiry into the Nature and Causes of the Wealth of Nations* [1776] (New York: Modern Library, 1937), 14.

2. R. Prebisch, "The Role of Commercial Policy in Underdeveloped Countries," *American Economic Review* 40 (May 1959): 251–73.

3. For instance, Ghana in the early 1980s declared that US$1 was equal to 2.75 cedis. When the value of the currency was later set by market forces, US$1 equaled 275 cedis. Thus, the exchange had been set at 100 times its market value by the Ghanaian government.

4. Albert Fishlow, "Brazilian Size Distribution of Income," *American Economic Review* 62 (May 1972): 391–402.

5. Simon Kuznets, "Economic Growth and Income Inequality," *American Economic Review* 45 (March 1955): 1–28.

6. Irma Adelman and Cynthia Taft Morris, *Economic Growth and Social Equity in Developing Countries* (Palo Alto, Calif.: Stanford University Press, 1973).

7. International Labor Organization (ILO), *Employment, Growth and Basic Needs: A One-World Problem* (Geneva: ILO, 1976).

8. International Labor Organization (ILO), *Employment, Incomes and Equality: A Strategy for Increasing Productive Employment in Kenya* (Geneva: ILO, 1972).

9. I. Little, T. Scitovsky, and M. Scott, *Industry and Trade in Some Developing Countries* (Oxford: Oxford University Press, 1970).

10. Irma Adelman, "Beyond Export-Led Growth," *World Development* 12 (1984): 937–49.

11. John Mellor, *The New Economics of Growth* (Ithaca, N.Y.: Cornell University Press, 1976).

12. Hollis Chenery et al., *Redistribution with Growth: An Approach to Policy* (Oxford: Oxford University Press, 1974).

13. Irma Adelman, "Growth, Income Distribution and Equity-Oriented Development Strategies," *World Development* 3 (February–March 1975): 67–76.

14. Paul Streeten and S. Burki, "Basic Needs: Some Issues," *World Development* 6 (March 1978): 411–21; Mahbub ul Haq, "The Crisis of Development Strategies," in *The Political Economy of Development and Underdevelopment*, ed. Charles K. Wilber (New York: Random House, 1973).

15. Dani Rodrik of Columbia University argues that initial conditions explain much, if not most, of the success in East Asia. See D. Rodrik, "King Kong Meets Godzilla: The World Bank and the East Asian Miracle," mimeo (New York: Columbia University, 1994).

16. A. G. Frank, "Development of Underdevelopment," in *The Political Economy of Development and Underdevelopment*, 4th ed., ed. Charles K. Wilber (New York: Random House, 1988).

17. C. Furtado, *Economic Development of Latin America: A Survey from Colonial Times to the Cuban Revolution* (Cambridge: Cambridge University Press, 1970).

18. V. I. Lenin, *Imperialism: The Highest Stage of Capitalism* (New York: International Publishers, 1939).

19. Lenin, *Imperialism*.

20. A. G. Meyer, *Leninism* (Cambridge: Harvard University Press, 1957), 185–216.

21. Charles K. Wilber, *The Soviet Model and Underdeveloped Countries* (Chapel Hill: University of North Carolina Press, 1969), chap. 5.

22. Over time, China developed its own version of socialism that was distinct from the Soviet model. For a discussion of this model, see C. Risken, *China's Political Economy* (New York: Oxford University Press, 1988), chaps. 6, 9, 10; F. Schurmann, *Ideology and Organization in Communist China* (Berkeley: University of California Press, 1968), chaps. 1, 4, 7; and Mao Ze Dong *A Critique of Soviet Economics* (New York: Monthly Review Press, 1977).

23. J. Ludlam, "Reform and the Redefinition of the Social Contract under Gorbachev," *World Politics* 43 (January 1991): 285–312. The Chinese seemed to recognize the importance of such a social contract following the death of Mao Zedong. Risken, *China's Political Economy*, chap. 11.

24. Wilber, *The Soviet Model*, 114, table VI-3.

25. Both China and the Soviet Union developed with low income inequality. In the early 1980s, China's gini coefficient (.33) was among the lowest in Asia and the world. The gini coefficient can range from zero (one person has everything) to one (all people have equal shares). Risken, *China's Political Economy*, 250. Income inequality was also low in the Soviet Union. A. McAuley, *Economic Welfare in the Soviet Union* (Madison: University of Wisconsin Press, 1979), 66, 359.

26. World Bank, *World Development Report 1994* (New York: Oxford University Press, 1994), 162.

27. Wilber, *The Soviet Model*, 118.

Part II

Macro Policies for Broad-Based Sustainable Development

Introduction to Part II

*B*ECAUSE WE ARE AT A POINT IN HISTORY where the role of national governments in development performance is so misunderstood, much of the rest of the book focuses on what governments must do to promote BBSD. In this part of the book (Chapters 4–6), we identify the macro (political and economic) policies that must be followed.

There is universal agreement across the political spectrum that good governance—the role of central government in creating the physical, legal, and social infrastructure that permits markets to function, private firms to operate, and community organizations to flourish—is a necessary precondition for development of any kind. In Chapter 4 we examine why this is so; we present and evaluate alternative routes to good governance and identify specific things governments must do to promote it. Contrary to those who promote minimalist government, governments must do many things and do them well if BBSD is to happen.

But the evidence is equally clear that although political stability and good governance are necessary for BBSD, they are not sufficient. A government's macroeconomic or economy-wide policies—exchange rate, fiscal, monetary, and credit policies—also matter. Chapter 5 identifies the economy-wide policies—stabilization and structural adjustment policies—necessary for BBSD; reviews developing country experience with those policies, particularly that of the highly successful East Asian newly industrializing countries (NICs); and critiques neo-liberal economy-wide policies pursued by donor organizations such as the World Bank and the U.S. Agency for International Development (USAID).

Three main points emerge from this chapter: (1) No developing country has been able to sustain economic growth in the absence of macroeconomic stability. (2) Macroeconomic stability and rapid economic growth do not automatically translate into rapid improvements in human development, low income inequality, or a low incidence of poverty. For this to happen, growth policies must increase the demand for those income-producing assets that are most equitably distributed (labor and land), and governments must invest in people, particularly their primary education and their primary health care. (3) The neo-liberal policies pushed on developing countries by donor organizations such as the World Bank and USAID are excessively ideological and inconsistent with the behavior of those countries that have come closest to achieving BBSD.

This part of the book closes with an examination (Chapter 6) of what reforming socialist economies (China and Russia) must do if they are to achieve both good governance and sound economy-wide policies for BBSD. The list of things that must be done and the differences in the sequencing and timing of political and economic reform in socialism's two giants show how difficult and contentious the process of reform is.

4

The Role of Governance

WHAT ARE THE PURPOSES OF GOVERNMENT? Those of us who have grown up in the United States tend to answer this question by referring to the Preamble to the U.S. Constitution:

> We, the people of the United States, in order to form a more perfect Union, establish justice, insure domestic tranquility, provide for the common defense, promote the general welfare, and secure the blessings of liberty to ourselves and our posterity, do ordain and establish this Constitution for the Unites States of America.

How do we achieve these ends through government? What does it mean to govern?

Government Functions and Governance Capacity

What does a government do when it governs? It chooses, implements, and enforces policies that are embodied in a system of laws and regulations. It produces routine regulatory actions. It issues licenses and permits; allocates access to government resources and subsidies; monitors compliance of companies, nongovernmental organizations (NGOs), and individuals; and intervenes to stop activities that do not meet regulatory standards. It either produces public goods and services itself—such as roads, schools, and clinics—or contracts for these goods and services. Then it distributes access to governmental goods and services among the citizenry according to its own criteria of need and program eligibility. *Effective governance* refers to the government's ability to do these things efficiently.

The current emphasis on the importance of effective governance to development comes partly from a recognition of government's vital role in creating the physical, legal, and social infrastructure that permits markets to function, private firms to operate, and community organizations to flourish. Even in a development strategy that expects the private and nongovernmental sectors to be the engines of growth, it turns out that effective government is a key prerequisite for that growth. Paradoxically, a strategy that de-emphasizes government as the source and means of growth ends up emphasizing the tasks the government retains.

We do not endorse a minimalist view of the role that government can and should play. It is nevertheless instructive to examine the free-market-oriented minimalist perspective, because this view turns out to endorse the idea of increased governance capacity in many areas of government in the developing world. If governments are to do what Adam Smith and Milton Friedman thought of as their minimal functions,[1] they must not reduce but rather expand their activities and capacities in key areas. These functions include (1) providing the physical and educational infrastructure necessary for a national economy; (2) establishing and maintaining the system of law that creates the societal rules of the game; (3) defending the law and order of this system against external military threats and internal illegality; (4) arbitrating disputes through a judicial system; (5) managing a sound system of currency that allows the economy to function without monetary disruption; (6) monitoring and adjusting the rules of the game to deal successfully with **market failures**; (7) dealing with natural monopolies to ensure that they are not run against the public interest; and (8) providing a safety net of last resort for the welfare of people unable to provide for themselves. Government must also do its part to establish and maintain a **societal infrastructure** without which no complex society can survive and no economy can function.

■ **market failure** *situation in which private firms cannot make a profit producing necessary goods or can increase profits by dumping their costs on the public*

■ **societal infrastructure** *physical transport and communications systems, institutions, and stable systems of rules and norms*

Stagnating societies are frequently those in which the government has been unable to make necessary improvements in the administration of key governmental functions and has tried to do many things that governments do not have to do—for example, running hotels, marketing boards, and fertilizer plants. As a result, the transport, power, and communications infrastructure is inadequate to support increased investment or production. The educational infrastructure is inadequate to provide the skilled labor for industrial expansion. The currency management system breaks down repeatedly, leading to rampant inflation; the resulting investment risks are so high that even local capitalist investors choose to invest their money outside of the country. Chronically poor societies will be able to develop only if their governments can dramatically improve their governance capacity.

Development disasters—societies that are moving away from BBSD rather than toward it, sometimes with cataclysmic speed—are societies in which the government has grown increasingly unable to provide one or more of these necessary elements. Frequently, the maintenance of law and order has broken down in the face of civil conflict, as demonstrated in Somalia, Cambodia, Lebanon, Rwanda, Liberia, Haiti, and Yugoslavia, among others. In development disasters, the first priority for reconstruction, after humanitarian relief has begun to meet basic human needs, is to reconstitute a government with the capacity to carry out its necessary functions. This is an extremely difficult job, calling for diplomatic, organizational, and managerial skills appropriate to the cultural and societal context. It is the area of development where the least is known and the applicability of generic how-to techniques is most open to question. But nothing is more essential for development. The realization of this fact on the part of development professionals and donor agencies has led to increased funding for governance projects in recent years, despite a lack of experience and the absence of a repertoire of tested interventions that are known to work.

Power, Legitimacy, and Governance

The new governance initiatives in many developing countries are beginning to build up a body of specific concepts about what it means to improve governance. But many of these findings are not intuitively obvious. To understand them, some basic political science concepts must be examined: how governments get the power to govern, and the role of legitimacy in maintaining that power.

The power pyramid is a conceptualization of the answer to what has been the basic question of political science since Machiavelli:[2] how do leaders get followers to follow their lead? When rulers set rules and issue commands, the rules must be respected and the commands obeyed, or the rulers will lose their ability to rule. Successful leaders have little trouble getting almost all people to respect almost all their rules and obey almost all their commands. They are routinely able to maintain and exercise their power. Unsuccessful leaders have a great deal of trouble getting anyone to respect any of their rules or obey any of their commands. They are rarely able to scrape together enough power to actually do any leading. What makes the difference? Max Weber, a founder of both political science and sociology in the 1890s, is the source of most of the concepts that modern social scientists use to address this question, which are summarized in Figure 4.1.[3]

The bedrock on which power rests is the ability to use force, and to maintain the credible threat of using force, to ensure that rules are followed and commands obeyed. Force is the basis for Weber's famous minimum definition of a government: that entity that has a monopoly over the use of force among a given population in a given territory. If a government loses its ability to enforce its rule over the population of an area, due to either a political insurgency or unchecked crime (gangs, bandits, warlords), then it ceases to be a real (de facto) government of that population, even if it hangs on to its international recognition as the nominal (de jure) government.

Although force is the indispensable minimum for successful rule, it is not very efficient. If compliance with every command requires enough physical coercion to keep the constant threat of force credible, then the ruler has to limit the number of commands issued, spend huge resources on military enforcement, or, most likely, do both. This describes the initial situation of a government based on conquest and military occupation of a hostile population. All its resources and energies must be spent merely to stay in power.

It is much more efficient to buy compliance with the hope of reward than to coerce compliance with the fear of force. That is what patronage systems do. They distribute access to government benefits (services, jobs, subsidies, contracts, and so forth) in such a way as to provide tangible benefits to those who respect and obey and to withhold benefits from those who are least cooperative. But a patronage-based system of government can work only if it violates some norms of universality (government benefits and services should be equally accessible to all citizens) and some norms of efficiency (government benefits and services should be distributed to maximize impact, meet the greatest need, and make the biggest difference).

Reformers have often scorned patronage-based governments, but they can be remarkably effective. When the population to be governed is ethnically diverse and culturally heterogeneous, or when the population is ■ statecraft *the art of* unused to dealing with a national level of government, or *conducting state affairs* when the government is new, patronage may be the best basis for **statecraft**. This was the case when urban political machines built city governments with immigrant populations during the industrializa-

Figure 4.1 The Power Pyramid: How Rulers Get the Ruled
to Follow the Rules

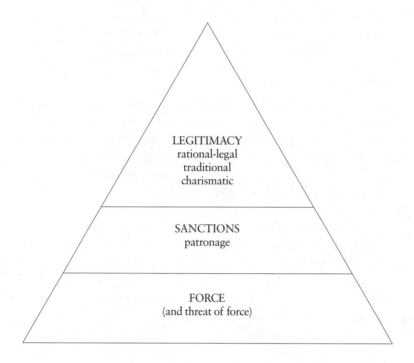

tion of the United States, and it was the case in Africa and Asia when
"big men" built multiethnic states in the early stages of postcolonial
political independence.

Patronage governments cannot continue to govern, however, in the
absence of rewards to distribute. Since they are, in essence, buying cooperation, they can govern only as long as they have resources. If the
resource base dries up, the ability to govern decays. When industries and
their tax revenues fled the American cities after World War II, heading
first for the suburbs and the rural south and then overseas, America's
urban political machines lost their support and collapsed. When in newly
independent Africa the traditional colonial-era export base declined from
lack of renewed investment, and the new government's export tax base
shriveled, the ruling "big men" looked smaller and their governments
collapsed.

If buying compliance is more efficient than forcing it, think how efficient it would be if compliance were free and voluntary. Free and voluntary compliance is the great gift to government that legitimacy can provide. When citizens believe that a government has rightfully set a rule or rightfully issued a command, they also believe that the only acceptable response is to respect the rule or obey the command. In such cases, citizens comply with the government because they think that they should. In the eyes of these citizens, the government has legitimacy.

Since legitimacy is such a boon to those who would govern, all leaders seek it. They do so by appealing to the citizens on one of three grounds: tradition or habit, charisma, or rational legality. Often, a leader makes all three appeals, emphasizing different ones to different constituencies. Legitimacy cannot be asserted; it is not a property of government. Rather, it is a belief or attitude of citizens about the government. Therefore, a government may be legitimate in the eyes of some citizens and not in others.

The oldest, and still the most common, form of legitimacy is traditional or habitual legitimacy. It is present when a ruler has taken power in the traditionally accepted way (for instance, by inheritance from the previous ruler) and when the ruler follows tradition in the setting of rules and the issuing of commands. In this case, compliance can become uncritical and even habitual. The rules are familiar, and obedience to them is an unquestioned way of life, like driving on the right side of the road. In well-ordered societies, habitual legitimacy is the source of much of the order. But as a source of innovation and change, it is useless. If a traditional leader starts issuing new rules and unconventional commands, the citizens will think them illegitimate. Not only that, but the citizens will start questioning the legitimacy of all the other rules and commands as well, because the habit of unquestioning compliance has been broken.

Historically, traditional legitimacy has been the most durable type. Any leader who stays in power long enough will acquire some measure of it. But the modern era of global information is not a hospitable time for traditional legitimacy. Citizens who are exposed to political traditions other than their own—as all are today—are less likely to assume that their government's way of doing things is the only way that things should be done.

Charismatic leaders can make their own legitimacy. Leaders are charismatic to the extent that they articulate the sense of identity and the deep aspirations of their followers. Political charisma is a secularized version of religious charisma. When people look at a charismatic political leader, they see not the essence of God but the essence of their own identity. To the followers, a charismatic leader is a living embodiment of their collective self. Unlike tradition, charisma puts no limit on its legitimacy. Followers freely and voluntarily respect any rule and obey any command the charismatic leader makes, because they own the rules and commands as if they were theirs. Leaders of revolutions in the twentieth century are remarkable examples of charisma at work: Lenin in the USSR, Hitler in Germany, Mao in China, Castro in Cuba, and Mandela in South Africa.

Although charisma puts no limits on legitimacy, charisma itself is limited in scope and transitory in time. Charisma does not travel well across ethnic or cultural lines. The very forces of personality and style that make a leader charismatic within one culture make the same leader seem alien and uncongenial in another cultural context. Charisma is also subject to what Weber called *routinization*. It can never be handed on to a successor, and even the original leader loses charisma over time as routine administrative decisions are made about resource allocations. There is no way for a leader to decide which neighborhoods get a sewer this year and which ones will have to wait without dissipating some of his or her charisma.

Although it seems at first that charisma is not a learned trait—either you have it or you don't—this is not true. It is possible for a leader to create a situation in which citizens are more likely to perceive him or her as charismatic. The way to do this is to heighten the sense of ethnic national identity. The more fervently nationalist the population, the more charisma the people are likely to perceive in their national leaders. Since nothing builds nationalism like a strong external threat, it is possible for military leaders who face genuine external threats—like Park Chung Hee in South Korea, Chiang Kai-shek in Taiwan, or Fidel Castro in Cuba—to maintain a nationalist charismatic legitimacy over quite a long time. Historically, this is one of the two most important sources of change-oriented durable legitimacy.

The other source of change-oriented durable legitimacy is constitutionalism. A government can appeal for rational-legal legitimacy if it can show that its rules and commands are legal. Two kinds of legality are required. First, the rules and commands must be issued by the constitutionally authorized leaders following constitutional procedures. Second, the content of the rules and commands themselves must fall within a rational interpretation of what the constitution mandates. In other words, rational-legal legitimacy can exist when a prior constitution or social contract exists and when the current government can successfully invoke prior agreement as the authorization for its current commands.

In European political history, constitutions or social contracts replaced divine right as the basis of legitimate government. By their nature, they are, at least in principle, somewhat democratic, since constitutions reflect agreements reached between at least one group of people and the government. Generally, the group that makes the social contract is not the entire population of the country to be governed. The citizens whose representatives approved the U.S. Constitution, for example, included all residents of the colonies who were free, white, male, and property owners. Then, as now, they were only a small minority of the total population that came under the rule of the new government. Yet the Constitution was and still is a sufficient basis for almost all the population to view succeeding governments as having rational-legal legitimacy.

Everywhere in the world today, the core social contract between a government and its citizenry is that the people expect the government to produce development. Governments that are able to bring about development can gain increased legitimacy from their performance. Conversely, failure to produce development eats away at rational-legal legitimacy. Even constitutionally elected governments that are unable to provide development for their citizens find themselves resorting increasingly to patronage and force to maintain their hold on power, while growing more vulnerable to an unconstitutional overthrow. Even in a culture like the United States—where the idea of a smaller and less obtrusive government is popular, and cynicism about government's importance is everywhere—local, state, and federal officials are judged overwhelmingly on their ability to bring economic development to their constituents. The legitimacy of governments in developing countries is even more dependent on their ability to produce development.

The traditional politician's instinctive response to improved governance—and, not coincidentally, to increased power—is to try to move up the power pyramid. Political leaders seek to expand the proportion of the population that views the government as legitimate. To the extent that they are successful, patronage resources are freed up for use among hostile segments of the population that have previously cooperated only from fear of force. To the extent that patronage motivates new obedience to the government's policies, police and military resources can then be concentrated where they are most needed to extend the government's rule among populations that are most hostile to it.

To increase a government's legitimacy is to increase its governance capacity. Increased legitimacy means that policies can be more easily implemented, with fewer resources devoted to monitoring and enforcing obedience to the regulations. The greater a government's legitimacy, the larger the number of policies it can support. Decreasing legitimacy quickly results in decreasing governance capacity. Therefore, policies that fail to deliver development, thereby reducing rational-legal legitimacy in growing sectors of the public, result in decreased governance capacity, and a downward spiral of development failure can result.

Dimensions of Effective Governance

Some ingredients of effective governance are systemic to the whole government and the way it relates to people and organizations in the country. Reforms in these areas could improve governance in all government agencies. The payoff from these systemic reforms is potentially much greater than improving the skills of one manager at a time or improving the manageability of one agency at a time. The World Bank's report on governance identifies these areas as technical expertise, organizational effectiveness, accountability, rule of law, and transparency.[4]

Technical Competence and Expertise

One obvious source of effective governance is the technical knowledge and skills of the people in the government who make and carry out the decisions. Do the managers of the finance ministry have the necessary knowledge of economics? Does the justice ministry know law? The agricultural ministry farming? The educational ministry teaching? For two generations, development agencies have concentrated on providing training and technical assistance to expand the knowledge base of government officials in developing countries. As a result, the knowledge gap between experts in the industrialized countries and their counterparts in many developing countries has been greatly narrowed. Around the world, people with college degrees are increasingly likely to have similar technical training. Technical expertise remains a critical factor in effective governance, but it is less likely to be the decisive governance constraint in poor countries that it once was.

In formerly closed societies, where faculties and students in institutions of higher education were relatively unaffected by new ideas and new knowledge in their fields, technical training may be important. Under these conditions, which include most countries emerging from the Soviet system, the knowledge gap is obvious; it is perceived by all concerned, and the thirst for technical training is great. Professional training of government employees in these circumstance can be money well spent.

Organizational Effectiveness

Another technical obstacle to effective governance may be the organizational and managerial structure of the government. Even if managers have the technical training to decide what actions should be taken, do their organizations have the capacity to follow through on these decisions? Do the management systems, the incentive systems, and the communications systems of the agency encourage the rapid identification and solution of problems, or do they tie the agency up in endless red tape or battles over turf? Organizational effectiveness or manageability, as it is sometimes called, is another obvious key to effective governance. Here too, the gap between most industrialized and developing societies might not be great, because most countries in the world consider the issue of reinventing government or increasing the effectiveness and productivity of government agencies to be a major problem.

It is ironic, though, that one of the keys to increased organizational effectiveness in many government agencies of the developing world is increased bureaucratization. Bureaucracy is a form of organization, first developed in the world's most modern military systems, for the mass production of routine services (such as unemployment compensation payments) and routine decisions (such as building permit approvals). Bureaucracies are characterized by a specialized division of labor, a system for classifying the infinite number of individual clients or applicants into a finite number of types of cases, a set of procedures for treating each type of case in the same way, and meticulous record keeping so that the file for each case can be passed from one department to the next until the process has been completed and the service provided or the decision made. Cases are processed in a bureaucracy like cars on an assembly line, and the result is more decisions made or services provided than could ever be accomplished if each case were handled individually. Bureaucracies are impersonal, but the impersonality can result in decisions that are fair and universalistic—citizens do not have to know somebody or pay a bribe to get services. Bureaucracies are unable to deal with truly unique cases, but these can be handled by more skilled and knowledgeable employees in a special process for exceptions to the normal rules. The problem in many bureaucracies, especially in developing countries, is that every case processed is treated as an exception, and the routine cases (of applicants or clients with no money or influence) pile up and are never processed.

Accountability

Accountability means holding people responsible for their performance and holding managers responsible for the results of their decisions. Accountability can range from the narrow, technical concept of financial accountability, which holds people responsible for correct handling of the money they control, to the broad concept of political accountability, which holds officials responsible for living up to the expectations they created while campaigning for election. In analyzing accountability, it is necessary to consider (1) who is being held responsible (2) to whom they are being held responsible and (3) how they are being held responsible.

The minimum core of effective accountability is a form of organization with a functioning division of labor and definition of management responsibilities. It is present in an organization to the extent that all important responsibilities are assigned to specific individuals, there are positive or negative consequences for those whose responsibilities are fulfilled or not, and individuals know to whom they report in the carrying out of their responsibilities.

Democracy and political participation are increased when accountability is supplemented by additional lines of responsibility to create a built-in system of checks and balances. This happens when government officials are responsible not only to their bureaucratic superiors on the organizational chart but also to a political party or constituency organization that they must keep satisfied and to a professional association that insists on its own standards for their performance. Thus, a lawyer working in an environmental protection agency may have to account for her actions not only to her own direct superior but also to environmental monitoring groups and to the standards of professional competence and ethics of the bar association.

This may slow down an agency, as conflicting demands must be worked out to the point where an operational consensus is possible, but it also greatly increases the visibility of the agency's performance and reduces the likelihood of graft and corruption. Some of the most effective governance development projects have focused less on managerial reorganization within the government and more on strengthening professional and civil society organizations that hold government agencies accountable.

Rule of Law

Governance is enhanced to the extent that there exists a functioning and effective rule of law. The rule of law refers not only to the actual content of regulations but, more importantly, to the institutional process by which rules are made, amended, interpreted, and enforced. An effective rule of law is conducive both to democracy and to rational-legal or constitutional legitimacy. Its role in development is to maximize the ease with which private firms and NGOs can assess the legal risks associated with their plans of action, thus maximizing the likelihood that firms and NGOs will be innovative and active. Stability is key to an effective rule of law. But since no system of rules can be literally stable and unchanging in a dynamic environment, the stability must come from an open and predictable process for changing the rules.

Transparency and Open Information Systems

Both accountability and an effective rule of law require open and public procedures—in other words, transparency. They also require that information about the economy and society be regularly and objectively collected and widely published. Without information about policy and program results, policy and program accountability is almost meaningless. Transparency and good information systems are thus two additional characteristics of a system of effective governance.

Measuring Governance

There have been no successful systematic efforts to measure governance quantitatively. The absence of effective governance is readily apparent: public resources are diverted to private ends, laws are not widely publicized at the time they are implemented, laws are enforced arbitrarily or not at all, and no honest data are publicly available. Everyone agrees that governance is an important component of BBSD, but nobody claims to know how to measure it or how to tell whether governance in a particular country is growing marginally better or marginally worse from one year to the next. It is possible to compare the annual performance of particular agencies in terms of cost-effectiveness and efficiency. In essence, this requires keeping track of the agency's output (immunizations by the public health department, miles of road repaired by the highway department) and comparing the ratio of those outputs to the expenses involved. But these measures are unique to each type of agency. They cannot be meaningfully compared or aggregated to get an overall picture of governmental effectiveness.

One increasingly common approach to measuring and monitoring governmental effectiveness is through public-opinion polls. This is not a precise measure of actual governmental performance, but it has several advantages. It can measure legitimacy very effectively, and it can increase democratic accountability if the opinion polling is performed regularly and independently and if the results are announced publicly. Thanks to new computer and communications technology, opinion polling is cheap and easy and its practice is growing throughout the world.

Notes

1. Adam Smith, *An Inquiry into the Nature and Causes of the Wealth of Nations* (New York: Modern Library, 1937); Milton Friedman, *Capitalism and Freedom* (Chicago: University of Chicago Press, 1962).
2. Niccolo Machiavelli, *The Prince* (New York: Heritage Press, 1954).
3. Max Weber, "Class, Status and Power," in *From Max Weber*, ed. Hans Gerth and C. Wright Mills (New York: Free Press, 1948). This essay is an excerpt from the three-volume masterwork *Economy and Society*, from which the concepts in much of the following discussion are drawn.
4. World Bank, *Managing Development: The Governance Dimension* (Washington, D.C.: World Bank, 1991).

5

Economic Policies

CLEARLY, THE EVIDENCE IS PERSUASIVE that political stabil-ity and good governance are essential prerequisites for development. Without them, development of any kind is impossible. But these neces-sary conditions are not sufficient conditions. In addition, macroeconomic policies play an important role in achieving broad-based sustainable development (BBSD). The purpose of this chapter is to describe these macroeconomic policies—stabilization and structural adjustment. We conclude with a discussion of the linkages between macroeconomic poli-cies and mobilization of the people at the grassroots.

Experiences of developing countries suggest that there are substantial social, political, and economic benefits to be gained by actively partici-pating in the world economy. With the collapse of socialist and inward-looking models of development, it has also become clear that the costs of isolation tend to be more than most countries can afford. Although we are strong proponents of openness in economics and politics, it is impor-tant to recognize that economic participation in the world economy both enhances and constrains national choices and independence. Participation in the international economy must be structured in ways that enhance the prospects for BBSD.

Achieving these goals is not easy. Very few countries have been consis-tently successful for long periods of time. In the first section of this chap-ter, we draw on the lessons of that experience to delineate what developing countries need to do in managing their economic interactions with the rest of the world.

Macroeconomic Stabilization

We measure a country's economic activity with the rest of the world by the balance of payments. Because developing countries have low incomes and economies that are very dependent on imports, most run a deficit in their **balance of trade**, that is, they buy more goods and services (imports) from the rest of the world than they sell to the rest of the world (exports). This is not a problem as long as they can finance these deficits. But how do developing countries normally finance these deficits?[1] They borrow from suppliers, commercial banks, international financial organizations, and multinational corporations.[2] As long as the bor-rowed capital is invested wisely so that it increases growth and generates sufficient income to pay back accumulated foreign debt, countries can sustain balance-of-trade deficits. But if borrowed funds are spent on consumption or, worse yet, wasted, countries can find themselves unable to service their foreign debts or unable to meet their import needs. Eventually, suppliers stop making credit available, and lenders stop lending money. When this happens, countries have to reestablish a balance between what they are earning abroad and what they are spending abroad. They must achieve a sustainable balance of payments.

■ **balance of trade** *relationship between the value of goods and services imported and the value of those exported*

In order to do this, they have to change domestic macroeconomic poli-cies. They have to slow the rate of growth of the money supply, reduce the size of the government's fiscal deficit, and devalue the exchange rate. This requires sacrificing domestic economic objectives such as full employment, rapid economic growth, or expansion of the public school system in the short run to meet balance-of-payments objectives. This set of policies is called *stabilization*.

It is important to recognize that no country since 1950 has been able to sustain development of any sort without prudently managing the macroeconomic policy or maintaining macroeconomic stability. Poor macroeconomic management is rampant in both developing and indus-trialized countries, including the United States. The most serious prob-lems are rapid growth in the money supply and high inflation, large government fiscal deficits, and overvalued exchange rates. These lead to unsustainable, or unfinanceable, current account deficits for all countries except the United States, which is the only country that can pay its foreign bills with its own national currency.

When current account deficits are unsustainable, countries inevitably run out of foreign currency to pay off foreign debts and to import the things they need for development.[3] At this point, the country turns to the International Monetary Fund (IMF) as the lender of last resort, which requires as a condition for the loan that the government change its macroeconomic policies.

There are two techniques for resolving the problem of unsustainable balance of payments deficits: expenditure reduction and **expenditure switching**. Virtually all IMF agreements have both an expenditure-reducing and an expenditure-switching component.

Countries must reduce expenditures if they are going to bring their demand for foreign goods into balance with their ability to pay for those goods. The IMF advocates two methods of reducing spending. The first

■ **expenditure switching** *spending less on imports, spending more on locally made import substitutes, and producing more goods for export*

is to reduce the growth of money and credit, particularly to the public sector. The second is to get government to reduce the fiscal deficit—the gap between government revenues and government expenditures. Quite often, public-sector borrowing from the central bank and public-sector deficits contribute heavily to the current account deficit. Limits are placed on how much credit can be increased, which restricts business activity. Limits are also placed on how much of the credit can go to the government. If no limits are established on government borrowing, the government will borrow all the credit available, and the private sector will be crowded out.

The problem with these policies is that a recession results. For this reason, IMF programs are referred to as *austerity programs*. Government spending and private spending are reduced. People lose their jobs, and incomes fall. This is a painful process, and countries are urged to avoid this problem if they can. Usually, IMF support is not requested until a country has no other alternative. When this happens, the country's macroeconomic position is usually desperate, and the country is forced to sacrifice a significant amount of national autonomy over economic policymaking. But this is not always the case. A number of countries in East Asia, including South Korea, repeatedly use the IMF to help them solve short-run balance-of-payments problems. When IMF assistance is used this way, countries can preserve more autonomy of action.

Expenditure switching means to devote more of a country's resources to producing goods for export and to producing goods that compete with imports. If this happens, imports fall and exports rise, and the balance-of-trade deficit is reduced. But how can we get people to switch

■ **devalue** *to reduce the value of a currency relative to other currencies*

their expenditures in this fashion? The easiest way to bring about expenditure switching is to **devalue** the currency. Let's say the exchange rate of the Tanzanian shilling is Sh200 = US$1. If we devalue to Sh400 = US$1, what will be the effect on exports and imports? Imports that had cost US$1 will now cost Tanzanians Sh400 instead of Sh200. The price of imports has just doubled. What will Tanzanians do? Import less. They will switch to domestically produced goods if such substitute goods are available. What about exporters? They previously got Sh200 for each $1 they earned for their exports. Now they will get Sh400 for each $1. What will they do? Export more. And that is exactly what we want to happen. Imports go down. Exports go up.

Why are countries so reluctant to undertake devaluation, if it is so effective in switching expenditures? There are many reasons. It is inflationary. Import prices go up, and this causes other prices to go up. However, if the central bank does not increase the money supply, the amount of inflation can be limited. There is also a prestige factor at work. Governments hate to have to devalue their currency. It implies a weak economy. Some people, particularly social, economic, and political elites, benefit from low local currency prices of the dollar. For those elites who can get foreign exchange at this price, it is a real bargain. They lose from devaluation.

What do we know about the effectiveness of stabilization policies? There have been many statistical studies that try to answer this question. Because economics and economic policy are not laboratory sciences, it is difficult to separate the effects of policies on outcomes from the influence of other events (such as a decline in the terms of trade). Despite this problem, evidence from a number of studies suggests that, taken together, expenditure-reducing and expenditure-switching policies bring the balance of payments back into a sustainable position. There is less agreement about the impact of stabilization on inflation, investment, growth, poverty, and income distribution.[4]

Macroeconomic Policies

Macroeconomic stability must be followed by correct macroeconomic policies. Before turning to those policies, it is necessary to review some basic arguments about the relationship among economic growth, income inequality, and the incidence of poverty.

Rapid economic growth does not automatically translate into rapid improvements in human development, income inequality, or the incidence of poverty. Sometimes, as in Brazil, growth is very unequal. But sometimes, as in Indonesia or Korea, it results in low inequality and rapid declines in the incidence of poverty. It is also clear that it is difficult to improve life expectancy, literacy, and infant mortality rates and achieve a low incidence of poverty in the absence of economic growth. This means that it is important to strive for a particular kind of economic growth, one that contributes to broad-based development.

As Table 5.1 shows, the countries in East Asia have been most successful in achieving such growth. How have they done this? The answer depends on three factors. The first is the initial distribution of income-producing assets—land (including natural resources), labor (including educated labor), and capital. If those assets are more rather than less equitably distributed at the beginning of the development process, growth will be more equitable and have a larger impact on reducing poverty. If those assets are inequitably distributed, growth will be more inequitable and have less of an impact on reducing poverty.

The second factor is that growth contributes more to income equality and poverty reduction if it increases the demand for those income-producing assets that are most equitably distributed. Whether this happens depends on government policies. If those policies promote an employment-generating growth process, income inequality and poverty will be lower than if those policies promoted use of capital rather than labor. Similarly, if government policies increase the productivity of small farmer agriculture, growth will result in less income inequality and less poverty. But if those policies promote plantation and mechanized agriculture, growth will be more unequal and result in more poverty.

Finally, growth results in less inequality and less poverty if governments invest in people, particularly in their primary education and their primary health care, which will make them more productive workers. But if government policies favor higher education for the few at the expense of primary education for the many, or if they favor curative health care in the urban areas at the expense of preventive health care in the rural areas, growth will be less equitable and will not reduce poverty.

What all this means is that macroeconomic policies for broad-based growth must focus on reducing inequalities in the distribution of income-producing assets and increasing the demand for those same assets. When this happens, we may get broad-based growth.

Unfortunately, colonialism led to extreme concentration of assets and incomes. And most postcolonial governments continued the policies followed by the colonial powers, with the benefits going to local elites. All too often, their agricultural, health, education, and macroeconomic growth policies only made the concentration worse.

Because most developing countries adopted policies to isolate the domestic economy from the international economy, they failed to take advantage of the gains from trade and foreign investment flows. The countries that did take advantage of those opportunities, especially those in East and Southeast Asia, grew faster, had the most rapid reduction in the incidence of poverty, and had the lowest income inequality.

What macroeconomic policy changes are necessary for growth to reduce poverty and contribute to low income inequality? An eclectic consensus about these issues is emerging among development economists. Although they tend to agree on what needs to be done, there is less agreement on how to do it. In what follows, we first describe what needs to be done. Following that, we turn to two different perspectives—one promoted by the World Bank, which we call neo-liberalism, and one promoted by a small but important community of academics, which we call neo-statist.

The Necessary Changes: Tearing Down the Walls

There is little disagreement about what needs to be done. This can be demonstrated with the help of a diagram (Figure 5.1). Consider an economy consisting of three spheres of economic activity: the informal sector, the formal sector, and the rest of the world. Most developing countries tried to develop by building two protective walls between a small formal sector, the rest of the world, and the informal sector. These walls were built to provide an opportunity for the small formal sector to grow and develop. The wall separating the formal sector from the rest of the world is made of quotas and tariffs, overvalued exchange rates, exchange controls, and investment codes that limit foreign investment to chosen sectors or limit the repatriation of profits or the percentage of foreign ownership allowed in firms. A second wall was constructed by restricting access of the informal sector and the bulk of the population to credit, foreign exchange, and other valuable inputs, such as fertilizer, technology, and markets.

The formal sector includes large public and private-sector firms with access to foreign exchange and subsidized credit from the government and that are taxed and regulated by the state. At the top of this sector we have the state, including state-owned enterprises. The state protects the formal sector by, among other things, regulating input, producer, and

Table 5.1 Regional Growth, Equity, and Poverty Performance

Region	Real GNP per Capita (US$ 1992)	Real per Capita GNP Growth Rate, 1980–92 (%)	Gini Coefficient[a]	Incidence of Poverty (Headcount %)
Sub-Saharan Africa	530	–0.8	0.44	47
South Asia	310	3.0	0.31	51
East Asia and Pacific	760	6.1	0.32	20
Latin America	2,690	–0.2	0.49	19

[a] The lower the gini coefficient, the more equal the income distribution.
Sources:
◆Per capita GNP data, World Bank, *World Development Report 1994* (New York: Oxford University Press, 1994), 163.
◆Poverty data, World Bank, *World Development Report 1990* (New York: Oxford University Press, 1990), 29.
◆Gini coefficient data, Michael T. Rock, "Twenty-Five Years of Economic Development Revisited," *World Development* 21 (1993): 1794.

consumer prices. For example, by the late 1970s, some 6,000 items were subject to price controls in Ghana. Governments subsidize credit and allocate import quotas to favored firms, allocate foreign exchange and access to foreign capital, set wages and interest rates and policies for the hiring and firing of workers, and have social insurance programs that add as much as 30 percent to the wage bill.[5]

Trade obviously takes place between the informal and formal sectors and between a particular country and the rest of the world. But the walls are there nevertheless, and trade between these sectors is limited. The walls were put in place and kept in place to provide an opportunity for an indigenous entrepreneurial class and a modern domestic industrial economy to grow. This set of policies was based on a perception that development was equated with industrialization. For many developing countries and for most of the industrialized countries, including the United States, protecting the modern formal sector of the economy from worldwide competition was an important first step toward development.

Initially, this protective system often resulted in economic growth. But over time, progress gave way to slower growth, inflation, and balance-of-payments problems. Because this system did not increase the demand for those income-producing assets (labor and land held by small farmers) that were more equitably distributed, it also led to high income inequality and a high incidence of poverty.

There were several reasons that these protective walls failed to generate lasting broad-based development. First, the protective system provided direct economic benefits to social and political elites, even if they were not economically efficient. Government allocation of foreign exchange and credit and import, export, and business licenses went to friends and relatives rather than to the most efficient users of resources. Second, in many instances, protecting domestic industrialists in the formal sector from international trade resulted in the production of high-cost, shoddy products that few people wanted. Third, protected industries were very dependent on imports. But the protective system reduced the incentive to export, thereby reducing export earnings and foreign exchange. This shortage of foreign exchange made it difficult for producers in the formal sector to produce and sell; as a result, economic growth declined.

This system also had a negative impact on income equality and poverty reduction. Governments provided credit to large firms at subsidized rates and provided foreign exchange at well below market rates. Barriers to labor mobility between the formal and informal sectors kept labor scarce and wages relatively high in the formal sector. This set of factor prices, high wages, and cheap credit and foreign exchange led firms to construct factories employing much capital and few workers. This meant that only a few laborers could find jobs in the relatively high-paying formal sector. In addition, policies in this protective system discriminated against agriculture.

The benefits of this kind of growth went to those who worked for the state, the few laborers who could get jobs in the formal sector, and formal-sector owners of capital. This occurred at the expense of small farmers and the rest of the labor force. Since these latter two groups constituted the bulk of the population, there was high inequality in income distribution and a high incidence of poverty.

If these protective walls between the formal sector and the rest of the world and between the formal sector and the informal sector are the problem, the obvious solution is to tear them down. But how is this to be done?

Neo-Liberal versus Neo-Statist Structural Adjustment

Proponents of neo-liberalism and laissez-faire, led by the World Bank, argue that the solution to this problem requires rolling back the role of

Figure 5.1 The Protective System

Informal Sector	Government Barriers to Entry into Formal Sector	Formal Sector	Government Policies to Limit Competition	Rest of the World
1. AGRICULTURE—RURAL AREAS Subsistence and near-subsistence farmers Landless workers Petty commodity producers—tools, beer, household goods, etc. Moneylenders Midwives—traditional medicine Retailers—shops in homes 2. URBAN INDUSTRIAL SECTOR Petty commodity producers—household goods, clothing, etc. Retailers—street vendors Transport—unlicensed taxis Moneylenders Urban squatters Black Marketeers, smugglers Midwives—traditional medicine 3. CHARACTERISTICS Low income Small scale Labor intensive Little formal education Capital from moneylenders High interest costs	1. License and permit requirements to operate a business—bureaucratic delays, red tape, corruption, bribes required 2. Legal system denies land titles to urban squatters for use as collateral for loans 3. No access to formal-sector credit or subsidized inputs, fertilizer, water, electricity 4. Building codes make legal housing prohibitively expensive 5. No access to foreign exchange or import inputs 6. Low prices for agricultural products 7. Unions closed to outsiders	1. STATE SECTOR Professional, managerial class Military Civil servants State-owned enterprises and banks Hospitals 2. INTELLECTUALS, ACADEMICS, MEDIA 3. INDUSTRIAL SECTOR Import-substituting industries Multinational corporations Labor unions 4. AGRICULTURAL SECTOR Commercial farmers Export agriculture 5. CHARACTERISTICS High income Access to foreign exchange Access to import quotas, licenses Access to subsidized credit Access to urban hospitals and higher education subsidies Regulated and taxed by government Much income from rent-seeking rather than production Capital intensive	1. Regulations to limit foreign ownership, to reserve certain industries to state and domestic ownership, and to restrict profit repatriation 2. Quotas and tariffs on imported goods to protect domestic firms 3. Control and allocation of foreign exchange to favored firms 4. Subsidized credit, low interest rates to favored firms 5. Government subsidies to state-owned enterprises 6. Tax holidays and loopholes for favored firms	1. Multinational corporations 2. Multinational banks 3. Agro-industries 4. Exporters and importers 5. International agencies

the state to get it to do only those things that states have to do and can do well.[6] This limits the role of government to providing those public goods that the private sector does not provide, including national defense, protection of persons and property, and enforcement of contracts. It also includes maintaining a sound system of money and credit, undertaking some public works and agricultural research, and financing (although not necessarily providing) public health and public education.

It is also necessary to open the economy to foreign competition.[7] This involves replacing quotas with tariffs and then harmonizing tariffs—that is, having the same tariff on all imports. The last stage is to gradually reduce tariffs.

In addition, countries must open their economies to competition from the rest of the world with respect to foreign investment.[8] There is a great need for investment in developing countries today and a shortage of capital to undertake it. This is particularly true in telecommunications, transportation, and energy. There are many multinational firms that would be willing to make investments in these sectors. But to encourage them to invest, developing countries must revise investment codes to guarantee repatriation of profits, allow majority foreign ownership, set up one-stop approval procedures, and take other steps.

Opening the domestic industrial sector up to foreign trade and investment is not sufficient, however. Governments not only protect the domestic economy from international competition, they also protect it from the informal sector. The informal sector includes economic actors that have no access to foreign exchange or subsidized credit from the government and are not subject to governmental regulation or taxation. It includes subsistence and small-scale farmers (especially food crop producers), small-scale enterprises, urban squatters, smugglers, and petty traders.

This sector of the economy is discriminated against, and this discrimination must be removed so that the informal economy is on an equal footing with the formal economy. This means extending property rights and the protection of the rule of law to those in the informal sector. It also means giving informal-sector actors access to credit and foreign exchange on the same terms as those in the formal sector.

The neo-statist approach to structural adjustment is very different. Neo-statists argue that neo-liberalism is too narrowly ideological and inconsistent with actual developing country experience, especially in East Asia.[9] Several examples make this clear. First, the standard approach to trade liberalization taken by the neo-liberals, the World Bank, the IMF, and most bilateral donors relies on a three-step process:

(1) eliminate quotas, (2) harmonize tariffs, and (3) lower tariffs. Although this is a clear sequence, it is inconsistent with what successful liberalizers actually did. In a World Bank study of successful liberalizers between 1960 and 1980, fully 40 percent failed to eliminate quotas. A similar percentage did not harmonize tariffs. In East Asia, successful trade liberalization did not attack the protectionist rents associated with tariffs and quotas. Instead, the successful trade liberalizers offered government subsidies to exporters, partly because it was politically difficult to reduce tariffs and quotas.

In addition, although neo-statists accept the importance of foreign investment, particularly foreign technology, for broad-based growth, they do not consider the neo-liberal solution of "free markets" to be the best way to achieve this. Rather, they perceive guided intervention by the state as critical. As a result, they are proponents of industrial policy—or a government policy of picking industries to support. South Korea did this in the mid-1970s when it subsidized the development of world-class shipbuilding and steel industries. In both instances, the government allocated highly subsidized credit to these sectors and kept foreign investors out.

How did firms in these sectors acquire state-of-the-art technology? The answer is through technology licensing agreements under which the state either permitted domestic corporations to participate in joint ventures with multinationals or purchased outright the right to use new technologies. This required the state to regulate what technology would be acquired and what relationship would be permitted between the domestic firm and the foreign partner. Sometimes this took the form of limiting how much of a joint venture could be owned by a foreign company. Sometimes this led to specification of the technology to be transferred, as well as provisions regarding the training of domestic personnel. Other times this led to limitations on how long a foreign corporation could operate in the country. After the time limit expired, the foreign corporation was required to sell its joint venture share to the domestic corporation.[10]

Foreign Aid and Structural Adjustment

Given the importance of macroeconomic policies for the achievement of broad-based growth, what can foreign aid donors do? During the 1980s, the international donor community created a special foreign aid instrument—structural adjustment loans (SALs)—to promote the adoption of these reform policies.[11] The loans provided quick-disbursing foreign exchange to be used for virtually any purpose other than the importing of military equipment. They were conditioned on an agreement about significant policy reform. SALs were designed to change microeconomic policies with respect to foreign trade, foreign investment, and competition between the formal and informal economies. Loans that targeted policy reforms at the sectoral level were called sector adjustment loans, or SECALs.

The World Bank has been the leader in providing adjustment loans. However, the IMF also moved into structural adjustment lending with the establishment of the Structural Adjustment Facility in 1986, followed by the Enhanced Structural Adjustment Facility in 1987, to provide additional support for low-income countries.[12] Most bilateral aid agencies, such as the U.S. Agency for International Development (USAID), also moved significant portions of their portfolios to policy-based assistance.

The reason that developing countries accepted SALs is clear. SALs were virtually the only source of quick-disbursing foreign exchange available after the debt crisis began in 1982, following Mexico's announcement of its inability to service its debt. Banks in industrialized countries drastically reduced the flow of commercial loans to developing countries. The international recession of the early 1980s, which led to sharply deteriorated terms of trade, higher interest on existing adjustable-rate loans, and a very strong U.S. dollar (the currency in which developing countries had to repay debts and purchase major imports such as oil), also contributed to a growing foreign exchange shortage in the developing world. The trade-off for developing countries gaining access to foreign exchange during this crisis was their agreement to reform policies.

Components of the Structural Adjustment Model

The first and most important component of SALs is realistic exchange rates.[13] Neoclassical economists disagree as to whether developing countries should use purely market-determined (floating) rates or fixed rates with provisions for changing them when circumstances dictate, but they all agree that foreign exchange rates should be as close to market-determined rates as possible.

When exchange rates are close to market rates, quotas are eliminated, tariffs are lowered, and foreign investment is encouraged, growth, equity, and poverty reduction can be promoted. These changes lead to increases in the domestic production of those goods in which developing countries have a comparative advantage, particularly labor-intensive manufactures. When these activities are promoted, the demand for labor rises, growth increases, and income inequality and poverty decline.

The next issue is improving the climate for private enterprise and tearing down the barriers between the formal and informal sectors of the economy. This requires removing price controls, reducing regulatory rigidity, eliminating legal monopolies, and improving the functioning of governments so that private enterprise can flourish.[14]

An important element in this reform is to change the relative prices of capital and labor so that interest rates are relatively higher and wages are relatively lower. This change, it was thought, would entice private owners of firms to economize on the use of capital and increase the use of labor. This would not only enhance economic efficiency and economic growth but also lead to less income inequality and less poverty, because it increases the demand for one of the income-producing assets that is equitably distributed—labor.

Fiscal policy must be reformed to reduce the fiscal deficit and economic inefficiencies in public expenditures and to redress the imbalances in public expenditures and taxation. The first will reduce inflationary pressures in the economy as part of macroeconomic stabilization,[15] and the second will improve economic efficiency. For example, subsidies on transportation, fuel, and fertilizer encourage firms to consume more of these. In addition, a significant number of studies have demonstrated that both public expenditures and taxes in developing countries dispropor-

■ **value-added taxes (VATs)** *tax on the extra value added to a product at each stage of production*

tionately favor the rich at the expense of the poor. On the expenditure side, public subsidies for health, education, energy, and food go primarily to the rich. On the tax side, the goal is to broaden the base, to require everyone to pay some tax, and to lower tax rates. **Value-added taxes** (VATs) are recommended because they can raise a lot of revenue and are fairly easy to administer.

Fiscal reform also promotes decentralization of government, allowing local governments to raise revenue and spend it for local infrastructure and services. Decentralization is an important part of fiscal reform, because local governments are far more effective in building and maintaining schools, roads, and health clinics than are central governments. And this infrastructure is absolutely necessary if agricultural transformation is to take place.

An important part of reducing the fiscal deficit is the closing, privatization, or reform of state-owned enterprises.[16] Privatization is meant to reduce economic inefficiency and income inequality. This has turned out to be an extremely difficult thing to do, and the international financial institutions (IFIs) have lost their early single-minded enthusiasm for privatization as they have come up against extraordinary obstacles. Instead of trying to privatize, the IFIs have moved to remove the monopoly status of state-owned enterprises and to allow private firms to compete with them. They have also introduced programs of reform for these institutions, including performance contracts for managers and bonuses for good performance.

Neo-liberalism also includes reform of the financial sector.[17] The growth of money and credit should be limited so that inflationary pressures are reduced. Real interest rates should be market determined and mildly positive, and the practice of directing credit to particular sectors should be ended. Prudent regulation of financial institutions is necessary. This reform of the financial sector should lead to significant reduction in the allocation of highly subsidized credit to social and political elites; it should also increase access to credit by those small enterprises and small farmers in the informal sector by establishing informal credit institutions, such as the Grameen Bank in Bangladesh. This should improve economic efficiency, increase economic growth, and reduce income inequality and poverty.

An Alternative

The economic policy reforms espoused by the World Bank and the IMF have not gone unchallenged. Those who were responsible for the economic policies that promoted broad-based growth in East Asia and those who have studied the East Asian approach have criticized the bank's model as being ideological and inconsistent with actual events in East Asia.[18]

Critics take exception to almost every aspect of the World Bank's structural adjustment model. They have demonstrated that except for Hong Kong, none of the highly successful exporters in East Asia liberalized its trade policies along neo-liberal lines. Korea is the most notable example. There, quotas were not eliminated, and tariffs were not reduced. Instead, the government countered protectionist, import-substitution industrialization (ISI) trade policies with large interest-rate subsidies for exporters that wanted to expand their production facilities. Access to these subsidies was limited to those firms that achieved high rates of growth in exports. The Korean government also followed a policy of "bleeding exporters," that is, it required exporters to keep export prices and profits on exports low. This helped Korean firms break into foreign markets. Since the firms exporting were the same firms practicing ISI, losses on exports were made up by high profits on domestic sales.

Several aspects of Korea's financial policies were also inconsistent with neo-liberal-style financial liberalization. First, in 1961, the government nationalized the entire banking system. Second, bank loans were directed by the government. During Korea's heavy chemical industry drive of the mid-1970s, the government allocated a significant percentage of bank credit to particular industries and firms. Third, this credit was highly subsidized. This targeting of subsidized loans to particular industries has been roundly criticized by neo-liberals.

A growing number of studies have shown that the Korean approach to growth with equity and a low incidence of poverty was not unique among the successful East Asian developing economies. Elements of it can be found in Taiwan, Singapore, Indonesia, Malaysia, and Thailand.[19]

Although it is now clear that the successful East Asian countries did not follow the neo-liberal model, two important questions remain: Why has government intervention in markets in East Asia not resulted in economic inefficiency and slow growth? How replicable is the East Asian model outside of East Asia? The simple answer to the first question is that the incentives provided by interventionist governments in East Asia rewarded results. Exporters were rewarded for export success; farmers were rewarded for growing food. In fact, the governments in Korea and Taiwan established elaborate mechanisms for tracking a firm's performance over time and rewarding it for success or punishing it (for example, through tax audits) for poor performance. This was possible because the governments saw export success and meeting food needs as critical to national survival; they had enough freedom from interest groups to design strategies that rewarded success, and they were characterized by relatively honest and competent bureaucracies. These examples demonstrate that when this combination exists, the alternative can work. But unless these conditions adhere, these policies are not likely to work. Since they are not found in very many places, this may limit the replicability of this approach to broad-based growth.

Final Thoughts on Efforts to Achieve Macroeconomic Stabilization and Adjustment

Although it is clear that macroeconomic adjustment is necessary, the economic policies that will bring about successful BBSD are still in dispute, and the transition is extraordinarily complicated.

The varieties of approaches used to achieve broad-based growth in East Asia are rich, yet donor-financed adjustment programs often ignore these important differences. Clearly, the countries of East Asia have experienced spectacular economic growth and have done so with extensive state intervention and without following the neo-liberal or laissez-faire policies being pushed by the IMF and World Bank, with the single exception of Hong Kong.

China, for example, has experienced successful broad-based growth in the 1980s and 1990s, and no one would describe it as a laissez-faire–free-trade regime. While borrowing money from the World Bank, the Chinese have assiduously avoided taking its advice. Korea is also widely known for the highly interventionist role its government played in its development. It must give us pause that most of the really successful economies followed policies quite contradictory to those being pushed by advocates of neo-liberal, laissez-faire structural adjustment.

The impact of adjustment on poverty is still contentious. Most observers agree that, in the long run, the reforms should benefit the poor. Early accusations that adjustment hit poorer groups disproportionately have not been substantiated. However, because of indications that the poor were suffering from the adjustment process in the short run, the donor community began to take income distribution and poverty into account in designing adjustment loans and designed compensatory programs for those who might lose in the short run.

The impact of adjustment on the environment is equally unclear.

In the end, although we see the need for adjustment, we remain agnostic concerning the impact of World Bank, IMF, and other donor-financed neo-liberal or laissez-faire structural adjustment on BBSD. The donor approach is unnecessarily ideologically biased, inconsistent with actual practices of structural reform in the highly successful East Asian NICs, and too unconcerned about the impact of adjustment on the poor and the environment.

Micro–Macro Linkages in Development

In the 1990s, there has been a clear rekindling of interest in participatory approaches to development. Beneficiaries' participation in designing and implementing projects, the empowerment of women and other disadvantaged groups, grassroots involvement in decision making and planning, and participatory rural appraisal are all the rage. Much to the chagrin of economists, macro policy, relative prices, and structural adjustment are decidedly out in the 1990s.

Interestingly, in the 1980s, macro policy, getting prices right, stabilization, and structural adjustment reigned supreme. In the 1970s, participation and empowerment of the poor, particularly in rural areas (integrated rural development), were popular, and macro policy and relative prices were forgotten. Those of us who can remember that far back ask, are we doomed to repeat history? Unless macro policymakers and grassroots activists develop more mutual respect and engage in dialogue with each other, the future seems grim indeed. The next downturn in the world economy or the next economic crisis in a developing country experiencing a participation explosion will probably be followed by the return of macro policy and a decline of participation. The cycle will start anew.

This cycle needs to be broken. It is important to foster dialogue between the two disparate communities of grassroots activists and macro policymakers and advisers, but it will not be easy. Policymakers, particularly economists, and grassroots activists have vastly different beliefs about what promotes development. Economists are prone to emphasize the influence of incentives, such as higher prices, on individual (for example, small farmer) behavior. Grassroots activists are more likely to emphasize the effect of structures and institutions on group (the landless, women) behavior and outcomes.

This difference in perspectives leads to radically different policy prescriptions. Whereas economists recommend restructuring incentives, activists emphasize the need for collective action. To the activist, the economists' incentives are part of the structure of domination that perpetuates poverty. To the economist, the grassroots activists' call for participation is doomed to failure.

Both groups are right and wrong. There is ample evidence that prices and incentives both matter. When governments practice confiscatory tax policies toward small farmers—either through overvalued exchange rates or by paying farmers a small percentage of the world price for their products—farmers do not produce for the market, and rural poverty results. But it is equally clear that unless those same small farmers find ways to solve collective problems, such as maintaining irrigation canals and ditches or farm-to-market roads, they will be unable to take advantage of market opportunities.

Both markets and organization matter. Macro policies have a better chance of success if micro practices reinforce them. Similarly, collective action has a better chance of success if macro policies are supportive.

This insight into the linkages between macro policies and micro collective action provides the basis for building a shared vision of development between these communities, one in which growth is equitable, poverty is reduced, and there is more rather than less participation.

Notes

1. What needs to be covered is the current account deficit. This includes the deficit on trade in goods and services; the deficit on payments to factors of production, such as capital; and the surplus on foreign aid grants or gifts.
2. Their borrowing from international financial organizations is referred to as foreign aid, borrowing from commercial banks is called foreign debt, and borrowing from multinational corporations is called direct foreign investment.
3. A simple rule of thumb is that the current account is unfinanceable if it exceeds 4 percent of gross domestic product.
4. Mohsin Khan, "The Macroeconomic Effects of Fund Supported Adjustment Programs," *IMF Staff Papers* 37 (June 1990): 195–231.
5. Bela Ballassa, "The Interaction of Factor and Product Market Distortions in Developing Countries," *World Development* 16 (1988): 449–63.
6. Clive Crook, "A Survey of the Third World," *The Economist*, September 23, 1989, 3–58.
7. World Bank, *World Development Report 1987* (New York: Oxford University Press, 1987).
8. World Bank, *World Development Report 1987*.
9. On the Washington policy consensus, see John Williamson, *The Progress of Policy Reform in Latin America* (Washington, D.C.: Institute for International Economics, 1990).
10. For a discussion of this, see R. Mardon, "The State and the Effective Control of Foreign Capital: The Case of South Korea," *World Politics* 43 (October 1990): 111–38.
11. James H. Weaver, "What Is Structural Adjustment?" in *Structural Adjustment: Retrospect and Prospect*, ed. Daniel Schydlowsky (Westport, Conn.: Praeger, 1995).

12. Mardon, "The State and Effective Control of Foreign Capital."
13. World Bank, *World Development Report 1983* (New York: Oxford University Press, 1983).
14. World Bank, *World Development Report 1988* (New York: Oxford University Press, 1988).
15. World Bank, *World Development Report 1988.*
16. World Bank, *World Development Report 1988.*
17. World Bank, *World Development Report 1989* (New York: Oxford University Press, 1989).
18. *The East Asian Miracle*, proceedings of the World Bank–Overseas Economic Cooperation Fund (OECF) Symposium, Tokyo, December 3, 1993 (Tokyo: Research Institute of Development Assistance, OECF, 1994).
19. Alice Amsden, *Asia's Next Giant: South Korea and Late Industrialization* (New York: Oxford University Press, 1989); Robert Wade, *Governing the Market* (Princeton, N.J.: Princeton University Press, 1990); and the special issue of the *Journal of International Development*, forthcoming, on Indonesia, Malaysia, and Thailand.

6

Transitional Socialist Economies: Russia and China

A S DEMONSTRATED IN CHAPTER 3, rapid growth and development in the state socialist countries, including Russia and China, ultimately gave way to severe economic, political, and environmental problems. For some time, governments in these countries were able to sustain the system. But since the collapse of Poland in 1989, a majority of the former socialist countries have turned away from socialism toward capitalism. This turn was precipitated by a popular upsurge that led to rapid collapse of the old political and economic systems.

In East Asia, China and Vietnam were able to avoid political rupture by liberalizing the economy while maintaining tight political control. As early as 1979, the Chinese started to experiment with pro-market economic reforms. Vietnam followed this approach beginning in the early 1980s. Thus, reform in these countries was led by economic liberalization. Compared with the Soviet Union and Eastern Europe, there was very little political liberalization. This difference provides an opportunity to observe how respect for human rights, democratization, and concern for the environment interact with market-oriented economic policy reform in reforming socialist countries.

Before comparing reform experiences in Russia and China, it is important to have some sense of how those governments initially responded to their economic crises and declining political legitimacy. The initial response was a typical mobilization designed to restart the engine of growth. Gorbachev's strategy for dealing with the crisis was a policy of *uskorenie,* or acceleration. The twelfth five-year plan (1986–90) sought to modernize industry by doubling the rate of retirement of machinery and equipment; creating a new agency, Gospriemka, to bring Soviet machines up to world standards; and increasing labor productivity by clamping down on wayward workers and launching an antialcohol campaign. Agriculture was expected to contribute to *uskorenie* after farmers were given a better deal.

The initial reforms in China (1976–79) were based on the assumption that China's political and economic problems were caused by the excesses of the Cultural Revolution. With the death of Mao Zedong in 1976, official ideology had all but lost its ability to achieve popular support. Soft-liners in the Party feared that unless the Party took action to reconcile itself with the population, it might risk popular unrest. This led the Party to construct an economic strategy aimed at restoring the stability and vitality of traditional Marxist-Leninist economic institutions. The reformers reasserted the primacy of the central planning apparatus, which had fallen into disuse during the Cultural Revolution. This led to a significant increase in the rate of investment, along with an effort to modernize industry by relying more on foreign technology.

In both countries, mobilization produced meager economic results. By 1989, it was clear that Gorbachev's strategy of acceleration was failing. Modernization of the machine tool industry achieved less than 50 percent of what had been planned.[1] The campaign to improve quality led to enormous rejection rates on first inspection without enhancing the quality of output. The clampdown on workers and the antialcohol campaign failed as Soviet workers turned to illegal brewing. The better deal for farmers was replaced by a remuneration policy based on the quantity of work done rather than the quantity of output produced.

In China, Hua Guofeng's New Leap Forward produced similar results. The restoration of central planning was followed by a rise in investment without any concomitant increase in the growth rate of the economy.[2] The attempt to modernize industry by relying on foreign technology resulted in a serious balance-of-payments problem. Post–Cultural Revolution urban wage increases, which were part of an attempt to regain Party support among urban workers, were not matched by an increasing supply of consumer goods.

Political and Economic Reforms

Reluctantly, reformers in both countries came to believe that they had reached a dead end. This led soft-liners among political elites in both countries to propose experimentation with political and economic liberalization. The reformist leadership in the Soviet Union cast the economic problem in terms of a need to reconstitute the relationship between society and the party-state.[3] Thus, reform in the Soviet Union was led by political liberalization from the top. Reformers in China viewed the problem in terms of a need to make a decisive break with the Marxist-Leninist economic model.[4] This led them to focus on creating a more market-oriented economy while maintaining Party control of the political system.

The failure of economic acceleration and accumulating evidence of the alienation of the population, particularly the educated elite, led Gorbachev to conclude that the human factor had become decisive. The focus on the human factor was an attempt to construct a new social contract based on the new social realities of Soviet society. By then, the population was primarily urban and well educated. Gorbachev believed that the old social contract failed to meet the needs of this rapidly changing social elite. The new elite was alienated, and this was politically and economically worrisome.

Perestroika became a search for a way to harness the initiative and creativity of this new social elite. Gorbachev believed that this could be done only by opening the political system. The process began with **glasnost**, especially regarding the errors of Stalinism.[5] This was followed by the encouragement of new political thinking that included open discussion of ideas and a recognition of the necessity of divergent opinions and diverse groups and interests in Soviet society.

■ **perestroika** *Soviet policy of economic and governmental reform*

■ **glasnost** *Soviet policy of public discussion and disclosure*

Reform in China took a decidedly different path. The modest political opening that accompanied Hua Guofeng's New Leap Forward unleashed a dissident movement. The Party responded with a series of campaigns to eliminate the possibility of a popular upsurge.[6] This tight control over political dissent stood in marked contrast to post-1979 liberalization of economic policies. The economic reforms were guided by a belief that private ownership and markets could occupy a useful place in the economy.[7] This led to a reduction in the role of the central planning system, rapid decollectivization of agriculture, increased business enterprise autonomy, and opening of the economy to international trade and foreign investment.

The economic command and control system that fixed prices and allocated inputs to meet state-determined output targets was dismantled in stages. In 1978, roughly 700 producer goods were subject to mandatory allocation by central planning authorities. By 1991, fewer than 20 products were subject to such mandatory allocation.[8] The number of products subject to state price controls also declined: price-controlled industrial products fell from 256 to 29, consumer goods from 85 to 37, and agricultural commodities from 113 to 25.[9]

Reform in agriculture began with a 40 percent increase in state-paid prices to farmers. At the same time, mandatory deliveries of farm output to the state were ended.[10] Under the Household Responsibility System (HRS), families were required to provide a share of the collective's agriculture tax and of its production quota and fees. Families were then free to use or sell their excess production as they wished.

Beginning in 1984, industrial enterprise managers were given greater control over what they produced, the prices they charged, and to whom they sold.[11] They were also granted greater authority over the hiring and firing, promotion, and remuneration of workers. Government ministries began choosing managers on the basis of efficiency; managers were fired for poor performance, and in some instances, managers' salaries were tied to economic performance.[12] Central planners eliminated the practice of requiring enterprises to remit profits to the state and replaced it with a system of enterprise taxes.[13]

China also opened the economy to foreign trade, aid, loans, and investment. It designated certain parts of the country as special economic zones to be front-runners in absorbing foreign technology, introducing foreign capital, and expanding Chinese exports. To promote openness, the Ministry of Foreign Economic Relations and Trade was stripped of its virtual monopoly control of exports and imports. By the late 1980s, about 2,000 separate channels linked Chinese buyers and suppliers with the rest of the world.[14] The Chinese also cautiously welcomed foreign investment, and by the late 1980s, virtually every sector of the economy and every part of China was allowed to receive foreign investment.

These limited political and economic openings created a host of problems. In neither country were the leaders fully aware of the problems they faced. Some sense of that can be gained by looking more closely at what political and economic reform required in the USSR.

Political reform required replacing an authoritarian one-party state that exercised tight control over independent groups in civil society; violated fundamental human freedoms and human rights; controlled the press, radio, and television; and outlawed independent political parties. Political reform required multiparty, freely contested elections. Rules that outlawed independent groups in civil society had to be replaced by rules that guaranteed individuals the freedom to organize. Fundamental violations of human freedoms and human rights had to be replaced by rules that guaranteed those rights. The tightly controlled mass media had to be guaranteed freedom of action. Since the people had virtually no experience with the institutions of democracy, it was not clear how to do this.

Should it be done all at once, or should political reforms be carried out in stages? If so, what should be done first, second, and third?

Changes in the economic sphere, in both Russia and China, were equally daunting. Laws protecting private property rights had to be enacted. A court system to adjudicate disputes over property rights had to be built. This required training judges and lawyers and creating rules of procedure. State-owned enterprises had to be valued and privatized. Rules for privatization had to be established. Rules for decollectivizing agriculture and privatizing ownership of land and implements had to be established. Laws and rules governing the creation of markets, particularly the labor market, had to be established and enforced. A social safety net had to be built that protected people from the economic disruption that followed such a radical transformation of the economy.

But this was not all that had to be done. A modern banking system that attracted deposits and made loans had to be created. This required laws governing rules of deposit, rules for making loans, and a regulation that guaranteed that banks would act in a prudent manner. The entire tax system had to be completely restructured.

Governments also needed to learn how to manage a large capitalist economy. This required building the central economic government agencies of capitalist economies—a central bank, a ministry of finance, a central budget authority, and an effective environmental regulatory system.

If democracy was to take root, each of these agencies would need to be accountable to elected governments. But each would also need enough political independence so that macroeconomic policy and environmental regulation were not totally dependent on the whims of elected officials. Achieving this delicate balance is not easy anywhere. It is particularly difficult to achieve in formerly authoritarian political systems. There was little experience that suggested how these things could be done.

Consolidating Reforms

In the Soviet Union, glasnost and perestroika led to a rapid and unexpected growth in nongovernmental organizations (NGOs) and a popular upsurge. In China, economic liberalization was followed by rising popular expectations, inflation, an increase in corruption, and a decline in the authority of the state. Despite these problems, leaders in both countries decided against reversing the reform process.

During the earliest stages of political activity from below in the Soviet Union, reformers in the Party and the intelligentsia assumed that independent social activism would remain within the confines of the program articulated by the Communist Party (CPSU). They believed that the Party could be the initiator and guide of political reform.

Those in political opposition also believed that it was impossible to contest the Party's fundamental right to rule, so independent social groups limited their goals to those that did not threaten this right. They did this by holding the government accountable in its own terms, by publishing the problems of society, and by relentlessly pursuing the truth.

This was particularly easy to do in the area of the environment. Officially, the government was committed to maintaining a clean environment. It had stringent environmental standards, but the gaps between standards and performance were large. To take but one example, in 1988, air pollution in 103 Soviet cities exceeded official standards by an order of ten, and air pollution in sixteen towns was fifty times the standard.[15]

The response to Gorbachev's call for social participation was surprisingly strong. Between 1986 and 1988, there was an explosion of independent group activity, with over 30,000 informal groups going public.[16] The political balance changed rapidly in the spring of 1988 when these independent and still illegal political groups openly resisted an attempt by Party conservatives to roll back the process of political reform. In May 1988, they formed a political party known as the Democratic Union. In the March 1989 elections for the Congress of People's Deputies, Gorbachev encouraged the informal organizations to help elect reform-minded candidates. In February 1990, the CPSU was forced to legalize opposition political parties.

This move toward democracy was followed by an economic reform program designed to create market socialism. The cornerstone of the program was a new law on state enterprises. The law abolished mandatory output targets and permitted enterprises to contract directly with suppliers and customers. Under the law, enterprise profits were to be taxed at reasonable rates, and workers were to be given an expanded role in the selection of enterprise managers. A policy of full self-financing permitted enterprises to adjust output in response to profits, keep a larger share of profits, and allocate part of these profits to wage increases. Limited price reforms gave enterprises the right to negotiate contract prices for new goods. A draft law on cooperatives gave cooperative (private) ownership equal standing with state ownership. Banking reform stimulated the emergence of private commercial banks. The government's monopoly on foreign trade was replaced with a system that granted enterprises the right to retain foreign exchange and to engage in importing and exporting. The net effect of these reforms was to reduce the role of the central authority in planning, allocating resources, and setting prices.

By 1990, it was clear that these reforms were failing. Despite efforts to replace state orders with business contracting between enterprise suppliers and customers, state orders continued to dominate industrial purchases. Although increased business autonomy led to significant increases in enterprise profits, state ministries continued to tax profitable enterprises arbitrarily. Also, the lack of business experience combined with newly gained independence backfired as many businesses granted exorbitant wage increases without realizing the long-term consequences.[17]

As more businesses became private, the government was less able to collect the revenues needed to run the state. When this was combined with increased state spending on investment, the result was predictable. The government deficit exploded, reaching 15 percent of gross domestic product (GDP) in 1988.[18] Most of this deficit was financed by the government's printing of money. The government faced enormous economic challenges. All the problems cited above led to rapid declines in GDP and the standard of living. Because Gorbachev's economic reform program ignored the environment, the country also faced horrendous environmental problems, symbolized by what happened at the Chernobyl nuclear facility.

The economic consequences of the Chinese pattern of reform were very different. Between 1979 and 1990, real GDP grew at more than 13 percent per year.[19] Industry grew by almost 20 percent per year.[20] The agricultural sector shared in this expansion. Between 1978 and 1986, agricultural output, including the output of rural, township, and village industries, grew at nearly 11 percent per year.[21] Likewise, employment in the 19 million rural industrial firms increased from 1.5 million in 1978 to 28 million in 1991. By 1991, these firms accounted for 40 percent of industrial employment, more than 25 percent of industrial output, and nearly a quarter of the country's exports.[22]

This stunning economic success contributed to a rapid decline in poverty and to significant increases in consumption. Because the benefits of this rapid economic expansion were distributed widely, the absolute number of poor people declined from roughly 250 million in 1978 to about 100 million in 1985. By 1988, the private sector produced almost one-half of China's gross national product (GNP) and the private industrial sector, with 118 million workers, employed 20 million more workers than state-owned enterprises.[23]

Problems of Reform:
Where We Stand Today

The transition from socialism requires change along two axes—one political, the other economic. By 1991, both the Soviet Union and China found themselves far along one axis but lagging behind in the other.

With the failure of the August 1991 coup in the Soviet Union, the breakup of the Union, and the election of a democratic government in Russia, the Russians began the difficult process of making democracy work in a largely unreformed economy with severe environmental problems. In China, the rapid growth of the private sector in agriculture and industry meant that the economy was largely market oriented, but this occurred within the context of Party control of the political system and severe environmental problems.

This very different order of political and economic liberalization leaves the governments and societies in these two giants with distinctly different problems. Leaders of Russia's fragile democracy confront enormous economic and environmental problems. How the country handles these problems will determine the success of Russia's transition. The Chinese must learn how to sustain and consolidate economic reform while cleaning up the environment. They must also learn how to cope with widespread alienation and distrust toward the regime. This will ultimately require some kind of sustained political liberalization.

Both will also have to figure out how to deal with the high social cost of the economic transition. Under the old order, health care, education, food, and old-age pensions were provided by work units in both agriculture and industry. With the collapse of state-owned enterprises and the dismantling of the communes, the traditional safety net has been shredded. As a result, the near universal access to highly subsidized health care, education, and food has all but disappeared, and unemployment has risen. In addition, inflation has eroded the purchasing power of pensioners. There have been numerous reports that approximately 100 million people in China are on the road in search of jobs. There have also been reports of increasing mortality, rising malnutrition among children and the old, and increasing income inequality.

The people with whom we have spoken in Russia and China emphasize the great gains of the reforms: the greater freedom, the increased economic opportunity, and rewards based on performance. But they have also spoken of the great losses, including the disappearance of relative equality. They speak with sadness of the return of homeless people, beggars, people obviously living in poverty, and the unemployed. They are terribly troubled by the return of corruption on a big scale. They universally complain about the high rate of crime and the lack of security and safety, which they had felt under the former system.

The new democratically elected government in Russia inherited several severe economic problems, including hyperinflation, a large external debt, a severe balance-of-payments deficit, and wages that are significantly higher than justified by **productivity**. The new government also faces a highly subsidized and economically inefficient state-owned industrial structure that continues to be a large polluter and is economically uncompetitive.

■ **productivity** *value of the output a worker produces per hour*

Leaders of Russia's fragile democracy must also cope with the consequences of the collapse of authoritarian rule. The parties competing for political power are left with no clear rules or guarantees about their place in the regime. Experience elsewhere suggests that once change occurs in this way, it is extremely difficult to routinize politics and reduce the high levels of uncertainty regarding the political rules of the game.[24] Yet unless this happens, it is difficult to see how Russian democracy can survive.

But even if this were to occur, the new regime would be caught in a difficult position. Leaders will face serious opposition as they take the steps necessary to overcome hyperinflation, an overvalued ruble, distorted wages, inefficient state-owned enterprises, and a severely polluted environment. Attempts to reduce inflation, stabilize the economy, make the exchange rate more realistic, and clean up the environment will reduce people's standard of living in the short run.

Leaders of China's gradual economic liberalization program face similar environmental problems but a significantly different set of political problems. In China, successful economic reform created a politically dangerous mix of rising popular expectations, high social cost, and an increase in official corruption. On several occasions, frustration over rising expectations and resentment about rampant official corruption have led to outbreaks of unrest. So far, the government has responded by brutally suppressing open popular unrest, as it did in the Tiananmen Square massacre in 1989. This only increased alienation and antipathy toward the regime.

What are the prospects for successful political, economic, and environmental transitions in Russia and China? It is too early to provide a definitive answer to this question. Several possibilities exist.

China's economic reform program was gradual. This permitted cautious experimentation, trying different things in different regions and different companies. Those that worked were extended, those that failed were dropped. Because the Chinese fear chaos, plunges, and great leaps, political liberalization is also likely to come by way of "crossing the river by feeling the stones underfoot."[25] But how is this to happen? The East Asian political transitions provide a road map for how China might build a democratic social compact.[26]

In the East Asian newly industrialized countries (NICs) of Korea, Taiwan, Hong Kong, and Singapore, substantial long-term increases in per capita income went hand in hand with the growth of an increasingly complex and differentiated social structure. Within two generations, largely peasant populations were transformed into urban industrial ones. This shift was accompanied by long-term rises in educational status, including universal secondary and mass higher education. It also included

■ **bourgeoisie** the emergence of a strong indigenous **bourgeoisie**. Over *capitalist class* time, the urban educated middle class questioned the restrictions of authoritarian rule. Authoritarian governments responded to urban middle-class and educated elite pressures for democratization with managed political openings. Those openings provided channels for political participation in business-dominated coalitions controlled by ruling elites.

Although this limited the political participation of popular groups such as labor, it also limited populist demands during the democratic transition. As a result, economic policy continued to be dominated by technocratic considerations. Consequently, the governments in East Asia avoided serious economic policy mistakes. This meant that the political transitions did not disrupt continuing economic successes.

These political transitions also resulted in the development of technocratic responses to difficult environmental problems. Environmental ministries were created and were granted the power to set environmental standards, monitor performance relative to the standards, and enforce the standards. This has contributed to a gradual but clear improvement in environmental quality, with minimal disruption of the economy.

The large size of the private sector in China suggests that an East Asian–style transition to democracy is possible. But it could take several generations of continuing success of the market-oriented reform program before the urban middle class and bourgeoisie are large enough and strong enough to pressure the authoritarian government into political liberalization. China's urban educated middle class is simply too small to produce a quick and sustainable middle-class-based democratic transition. The country lacks a tradition of free competition among autonomous groups that could challenge one another and the state. But if the Chinese maintain a high-performance, market-oriented economic reform program, all these things could change to such an extent that a bourgeois takeover of the economy could be followed by takeover of the polity.

One consequence of this would be a cleaner environment. But China does not have to wait for democracy to clean up its environment. Because the state remains largely independent of civil society, it can act now to build a strong environmental ministry with the power to set standards and to monitor and enforce them.

Russia's economic and environmental transition is not likely to be easy. Successful economic liberalization is dependent on the routinization of political rules of the game and the lowering of popular expectations. If this does not happen (and it is difficult to see how it could), the short-run costs of economic and environmental policy change are likely to be more than a fragile government can bear. The most likely outcome is a weak economic and environmental reform program that will contribute to the continuing decay of both the economy and the environment. Under these circumstances, it might not take much for this to degenerate into either an internal civil war, as in Yugoslavia, or an authoritarian turn and military coup.

It is not clear what a new authoritarian government in Russia might do. It might try to reintroduce the Marxist-Leninist party-state and economic policies. At best, it might use its leverage over political power to engineer a Chinese-like transition of the economy. This would reverse the current sequence of economic and political liberalization. If this occurs, it would lend great credence to the Chinese view that it is better to keep tight control over the political process as economic reforms are given a chance to work.

Many compare Russia today to Weimar Germany in the 1920s. Both lost a war, saw the military disgraced, lost vast territories, suffered from hyperinflation, and experienced rampant decadence and corruption. In both countries, some leaders blamed their problems on outsiders—in Russia's case, on the United States and Western European countries and their instrumentalities, the International Monetary Fund (IMF) and the World Bank.

Some in Russia are convinced that the United States and Western Europe want to turn the countries of the former Soviet Union into developing countries or semicolonies, as they were before World War I. They would produce and export petroleum, minerals, and low-wage goods and serve the interests of the industrialized capitalist countries. Others see the main objective of the United States and its European allies as making sure that these countries can never again pose a security threat. They are using their resources and influence, working through the IMF and the World Bank, to ensure the economic and political decline of the countries of the former Soviet Union.

In Weimar Germany, these conditions led to the rise of reactive nationalism and the peaceful rise to power of Hitler and the National Socialist or Nazi Party. In Russia in the 1990s, there are strong forces espousing nationalist and socialist messages. Will we see a return of national socialism in the former Soviet Union?

Notes

1. Organization for Economic Cooperation and Development (OECD), *A Study of the Soviet Economy* (Paris: OECD, 1991), 21.
2. Between 1967 and 1975, investment averaged 26.3 percent of gross domestic product (GDP), and real GDP grew at an annual average rate of 6.3 percent. The investment-to-GDP ratio increased to 31.4 percent of GDP between 1976 and 1979, and the growth rate did not change (6.1 percent per year). Investment-to-GDP data are from World Bank, *World Tables, 1988–89* (Washington, D.C.: World Bank, 1989), 62–63. Real GDP growth data are from International Monetary Fund (IMF), *International Financial Statistics, 1992* (Washington, D.C.: IMF, 1992), 148–49.
3. G. Lapidus, "State and Society: Toward the Emergence of Civil Society in the Soviet Union," in *Politics, Society and Nationality Inside Gorbachev's Russia,* ed. S. Bailes (Boulder, Colo.: Westview Press, 1989), 122.
4. H. Harding, *China's Second Revolution: Reform after Mao* (Washington, D.C.: Brookings Institution, 1978), 99.
5. Lapidus, "State and Society," 131–35.
6. Harding, *China's Second Revolution*, 182–89.
7. Harding, *China's Second Revolution*, 100.
8. "China: The Titan Stirs," *The Economist,* November 28, 1992, 7.
9. Harding, *China's Second Revolution*, 111.
10. Harding, *China's Second Revolution*, 102.
11. Harding, *China's Second Revolution*, 113.
12. "China: The Titan Stirs," 11.
13. Harding, *China's Second Revolution*, 116. Prior to the reforms, the state set output and input prices. This control over firms' revenues and costs implied control over the size of firm-level profits. These profits were normally collected by the state and were the dominant source of state revenue. With liberalization of input and output pricing, these administratively determined profits began to disappear. As a result, state revenues fell, and the state began searching for other sources of revenue.

14. Harding, *China's Second Revolution*, 137.
15. H. French, "Green Revolutions: Environmental Reconstruction in Eastern Europe and the Soviet Union," *Columbia Journal of World Business* 26 (Spring 1991): 31.
16. M. Weigle and J. Butterfield, "Civil Society in Reforming Communist Regimes: The Logic of Emergence," *Comparative Politics* 25 (October 1992): 15.
17. D. Lipton and J. Sachs, "Prospects for Russia's Economic Reforms," paper presented to Brookings Panel on Economic Activity, September 17–18, 1992, 10.
18. OECD, *Study of Soviet Economy*, 33.
19. World Bank, *World Tables 1994* (Washington, D.C.: World Bank, 1994), 204–5.
20. In addition, the incremental capital output ratio (ICOR) fell, and total factor productivity improved. The ICOR was 9.0 percent between 1966 and 1976, and it declined to 3.8 percent between 1979 and 1990. The ICOR was calculated from data in World Bank, *World Tables 1992* (Washington, D.C.: World Bank, 1992), 184–85. Between 1966 and 1976, total factor productivity in state-owned industry was virtually stagnant. C. Risken, *China's Political Economy* (New York: Oxford University Press, 1988), 265. During the 1980s, total factor productivity in state-owned industry increased by 2.4 percent per year. G. H. Jefferson, T. G. Rawski, and Y. Zheng, "Growth, Efficiency, and Convergence in China's State and Collective Industry," *Economic Development and Cultural Change* 40 (January 1992): 275.
21. Harding, *China's Second Revolution*, 107.
22. "China: The Titan Stirs," 11.
23. "China: The Titan Stirs," 4, and M. Pei, "Societal Takeover in China and the USSR," *Journal of Democracy* 3 (January 1992): 111.
24. T. L. Karl, "Dilemmas of Democratization in Latin America," *Comparative Politics* 23 (October 1990): 8.
25. "China: The Titan Stirs," 6.
26. See T. Cheng and S. Haggard, "Taiwan in Transition," *Journal of Democracy* 1 (Spring 1990): 62–74, and S. Haggard and R. Kaufman, "Economic Adjustment and the Prospects for Democracy," in *The Politics of Adjustment*, ed. S. Haggard and R. Kaufman (Princeton, N.J.: Princeton University Press, 1992), 332–36.

Part III

Sectoral Policies for Broad-Based Sustainable Development

Introduction to Part III

GOOD GOVERNANCE AND SOUND ECONOMY-WIDE POLICIES set the stage for broad-based sustainable development (BBSD), but these policies must be complemented by a host of sector-specific policies if we are to move toward BBSD. People everywhere in the world live and work in rural areas and agriculture as well as in urban areas and industry. They also work in and depend on a country's education and health care systems. Finally, much of what happens at household and national levels is profoundly affected by female fertility and population growth. This part (Chapters 7–11) examines what these various sectors look like as development proceeds and identifies sector-specific policies necessary to achieve BBSD.

We start with agriculture (Chapter 7), the dominant sector in most developing countries. Unlike in the United States, most people in developing countries live in rural areas and derive their living from agriculture. For most of human history, large numbers of people have worked and continue to work hard producing low incomes in agriculture. Agriculture has also been forced to absorb large increases in the labor force. Unless agricultural productivity can be increased, many people will be stuck in low productivity occupations—in poverty—even if there is good governance and sound macro policies. Chapter 7 examines what must be done (and has been done) to overcome these problems.

Cities and large urban industrial areas are the flip side to rural agricultural areas in developing countries. Chapter 8 looks at the role of cities and urban, industrial, and trade policies in achieving BBSD. We begin by pointing out that cities offer exciting opportunities and high-paying jobs, but they are also the site of overcrowding, pollution, and poverty. We examine why this is the case and what specifically can be done to increase the former and reduce the latter. This leads to a discussion of government policies that favor urban areas and industry over agriculture. We find that the urban bias of import-substitution industrialization plays an important role in the early development process, but at some point, urban bias slows and impedes development. Chapter 8 identifies what some countries have done to sustain BBSD after the early returns of urban bias fall.

Individuals in developing countries earn their livelihoods in agriculture and in urban industry. Productivity and employment opportunities in those sectors have a large influence on how well individuals and their families do. But even if governments promote high-productivity, labor-intensive policies, they will be insufficient unless governments also invest in the health and education of their populations. Chapters 9 and 10 describe what must be done in education and health policy if people are to be able to take advantage of the economic opportunities created by economic growth in rural and urban areas. We also show what can happen when governments fail to do this.

This part closes with a consideration of how population growth and family planning affect the ability to move toward BBSD (Chapter 11). The chapter places the post-1950 population explosion in developing countries in historical perspective, assesses the impact of that explosion on countries' ability to move toward BBSD, argues that we are on the precipice of zero population growth, and identifies what governments can do to slow population growth and facilitate the emergence of BBSD.

7

The Role of Agriculture and Rural Development

FOR THOSE WHO LIVE IN THE UNITED STATES, it may be surprising to learn that most people in developing countries still live in rural areas and derive their living from agriculture. Of the 3 billion people in low-income countries in 1992, more than 70 percent lived in rural areas.[1] In these countries, agriculture accounts for 29 percent of the gross domestic product (GDP), and more than 70 percent of the population works in agriculture.[2]

This combination tells us that large numbers of workers are working very hard but producing very little. It is difficult to generate jobs outside of agriculture rapidly, so unless agricultural productivity can be increased, large numbers of people will be stuck in low-productivity occupations. This translates into low incomes and a high incidence of poverty.

The purpose of this chapter is to examine what must be done in agriculture to overcome this problem. Before doing this, we examine agricultural policies pursued by countries following import-substitution industrialization (ISI). As we shall see, those policies perpetuate poverty and inequality and result in slow growth and environmental degradation.

The Importance of Agricultural Transformation

Why is it crucial to transform agriculture in order to achieve broad-based sustainable development (BBSD)? The answer seems obvious to us now, yet for four decades, governments of less developed countries ignored or squeezed agriculture in a mad drive to achieve ISI. Development economists and developing country governments did not fully understand all that was expected of agriculture. Because they equated development with industrialization and viewed agriculture as traditional and backward, many governments, advised by Western economists, focused attention on getting cheap food, foreign exchange, low-cost wage labor, and an investable surplus out of agriculture. Both capitalist and socialist governments in the developing world used similar means to achieve these goals, including pricing policies and the creation of special institutions to extract resources out of the agricultural sector. For much of the 1950–1975 period, these concerns dominated all other considerations in agriculture.

To begin with, governments monopolized agricultural input and output marketing. In the capitalist developing economies, government-controlled and -owned marketing boards were often holdovers from the colonial era. In socialist economies, these institutions were created by the state following successful socialist revolutions. Once input and output markets were controlled by governments, they set input and output prices. Subsidized prices for modern inputs, irrigation water, chemical fertilizers, and high-yielding seed varieties did not make up for low prices paid for agricultural output. This turning of the terms of trade against agriculture was justified on the grounds that agriculture was the only source of funds for industrialization.

In both capitalist and socialist developing economies, the early economic returns from this strategy were high. Rapid economic growth and the creation of large, modern, urban industrial systems followed. But over time, taking resources out of agriculture without investing in agriculture created a number of severe problems.

Low prices for crops discouraged farmers from increasing production. This led to lower exports of agricultural commodities, which limited the import of critical items to run the new factories in urban areas. Low prices for food crops meant slow increases in food production. This led to food shortages and rising food prices in urban areas. Low prices also limited new supplies of industrial raw materials, such as raw cotton. Since much of the early industrial development was in textiles, slow growth in raw material supplies left factories without inputs to produce output.

Governments in both capitalist and socialist economies responded to recurring crises in agriculture in several ways. Some increased producer prices paid to farmers, especially for food and agricultural raw materials used in industry. This was combined with government subsidies for urban consumers of food and for industrial users of agricultural raw materials. Although this increased the supplies of food and agricultural raw materials to urban areas, it drained national treasuries, caused large budget deficits, and destabilized economies. Some in the socialist world, particularly in the Soviet Union and China, turned to forced confiscation of food. When this happened, mass starvation in the countryside followed.

Still others turned to food imports to meet basic food needs. Unfortunately, this reduced the availability of foreign exchange for capital and technology imports, slowed growth, and aggravated the balance-of-payments problem. The net effect of these responses was slower growth, inflation, and balance-of-payments crises.

This set of extractive policies toward agriculture also had disastrous consequences for poverty, income distribution, urbanization, and the environment. Most of the rural population sought to make a living out of low-productivity agriculture. ISI policies reduced already low living standards, pushing many into poverty or keeping them from working their way out of poverty. Because the surplus extracted out of agriculture was used to develop modern urban industry, it contributed to high income inequality, because only a few could obtain jobs in the high-paying urban industrial sector. The large wage differential between urban and rural areas contributed to rapid rural-to-urban migration. But because there were few high-paying jobs available in urban areas, urban unemployment and urban poverty grew.

Poor farmers in rural areas, particularly in sub-Saharan Africa, were left with little choice but to withdraw from the formal economy that taxed them so heavily. They met their food needs by growing poor people's food—cassava, sorghum, millet—on poor soils. Because they could not afford to own animals or buy fertilizer, they soon exhausted the soils they worked. They met their fuel needs by cutting down forests. Both these actions contributed to environmental degradation, soil erosion, deforestation, and the loss of biodiversity.

By the 1970s, it was clear that the practice of extracting a surplus out of agriculture had failed. This experience led to a new appreciation of the role of agriculture in development. It also precipitated a search for a new agricultural development strategy.

The Role of Agriculture in BBSD

What role does agriculture play in BBSD? To be effective, agriculture must meet growing demands for food at stable prices; meet this demand in a way that does not do more damage to rural ecosystems; provide work for billions of people for the indefinite future at higher incomes; provide critical raw materials, such as cotton, for industrial processing; provide goods for export to earn foreign exchange to finance the capital imports needed to increase productivity in agriculture and to keep factories running at full capacity; provide taxes for the government; and provide an investable surplus and a reliable supply of low-cost labor to modern industry.

How can agriculture meet these expectations? Based on the experience of Taiwan, South Korea, and the Indian Punjab, John Mellor, among others, has argued that it is possible to achieve an agricultural transformation that meets these goals and distributes the benefits of productivity widely while supporting industrialization.[3] His model is predicated on two vital assumptions: that land is fairly equitably distributed, and that developing countries can export their products to the industrialized world and earn foreign exchange.

The core of this new strategy is the paradox of agriculture. Orthodox analysis, as articulated above, argued that development required extracting a surplus out of agriculture. No one disagreed with this. But the question was, how can low-productivity agriculture provide foreign exchange, raw materials, food, a labor surplus, and capital for industrialization? The paradoxical answer is that agriculture can do all this only after it has been turned into a high-productivity sector. This requires substantial public-sector investments in agriculture and turning the terms of trade in favor of agriculture.

How does this new strategy work? Government must pay for agricultural research to adapt new technology to local conditions. This new technology is biological in nature, and it requires high-yielding varieties of grain, fertilizers, pesticides, and herbicides.

These new technologies are adopted only by the more successful farmers who have the resources to pay for them, and only if it is profitable to do so. This means that government price policies must support the adoption of these new technologies. The result is an increase in the production and productivity of food crops and higher incomes for these better-off farmers. They spend their higher incomes on labor-intensive food products—dairy, fruits, and vegetables—which generates employment. They also spend their higher incomes on labor-intensive light manufactured goods, such as inputs for agriculture—hoes, plows, small tractors—and on labor-intensive consumer goods, such as transistor radios, bicycles, motorcycles, clothing, and improved housing. There is also a demand for labor in the food-processing industries that are induced to set up operations—grain elevators, flour mills, bakeries, dairies, chicken hatcheries, chicken processing plants, canning factories, and frozen-food-processing plants.

Much of this labor-intensive manufacturing takes place in rural areas, if policies are right, and generates off-farm employment and incomes for many people. These incomes are spent on food grains, thus stimulating further demand for such grains and greater incentives for more investment in new technology and increased production. The virtuous circle repeats itself.

The Government's Role in Agricultural Sector Reform

What roles must governments play in this strategy? First of all, macro-economic policy must be reformed to encourage agricultural transformation. Thus, governments must maintain a foreign exchange rate that gives agricultural exporters an incentive to grow export crops. This exchange rate will also discourage people from importing food and encourage them to consume locally produced food, for example, to switch from imported wheat to locally produced corn. It also means that governments must stop excessive taxation of export agriculture and let farmers keep enough of the export earnings to have an incentive to produce such crops. They must also adopt a series of other reforms, referred to as the rural reform *i*'s by Paul Streeten: incentives, investment, infrastructure, innovation, industry, institutions, and information.

INCENTIVES. First and most important, incentives must be reformed. Prices of export and food crops must be high enough to give farmers reason to grow their crops and market them. Farmers are responsive to higher prices for crops; the evidence of this is clear. It is also clear that government schemes to control production and pricing, particularly those that reduce farmer incentives, have all too often destroyed the incentive to grow food and fiber.

INVESTMENT. Investment in human beings is crucial for agricultural transformation. Without an educated rural population, agricultural transformation can not take place. In Chapters 9 and 10, we show that investments in the primary education and primary health care of rural people have very high rates of return. The rate of return on investment in education for farmers is particularly impressive. Even four years of schooling can increase farmers' productivity by as much as 20 percent, if they are also provided with complementary inputs.[4] Without this education, they are less willing to adopt new technologies and increase their productivity. One of the sad consequences of the economic crisis of the 1980s and 1990s in sub-Saharan Africa was that as incomes fell, the opportunity cost of sending children to school became higher, and many farm families kept their children at home to work rather than sending them to school.

INFRASTRUCTURE. Government must provide the labor-intensive infrastructure necessary for agricultural transformation. This includes farm-to-market roads, irrigation systems, schools, clinics, electrification, and telecommunications. Western Europe, North America, and Japan had vast rural infrastructure before development began. It was a sequential process; rural infrastructure came first, then development. India today has a fraction of the rural infrastructure that Japan and Taiwan had when they started development. Nigeria has only a fraction of the rural infrastructure that India has, and Nigeria is relatively advanced in this regard compared with the rest of sub-Saharan Africa. The part of agriculture that has access to rural infrastructure experiences growth; the part that does not have access is largely left out of the growth process.

INNOVATION. As has already been mentioned, government must finance the adaptive research necessary to obtain higher yields from new seeds. Agricultural research is a public good, which will not be undertaken by private actors. One of the tragedies of sub-Saharan Africa is that it is the only region of the world that has not had a **green revolution**. The green revolution technologies were designed for Asia, where there is an abundance of labor and water and a shortage of land. When these new technologies were imported into Africa, they didn't work, because Africa is characterized by a shortage of labor and water and abundant land. The world stands on the brink of breakthroughs in biological research and genetic engineering. African governments and international development agencies must ensure that this new revolution does not bypass Africa.

■ **green revolution**
increase in food grain production per acre due to the use of high-yielding varieties, pesticides, and improved management practices

INDUSTRY. It may seem strange to discuss industry in a chapter on rural and agricultural policies, but rural industrialization is key to agricultural transformation. Rural labor-intensive industries played a key role in Taiwan's development. There, processed agricultural crops such as asparagus and mushrooms were early sources of export earnings, which financed necessary imports for industrialization. Recent studies by Carl Leidholm and his associates at Michigan State University reveal that much of industry in developing countries is located in rural areas.[5] It is invisible, but it is there—women making beer in Africa, producing baskets, furniture, clothes, cooking utensils, dishes, soap—and it is growing.

As much as 90 percent of manufacturing in some developing countries is taking place in small-scale enterprises located in rural areas. Much of the income generated in rural areas is not from agriculture but from industry. It is a particularly important source of income for women. And it is clear that most farmers want to supplement their income from sources other than farming. Farm income is irregular and unpredictable. Farmers are subject to the vagaries of both the weather and the commodities markets. Insofar as they can diversify their income sources, they feel more secure. Ultimately, most of them hope to get out of low-income agriculture altogether.[6]

INSTITUTIONS. The last forty-five years of development experience has taught us that institutions—those that buy and sell inputs and output, provide credit, govern the ownership and distribution of land and the relationship between farmers and government (local and national)—matter. Either governments must break up state monopolies that extract too much surplus out of agriculture by controlling the buying and selling of farm inputs and outputs, or those monopolies must be reformed to provide effective services to farmers. If the latter is impossible to achieve, competition in marketing should be promoted as one way to protect incentives for farmers to grow food and fiber.

Land reform has been attempted in many countries but has been successful in very few, and then only after a major war or a successful social revolution. This was true of the smallholder agricultural countries in East Asia: Japan, South Korea, Taiwan, and the People's Republic of China. Although smallholder agriculture is an important element for achieving equitable and poverty-reducing rural growth, we are convinced that the threat of such reform merely keeps landowners from making investments without increasing the prospect for any real reform. Therefore, we have come to believe that security of tenancy is more attainable and just as effective.

A difficult problem exists in Latin America, where *latifundia* (large estates) prevail and most agricultural laborers have no claims on the land. In sub-Saharan Africa, there is a lack of titles to farmland. Land has historically been allocated by local groups. Clear titles have to be established if farmers are going to invest in the land and improve it. But people proposing to grant African farmers title to land must be aware of the problem posed for women in this process. For instance, in the Gambia, the regulations being drafted prohibit a married woman from initiating judicial proceedings against her husband to claim a right to his property, unless such property was wrongfully taken by the husband when leaving or deserting his wife.[7]

Another necessary institutional change is decentralization of government services and taxing authority. Local governments are far more effective at building and maintaining local schools, clinics, and farm-to-market roads. These governments need to be given technical assistance in the provision of these services, and they must have the capacity to tax and to assess user charges so as to be able to raise the revenue to pay for these services.

Because government credit policy often discriminates against agriculture, reform of credit institutions is also required. Under ISI policies, either credit was rationed to industrial users or those users received large credit subsidies. When this happened, little credit was available for agricultural investment, and what little did exist was at high rates. This discouraged investment in land, agricultural implements, high-yielding technologies, and irrigation systems. The goal is to create opportunities so that agriculture can compete for credit either on the same terms as industry or on more preferential terms.

Provision of credit requires new institutional forms. In the past, when governments set up agricultural credit banks to channel loans to farmers, most of these loans went to well-off farmers, many of whom never repaid the loans. Now many of these agricultural credit banks are bankrupt. Recently, the Grameen Bank in Bangladesh and its imitators have demonstrated that credit that is not backed by collateral, but is given to groups that are collectively responsible for repaying the loans and whose members police one another to make sure that they repay, has been amazingly successful in stimulating economic activity. These kinds of institutions need to be duplicated widely throughout the developing world.

INFORMATION. Unless farmers know what prices are and know of the availability of new high-yielding seeds that work, they cannot take advantage of them.

Prospects for Success

How do we know whether this agricultural development strategy will work? In truth, we do not know that it will work everywhere, but we do know that it was highly effective in promoting broad-based poverty-reducing growth in East Asia. Two examples should make this clear.

In Taiwan, agricultural output increased at 3 percent per year between 1911 and 1955. Despite an increase in population from 2.1 million to 5.2 million during this time, Taiwan was able to meet its food needs and finance industrialization. How did it do this? Initial conditions and several elements of the strategy were critical to Taiwan's success. First, the Japanese, who annexed Taiwan as a colony during the early part of the twentieth century, carried out a thorough land reform that created the basis for a highly productive smallholder agriculture. This was followed by massive investments in rural infrastructure—roads, electrification, and irrigation. Third, the terms of trade favored expenditures by small farmers to increase agricultural productivity. In fact, their purchases of current inputs, particularly fertilizer, increased from about one-fifth of on-farm costs in 1911–15 to about one-third in 1950–55.

Throughout this entire period, somewhere between 20 and 30 percent of the annual value of farm output was transferred out of agriculture. Because the absolute size of the agricultural sector was growing by 3 percent per year, the absolute size of the transfer of resources out of agriculture tripled between 1911–15 and 1966–69. How was income transferred out of agriculture? Up until 1940, 75 percent came from land rent and interest charges. Following another land reform in 1953, most of the extraction came from direct taxes on output and irrigation fees. During the 1960s, fully two-thirds of the resource transfer came from the voluntary savings of rural farm households. All this occurred while rural household consumption was rising at a steady rate of 1 percent per year between 1915 and 1965.

This process was similar to that in South Korea. Japan annexed Korea in the early part of the twentieth century and carried out a land reform that created the basis for a highly productive smallholder agriculture. This was followed by heavy investments in rural infrastructure, particularly irrigation, agricultural research and extension, and rural education. After independence, reasonably favorable agricultural prices led fertilizer use to increase by 9 percent per year between 1956 and 1970. Interestingly, the Korean government captured much of the productivity increase in agriculture by purchasing agricultural output at less than market prices. As a result, even though the incidence of rural poverty fell, overall rural incomes stagnated and rural residents migrated to urban areas. Because government policy in urban areas favored a labor-intensive industrial development strategy, employment and real wages grew rapidly, absorbing this labor into higher-productivity jobs. This contributed further to broad-based poverty-reducing growth.

Although this process worked in East Asia, there are two reasons to believe that the challenge facing agriculture in currently developing countries is much greater than that faced by countries that experienced agricultural transformation earlier. First, agricultural growth in East Asia relied heavily on irrigation, agricultural chemicals, inorganic fertilizers, pesticides, and insecticides.[8] There were large subsidies on their use. This subsidized chemical- and water-intensive agriculture resulted in environmental degradation through soil erosion, waterlogging and salinization of irrigated areas, runoff of agricultural chemicals, and human health effects caused by inappropriate handling of chemicals, particularly pesticides.[9]

As a result of this outcome, by 1990, the green revolution's impact had come to be viewed more skeptically. Lester Brown of the Worldwatch Institute, who had done much to publicize environmental resource limits in the 1970s, published new studies showing that the hope of the green revolution had proved illusory. He argued that it generated significant environmental costs and that continuing research had not been able to generate new food yields. He now predicts that global food shortages are again imminent.[10]

Brown is right that world agricultural research has not resulted in dramatic new breakthroughs since the 1960s. He and all the other environmentalist critics are right in arguing that the original green revolution technologies and massive irrigation had intolerable long-run effects on soil and water contamination. But does this mean that there is no hope for future agricultural technology breakthroughs, particularly ones that are less environmentally harmful? We think not.

The environmental consequences of East Asia's high-input chemical agriculture have only recently attracted the attention of donors, governments, and researchers.[11] As a result, hard data and firm conclusions are difficult to find and reach. Although it is not conclusive, a small but growing body of research suggests that the negative environmental outcomes may not be a necessary consequence of intensification of smallholder agriculture. Rather, they appear to be the result of policy failure, including the failure to account for the environmental damage done by chemical- and water-intensive agriculture. For example, Larson and Knudsen demonstrated how incentives and a public-sector institutional structure reinforced environmentally destructive chemical-intensive agricultural practices in the United States.[12] This is consistent with arguments by Repetto and Barbier that government policy failure (especially with respect to pricing policies for fertilizer, water, and pesticides in East Asia) rather than agricultural intensification policies per se was responsible for much of the environmental damage. More recent research by Rola and Pingali on pesticide policies confirm this by demonstrating that under full-cost pricing of agricultural chemicals, which includes the environmental costs of pesticide use, it pays profit-maximizing small farmers to shift to alternative and less polluting control technologies.[13] Evidence from Indonesia suggests that it may be possible to sustain high agricultural yields while shifting from pesticide-intensive practices to integrated pest management, which can significantly reduce pesticide use.

These findings suggest that it may be possible, in most places, to generate high agricultural yields without subsidizing heavily polluting chemical inputs. But we fear that this may not be true for countries in sub-Saharan Africa. We come to this conclusion because yields there are exceedingly low and highly variable. Under these conditions, risk-averse farmers are, for good reason, unwilling to go into debt to buy chemical inputs that may not yield a fair rate of return. This suggests that the World Bank's solution of relying on markets to get prices right may not work to increase agricultural yields in Africa. It also suggests that subsidies of chemical inputs may be an important part of a successful green revolution in Africa. If this proves to be the case, it may be difficult to achieve yield increases without accepting some chemical pollution.

Because of this, we now recognize that future agricultural research breakthroughs will have to come from new genetic engineering technologies. The nearest and most important of these is probably nitrogen fixation. Legumes, such as beans and peas, draw nitrogen, a crucial nutrient and the principal ingredient in chemical fertilizers, from the air to replenish nitrogen levels in the soil. Nitrogen fixation gives that ability to other food crops such as corn and wheat. With this and other technologies, such as less water-intensive varieties of rice and wheat, modern agriculture will probably be able to produce more food on less land, with less damage to our soil and water resources. This will add other virtues to the original environmental virtue that intensified agriculture has always had—freeing marginal farmlands for expansion of forest, savannah, and wetland habitats.

These preliminary findings are important because equitable growth in rural societies appears to depend on high-productivity smallholder agriculture, and because population growth forces policy-makers to decide how to meet the rising demand for food and fiber. At the national level, some demand can be met from imports, some from intensifying production on existing land, and some from **extensification**. At a global level, choices are restricted to

■ **extensification**
bringing more land under cultivation

intensification or extensification. The latter can come only at the expense of forests and biodiversity. Because of the global distribution of unconverted forest and pastureland, extensification can come only at the expense of much of sub-Saharan Africa's and Latin America's remaining forests and pastureland.

The second reason to believe that currently developing countries face a greater challenge in transforming agriculture is historical evidence that the demand for food in those countries will grow by at least 3 percent per year. It is difficult, even under the best of circumstances, to get food supply to keep pace with such fast-growing demand. This growth in demand is much higher than it was during the industrial revolution in Japan, the United States, and Western Europe. In each of these places, population and income growth were lower and exerted much less pressure on agriculture. In short, it has become harder for agriculture to fulfill one of its most important development missions. Thus it is not surprising that net imports of food have been increasing in the developing world.[14]

The population momentum attending the end of the population explosion will place severe strains on our capacity to eliminate world hunger. How severe will those strains be? Projections of the world demand for food grains suggest that food needs will grow by about 55 percent, or 780 million tons, between 1995 and 2025. During the green revolution period from 1970 to 1994, food grain production increased by about 780 million tons, or 79 percent.

Does this mean that the task before us is unachievable? Probably not, but it will not be easy. We achieved the initial increase of 780 million tons between 1970 and 1994 by investing in the greatest expansion of irrigated area in world history. We also invested heavily in yield-increasing food grain varieties, which led to a doubling and tripling of agricultural yields from very low levels. The slowing of irrigation investments and the leveling off of green revolution yield increases suggest that it is going to be very difficult to produce an additional 780 million tons of food grain by 2025.[15]

Doing so will require doing more of everything. We will need substantial investment in new water-saving drip systems of irrigation, which use water more efficiently, lower water tables less, and create fewer problems of salinization of the soil. We will have to invest more in new forms of high-yield–low-input agricultural technology, and we will have to put more money into biogenetic and other new types of agricultural research. All this will have to be done in a more environmentally sustainable way than it has been in the past.

But it is important not to give up. If we do what is necessary, world population will peak at about 8 billion in 2025. This means that we have to push hard for only a few decades.

So what is the likelihood of successful agricultural transformation? The question is asked against a backdrop of miserable performance in food production in most poor developing countries in the period from 1979 to 1992. China and India were the striking exceptions. Per capita food production grew 2.9 percent per year during this period in China, which was a spectacular increase; it grew by a respectable 1.6 percent per year in India. But in twenty-seven of the forty remaining low-income countries, food production per capita actually fell between 1979 and 1992.[16]

What are the chances that these trends can be reversed? The answer to this question depends both on the international environment and on developing country policies. Unfortunately, the international environment is quite inhospitable to agricultural transformation in developing countries.

There is no shortage of food in the world. There is a surplus. We could end world hunger tomorrow if we chose to do so. It is not a problem of production but a problem of distribution. Poor people do not have the incomes to buy the food that is available. They are hungry because they are poor, not because there is not enough food. Evidence of surplus food is all around us. Real prices of agricultural commodities fell more than 1 percent a year between 1950 and 1984. Prices of beverages—coffee, cocoa, tea—which are crucial exports for many developing countries, fell by 1.13 percent per year; cereal prices fell 1.3 percent, fats and oils 1.3 percent.[17] This trend continues.

Countries exporting agricultural goods can expect to continue to experience declining terms of trade. Thus, any country that relies on agricultural exports to earn foreign exchange to finance development must recognize the fact that each year it must transfer more of its agricultural production to the rest of the world just to sustain existing imports.

There is the persistent **dumping** of agricultural commodities by the industrialized countries, particularly the European Union and the United States. This makes it hard for developing countries to produce these commodities at competitive prices, and it makes it almost impossible for them to break into international export markets.

■ **dumping** *selling products at less than their cost of production*

Industrialized countries also discriminate against processed agricultural commodities from developing countries. For example, if cocoa beans are imported into industrialized countries, the tariff rate is only 2.6 percent; if processed cocoa is imported, the tariff rate is 4.3 percent;

and if chocolate is imported, the tariff rate is 11.8 percent. This is also true for coffee, oil seeds, rubber, and many other commodities.[18] This is done to protect the processors of such products in the industrialized countries. If this looks like an attempt to keep the people in developing countries hewers of wood and drawers of water in perpetuity, that is exactly what it is. Most parties would benefit if coffee, cocoa, and rubber were processed in developing countries where wages are lower, so they could be imported and sold in industrialized countries at lower prices. Only the people engaged in processing these raw materials in the industrialized countries would lose. Programs should be designed to help them find other employment, relocate, or go into self-employment, but politically, this is very difficult to do.

The Uruguay round of the General Agreement on Tariffs and Trade (GATT) negotiations (which took years before finally producing a new treaty in 1994) demonstrated the power of vested interests in rich countries to block trade policy changes that would be beneficial for most of the people of the world. So there is little hope of changing the international climate for developing countries trying to transform their agriculture.

The domestic politics of agricultural sector reform in developing countries are also problematic. In most developing countries, there is a strong urban bias in development policies that discriminates against farmers and the rural economy. Urban consumers are politically powerful and resist efforts to let food prices rise as a stimulus to food producers. Government bureaucrats resist efforts to stop taxing export crops and cut off their source of income and power. Urban dwellers resist efforts to reallocate school and health spending to rural areas.

How and whether these challenges are met will have a great influence on growth, inflation, the balance of payments, the incidence of poverty, income distribution, and the environment. If agriculture fails to earn sufficient foreign exchange or meet domestic food needs at stable prices, inflation and balance-of-payments problems will follow. If it fails to provide cheap labor, an investable surplus, or sufficient raw materials for industrial processing, industrial growth will falter. If countries try to meet the demands placed on agriculture without sufficiently investing in agriculture, growth will be self-limited, the rural environment will deteriorate, and the incidence of rural poverty will be high. If governments try to meet these demands with high inequality in the distribution of ownership of land, high income inequality will follow. If they try to meet these demands by relying on chemical- and water-intensive practices, environmental degradation will follow.

We have made the strongest case we can for the absolute necessity of transforming rural and agricultural sector policies if countries are going to move toward BBSD. We have presented the difficulties involved in implementing these policies very briefly. We acknowledge how great these difficulties are, but developmental growth will be slowed and developmental equity denied unless these policy changes are made.

Notes

1. World Bank, *World Development Report 1994* (New York: Oxford University Press, 1994), 222.
2. World Bank, *World Development Report 1994*, 166.
3. J. Mellor, *The New Economics of Growth* (Ithaca, N.Y.: Cornell University Press, 1976), and J. Mellor, "Agriculture on the Road to Industrialization," in *Development Strategies Reconsidered,* ed. John Lewis and V. Kallab (Washington, D.C.: Overseas Development Council, 1986), 67–89.
4. World Bank, *World Development Report 1980* (New York: Oxford University Press, 1980), table 5.3.
5. C. Leidholm and E. Chuta, "Rural Nonfarm Employment: A Review of the State of the Art," Department of Agricultural Economics, Rural Development Paper No. 4 (East Lansing: Michigan State University, 1979).
6. Ken Kusterer, "What Do Small Farmers Want?" *American Inquiry* 2 (1988): 53–56.
7. Carolyn Barnes, "A Strategic Evaluation of Gender and USAID's Private Sector Program in the Gambia" (Washington, D.C.: Management Systems International, 1994), 60.
8. For example, fertilizer consumption per hectare of arable land in East Asia and the Pacific is about twice the consumption in the United States. World Bank, *World Development Report 1993* (New York: Oxford University Press, 1993), 245.
9. For a discussion of these problems in East and Southeast Asia, see C. Brandon and R. Ramankutty, *Toward an Environmental Strategy for Asia,* World Bank Discussion Paper No. 224 (Washington, D.C.: World Bank, 1993), 115–58; A. Rola and P. Pingali, *Pesticides, Rice Productivity, and Farmers' Health: An Economic Assessment* (Manila, Philippines: International Rice Research Institute, 1993); R. Repetto, *Paying the Price: Pesticide Subsidies in Developing Countries* (Washington, D.C.: World Resources Institute, 1985); and E. B. Barbier, "Cash Crops, Food Crops and Agricultural Sustainability: The Case of Indonesia," *World Development* 16 (June 1989): 879–95. For discussion of the environmental consequences of similar policies in the United States, see B. Crowder et al., "Agriculture and Water Quality," Agriculture Information Bulletin No. 548 (Washington, D.C.: U.S. Department of Agriculture, Economic Research Service, 1988).

10. Lester Brown et al., *Vital Signs: 1994* (New York: W. W. Norton, 1994).
11. See, for example, Brandon and Ramankutty, *Toward an Environmental Strategy for Asia*, and World Bank, *Indonesia: Integrated Pest Management Training Project*, Staff Appraisal Report No. 11377–IND (Washington, D.C: World Bank, 1994).
12. B. Larson and M. Knudsen, "Whose Price Wins: Institutional and Technical Change in Agriculture," *Land Economics* 67 (May 1991): 213–24.
13. Rola and Pingali, *Pesticides*, 6.
14. In sub-Saharan Africa, food imports have increased 9 percent per year for the last thirty years. Today, imports make up almost 20 percent of Africa's food supply.
15. "Water Strategies for the Next Century: Supply Augmentation vs. Demand Management," Irrigation Support Project for Asia and the Near East, U.S. Agency for International Development, September 26, 1994.
16. World Bank, *World Development Report 1994*, 168.
17. World Bank, *World Development Report 1986* (New York: Oxford University Press, 1986), 7.
18. World Bank, *World Development Report 1986*, table 6.7.

8

The Role of Urban, Industrial, and Trade Policies

THE LAST SEVERAL DECADES HAVE WITNESSED rapid urbanization in most of the developing world. Cities offer exciting opportunities and high-paying jobs, but they are also the site of enormous problems: congestion, crowding, pollution, and poverty. The great cities—Mexico City, Bangkok, Rio, Cairo, and Nairobi, to name a few—are paradoxes. Alongside great wealth, there is great poverty. Alongside high-paying jobs, there are masses of unemployed persons. Alongside beautiful housing and access to what money can buy, there are shantytowns.

Urban migration increases real income. Urban dwellers are more productive than rural people because they have more capital with which to work. Higher productivity in urban areas leads to higher wages. This causes people to migrate to cities. Developing countries cannot keep people out of cities. Only South Africa and China have been successful in doing so by using coercive and abhorrent policies.

Despite the fact that people can increase their incomes when they move from rural to urban areas, there is tremendous poverty in cities. A combination of rapid population growth, dramatic urban migration, and inadequate facilities to provide housing, sanitation, safe water, health care, education, and training leads to a lack of human capital, which leads to low labor productivity. This leads to massive urban poverty. **Urban bias** reinforces this process, engendering more rural-to-urban migration, ■ **urban bias** *inequitable distribution of benefits, goods, and services in favor of city dwellers* greater rural-urban and hence national inequality, and higher incidences of both rural and urban poverty. Unless urban bias is addressed, it will be impossible to achieve broad-based sustainable development (BBSD).

What role do cities play in BBSD? Are there ways to overcome urban problems, or are urban blight, poverty, and degradation part of the development process? These are the questions addressed in this chapter. We review the role of urban areas and cities in development and examine the emergence of urban bias and its impact on BBSD. Then we describe what must change so that urban areas can contribute to BBSD. Finally, we present the Taiwanese experience as a case study in urban development.

Cities and Development

Theorizing about the role of urban areas in development has gone through several stages. In the 1950s and 1960s, modernization theory placed great emphasis on cities as modernizing forces. Following the failure of macroeconomic growth to trickle down, focus in the 1970s shifted toward achieving growth with equity, especially in rural areas. This required a shift in emphasis away from large urban areas and toward promoting integrated rural development. During this period, there was little discussion of the role of large urban areas in development. Then, with the slowing of the engine of growth in the 1980s and the difficulties associated with reaching the poor in rural areas, attention shifted once again to urban areas. This time the emphasis was on removing urban bias.

Modernization Theory

According to modernization theory, there are two types of societies in the world: modern and traditional. The change from traditional to modern occurs through the diffusion of capital, technology, values, institutional arrangements, and political beliefs from modern societies to traditional ones.[1] Large cities are one of the main vehicles for this diffusion. The positive, diffusing influence of the city acts on the countryside as a catalyst of transformation. Cities are the dynamic, job-creating, trade-creating centers that trigger the growth of nations.

Jane Jacobs is the most forceful spokesperson for this view. She argues that the city is active and that "the dense, central areas of great cities are the indispensable hatcheries of new jobs for society."[2] Jacobs's idea of great cities is rooted in an ecological model. Societies are good when they are complex, resilient, and creative, like nature's mature forest ecosystems.[3] The diversity versus stagnation theme from ecology allows Jacobs to define a number of other basic concepts:

> One of them is the contrast between new work and old work. New work consists of young enterprises that the city's multitude of small

entrepreneurs start. It is society's dominant source of new jobs and economic progress. The city, with its density of labor, capital, expertise, leadership, shelter, material resources, and experimental markets, is the unique birthing area for new work.[4]

Jacobs also explains the stages by which noncity areas evolve into diverse cities by acquiring new work. The process centers on what she terms *import replacement.*[5]

> Towns that aspire to become cities focus the attention of their small entrepreneurs on what she calls breaking away new work from old and beginning to do locally the work that produces things which previously had to be imported from more developed cities. . . . With new capital available, the town can then import more complex and exotic products, which it subsequently can replace and export. The town keeps repeating the process, creating a multiplier effect until explosive growth in the town's diversity occurs. Ultimately, the town becomes a city and begins trading with other cities on an international scale.[6]

Jacobs is also aware that the socioeconomic dynamism of cities and new work can fall prey to antidevelopmental tendencies. Large, mature, bureaucratized, conservative business organizations, which began in cities, can become complacent. These organizations fear the healthy city's ability to create competitive products and therefore tend to try to control city diversity by relying on politics to freeze existing economic structures in place.[7]

Although not quite the same, Jacobs's theory can be used to understand both the positive and the negative roles of urban-based import-substitution industrial policies. After World War II, most developing countries tried to modernize their cities by making them centers of industrial activity. This followed directly from modernization theory, which saw urban industrial activities as modern and everything else as backward and traditional. In the early stages of import-substitution industrialization (ISI), cities in developing countries did become centers of economic dynamism and indispensable hatcheries of new jobs. They did so by diversifying and acquiring new work through import replacement. But by the late 1960s, the economic returns from these policies declined. The large, mature, bureaucratized, conservative business organizations that had emerged began to resist change, with the result that economic structures were frozen in place.[8] When this happened, many cities stopped being dynamic job-creating centers. Instead, they became bases for corrupt public-sector elites engaged in rent-seeking activities. DeSoto described this process in Lima, Peru.[9]

Because ISI was capital intensive, few jobs were created, and urban unemployment and underemployment were high. Cities inevitably experienced the growth of poor squatter populations housed in hovels and lacking access to basic city services such as potable water, adequate sanitation, and electricity. The urban poor also lacked access to basic education and primary health care. Congestion and pollution reached horrific levels. This urban, rent-based, distorted development bypassed much of the rural population, increasing inequality and poverty.

Attacking Urban Bias

As the contradictions of the pattern of socioeconomic development associated with ISI became more obvious, the problems of reducing rural poverty and reaching the poorest of the poor replaced concern for developing large central cities. Several theorists, such as John Mellor, argued for an agriculturally led development strategy that would generate broad-based increases in rural incomes. Those incomes could then become the basis for development of small towns and secondary cities.[10]

Later, theorists in developing countries, such as Hernando deSoto, pointed out to policymakers that the large informal sectors in the developing world's large cities were the real indispensable hatcheries of new jobs. They also pointed out that the formal sector was not creating many jobs.[11]

Dependency and World System Theories

Dependency theory and world system theory analyzed cities in developing countries from a different angle. Dependency theorists argued that development in rich countries and underdevelopment in Africa, Asia, and Latin American were two sides of the same phenomenon. Development in rich countries came at the price of underdevelopment in poor countries.

The vehicle for keeping poor countries poor was the city, which extracted the wealth from developing countries. This facilitated underdevelopment. In this vision of internal colonization, cities and urban elites in the Third World extracted the wealth and income out of the rural sector. As a result, cities were not the source of development; rather, they acted like parasites that removed the surplus from the rural sector and blocked the rural sector's ability to transform itself.[12]

The world system approach, unlike dependency theory, allowed for the possibility of capital accumulation and growth within cities, but this did not change the negative role of cities in development. The new factor that made it possible for cities to keep some of the surplus they extracted from their workers and their rural areas was the multinational corporation (MNC). With the advent of MNCs that located in developing countries, cities themselves were able to exploit labor in the periphery and skim off the surplus. By virtue of foreign investment, the city could become a location for the accumulation of capital.

Although this permitted limited or dependent development, it blocked real development. It led, among other things, to the creation of an urban hierarchy organized on a global scale. World cities sit at the apex of this global urban hierarchy. World cities are the control centers of the international corporate economy, and they have emerged in both the core and the semiperiphery.[13] The central point of this analysis is that world cities such as Hong Kong and Singapore do not chart their own courses. Instead, they are used by the richer core economies to extract surplus from these cities' labor as well as from the periphery. The fact that some capital remains under the control of these cities does not detract from the larger point that a far larger share of this capital is flowing back to the richer core.

Cities as Nodes of Development versus Cities as Vehicles of Poverty Perpetuation

There is little doubt that cities can be and have been dynamic centers of activity with the potential to help developing countries attain BBSD. Singapore and Hong Kong are two good cases in point. But we agree with dependency theory when it suggests how and why cities became vehicles for the extraction of surplus and the development of national underdevelopment. We also agree with those who argue that many Third World cities, such as Bangkok, Thailand, have become vehicles for internal colonization. Urban bias that went hand in hand with ISI policies ultimately promoted slow growth, high poverty, high income inequality, and a redistribution of income and power away from the bulk of the population in rural areas to a small elite in urban areas. Sometimes, as in much of sub-Saharan Africa, this ISI elite was a public-sector elite. In other instances, particularly in Latin America and the Caribbean, public-sector elites worked closely with indigenous business elites and a small labor aristocracy in the ISI sector. In some instances, elites worked closely with the representatives of multinational capital.

But we also agree with Jacobs: the failure of nations to grow and of cities to thrive is not due primarily to the global order of capital-labor relations but rather to how countries choose to deal with cities. The independence of virtually all developing countries provided real opportunities for them to create their own destinies. Hong Kong, Singapore, and Taiwan show that it is possible to devise urban policies that promote more broad-based and sustainable development.

Urban Sector Reform

By the 1980s, many developing countries were still pursuing ISI and had substantial urban bias. Policies of urban bias favored urban import-competing industries in the formal sector, extracted a surplus out of rural areas, and skewed the benefits of public expenditure and tax policy to favor privileged urban residents at the expense of everyone else. This set of policies contributed to slow growth, recurrent balance-of-payments problems, high income inequality, and a high incidence of poverty.

Because these policies and their outcomes are so closely intertwined with cities and their problems, urban sector reform has become essential. But what should urban sector reform include? Some insight into this question can be gained by looking at the economic and urban policies of the East Asian newly industrializing countries (NICs).

Starting in the 1960s, each of these countries focused on identifying ways to increase productivity and economic growth in cities. Because several of these countries were city-states, what happened in urban areas determined the overall pace of development. This is no less true for most of the developing world. More than half the gross domestic product (GDP) in developing countries is generated in urban areas. In Latin America, it is more than 80 percent. Even in sub-Saharan Africa, agriculture and the rural sector's contribution to GDP is declining.

How did the East Asian NICs make their urban economic bases strong and vibrant? They did this by adopting trade and industrial policies that promoted increased productivity and rapid employment growth. This rapid growth provided the solution to many of the problems Third World cities face. For example, if many new jobs are being created, as happened in these countries, vast numbers of urban migrants can be gainfully employed. This contributes to less poverty and less inequality. It can also provide the income for city residents to pay for city services and a tax base for city governments to tackle urban problems, such as the need for more physical infrastructure (transportation, power, and telecommunications), social infrastructure (schools and clinics), and environmental infrastructure (facilities to deal with urban pollution, urban garbage, and sewage).

Trade and Industrial Policy

The macroeconomic trade and industrial policies adopted by the East Asian NICs were particularly important. Instead of promoting a small, protected ISI sector that created few jobs and little tax revenue for city governments, these policies promoted economic efficiency and rapid growth by encouraging the private sector to economize on the use of capital and to use the resource that was in abundance—educated and skilled labor. This was accomplished by promoting exports, especially of labor-intensive manufactures, and by opening the urban economy to foreign investment and foreign technology. This plan was highly successful.

Experience in Asia suggests that two types of trade and industrial policies can be successful: laissez-faire and statist. Hong Kong followed laissez-faire trade and industrial policies. This meant that the exchange rate was determined by market forces; foreign trade was virtually free, because there were no tariffs or quotas on imports; foreign capital was granted unrestricted access to the domestic economy; credit was allocated by private commercial banks on the basis of the expected profitability of projects; and no sector or industry was favored over another. Most of the other countries in East Asia, particularly Singapore, Taiwan, and South Korea, achieved the same end by a more statist and interventionist means.

South Korea is the most statist. Its trade and industrial policies also favored the export of labor-intensive manufactures, but this was done by relying on a government-controlled multiple exchange rate that favored exports and exporters, using import quotas and tariffs to protect industry while at the same time subsidizing exporters, relying on a state-owned banking system that allocated heavily subsidized credit to exporters on the basis of their export performance, and using industrial policies to target industries for development. This statist approach to the promotion of labor-intensive manufactured exports was centralized in the office of the president. It also depended on collaboration between private-sector exporters and government agencies. Those agencies, working with exporters, set export targets for exporters, tested exports prior to shipment to ensure their quality, marketed exports worldwide, and searched for new technologies for exporters.[14]

Fiscal and Financial Policies

In addition to trade and industrial policies, East Asia also paid attention to the fiscal and financial problems of cities. Most cities in developing countries face severe fiscal problems. Most lack the capacity to tax and collect revenues. Thus it is not surprising that a large proportion of government fiscal deficits in the developing world has its origin in the deficits of cities. This is mostly because developing country governments are over-centralized, which means that revenues go to national treasuries while local governments, including city governments, are often starved for money. Because cities lack revenues, it is difficult for them to provide essential city services—sewage treatment, garbage collection, education, health care, crime prevention, and services to the urban poor. Unless reform of the fiscal sector addresses this problem, city governments and cities are doomed.

Financial issues are no less important. Investment in cities, especially urban infrastructure and housing, is long term and expensive. It cannot be financed out of current income. Unless ways can be found for local governments to mobilize savings to finance urban infrastructure, that infrastructure will be inadequate. When this happens, roads become overly congested, garbage does not get collected, and untreated sewage gets dumped into streets, rivers, and oceans. Power and telecommunications are inadequate to meet the needs of the private sector.

Governments in East Asia figured out how to get financial institutions to mobilize savings from urban residents that were tied to priority uses. Housing banks, education savings accounts, and provident funds generated vast resources. This was particularly true in Singapore.[15]

Governmental Reform

In many developing countries, urban governments tend to be technically weak. Institution building is needed on a vast scale to help local governments perform their necessary functions. Part of this should involve granting the private sector a much larger role in providing urban services. Many cities are now experimenting with private provision of urban services such as transportation, education, and garbage collection.

Urban governments need help with their enormous environmental problems. The urban environmental agenda of developing countries is a large one focused on poor water and air quality and dealing with wastes. There is a desperate lack of sewage facilities; open sewers run through many major cities of the world. There is concern about the lack of open space around factories, which has all been settled by squatters who are desperate to find places to live. As a result, when the Bhopal accident occurred in India, thousands of people were killed. The health of workers is severely affected by lack of sanitation, safe water, and clean air.

Several studies demonstrate that the latest technologies in Japan and Germany, which have tough environmental regulations, pollute less and are more efficient. It appears that one no longer has to choose between preserving the environment and increasing productivity. If these technologies are appropriate for use in less developed countries, which typically have more labor and less capital than developed countries, they should be adopted.

Case Study: Urban Development in Taiwan

Since its first four-year economic development plan in 1953, Taiwan has achieved a high rate of economic growth and transformed its economy from an agricultural to an industrial one. Large numbers of people have moved from rural areas to cities, contributing to the rapid growth of Taiwan's urban population. Between 1953 and 1983, the urban share of population increased from 29 to 70 percent.[16] The spatial distribution of Taiwan's population, however, is less concentrated than that of South Korea, Thailand, or the Philippines, and it is manageable. So Taiwan's rapid economic development and urbanization did not result in a high concentration of population in primary cities, as occurred in many developing countries. How did this happen?

The government did not seriously consider population distribution prior to 1970. But even though there was no explicit policy before then, many of the government's development policies influenced the spatial distribution of Taiwan's population. The major policy initiatives that affected population distribution included agricultural land reform, transportation development, public facility development, educational development, industrial estate development, and the dispersion of industrial establishments.

The agricultural land reform program was launched in 1949. It significantly reduced land rent, sold public land to tenant farmers, and allowed other farmers to purchase the land they tilled. This program created a large number of new owner-farmers and greatly increased job opportunities in the rural sector. This effectively restrained out-migration to the cities.[17]

The government adopted a series of policies that encouraged local autonomy for cities and counties. Starting in 1950, the central government decentralized several government functions.[18] It also encouraged the development of secondary cities outside the core region. As a result, a diffuse pattern of urbanization was promoted.[19] Transport development also received substantial attention. Between 1950 and 1970, the government improved the island-wide highway and rail systems, a system of international airports, and the intercity and rural road systems. These transport networks were evenly distributed over the island, and this favored the dispersion of industrial establishments. This dispersion contributed to the balanced growth of cities of various sizes. Subsequently, these cities absorbed a substantial portion of the population from rural areas.[20]

The government also spent heavily on public utilities: piped water, electricity, and telephone service. The spatial distribution of public facilities corresponds to the distribution of population and economic activities. It is fairly decentralized. Public utilities are available throughout most of the island.[21] Provision of public utilities was combined with forty-one widely dispersed **industrial estates**, which fostered industrial development.[22] Population dispersion followed.

■ **industrial estates**
places where utilities and other services are provided to encourage industry to locate there

With all these programs, Taiwan's economy was export oriented, and Taipei and Kaohsiung had locational advantages for industrial development. However, the social and environmental costs of rapid development there—traffic congestion, air and water pollution, and the improper use of natural resources—were high.[23] To reduce these regional disparities, a comprehensive physical plan was drafted in 1971 and adopted in 1979. In the less developed regions, top development priority was given to industries with strong income and employment multiplier effects. Infrastructure (for example, transportation and industrial estates) was improved in these regions to reduce disparities in the investment environment. Indigenous resources and related industries were developed, and industries producing goods that were being imported from other regions were actively promoted. Finally, incentives were provided to induce investment in selected industries in designated localities.[24] Although the island-wide plan was not officially approved until 1979, it has been functioning since 1971 and has served as a policy guideline for physical development programs.[25]

Taiwan demonstrates how both macro and urban policies can be employed to move toward urban development that is broad based. But environmental sustainability was not a strong component of the 1970s plans, and this remains a severe problem on the island. Air pollution is particularly bad, both from vehicle exhaust and from factories and production facilities. The government has begun to recognize environmental quality as one of its most severe development problems.

What is needed is a series of strong regulatory actions to gradually reduce vehicular and factory-generated air pollution. Although Taiwan has allowed its air quality to deteriorate far below any acceptable level, the government has demonstrated that it has the technical and governance capacity to implement the necessary regulatory system (see Chapter 16, where environmental quality issues are dealt with more specifically).

Notes

David Brat served as coauthor of this chapter.

1. David Drakakis-Smith, *Urbanization in the Developing World* (London: Croom Helm Press, 1986).
2. David Hill, "Jane Jacobs' Ideas on Big Diverse Cities: A Review and Commentary," *Journal of the American Planning Association* 54 (Summer 1988): 302. In this article, Hill reviews Jane Jacobs, *Cities and the Wealth of Nations: Principles of Economic Life* (New York: Random House, 1984). See also Jane Jacobs, *Economy of Cities* (New York: Random House, 1969).
3. Hill, "Jane Jacobs' Ideas," 303.

4. Hill, "Jane Jacobs' Ideas," 304.
5. Or, in the terminology used in this book, import-substitution industrialization.
6. Hill, "Jane Jacobs' Ideas," 304.
7. Hill, "Jane Jacobs' Ideas."
8. Hill, "Jane Jacobs' Ideas."
9. Hernando deSoto, *The Other Path* (New York: Harper and Row, 1989).
10. John Mellor, *The New Economics of Growth: A Strategy for India and the Developing World* (Ithaca, N.Y.: Cornell University Press, 1976).
11. DeSoto, *The Other Path*.
12. Andre Gunder Frank, "The Development of Underdevelopment," in Robert Rhodes (ed.), *Imperialism and Underdevelopment* (New York: Monthly Review Press, 1970), 4–7.
13. Frank, "The Development of Underdevelopment," 7–13.
14. For a discussion of this statist export system, see M. Rock, "Public Sector Marketing and Production Assistance to South Korea's Manufacturing Exporters: Did It Make a Difference?" *Development Policy Review* 10 (1992): 339–57.
15. Roland J. Fuchs, Gavin W. Jones, and Ernesto M. Pernia, *Urbanization and the Urban Policies in Pacific Asia* (Boulder, Colo.: Westview Press, 1987), 267.
16. Fuchs et al., *Urbanization*, 218.
17. Fuchs et al., *Urbanization*, 218.
18. Fuchs et al., *Urbanization*, 218.
19. Fuchs et al., *Urbanization*, 218.
20. Fuchs et al., *Urbanization*, 218.
21. Fuchs et al., *Urbanization*, 219.
22. Fuchs et al., *Urbanization*, 220.
23. Fuchs et al., *Urbanization*, 224.
24. Fuchs et al., *Urbanization*, 224.
25. Fuchs et al., *Urbanization*, 225.

9

Policies in Education

WE HAVE ARGUED FOR BROAD-BASED DEVELOPMENT that distributes the benefits of growth widely and equitably. This is the most effective and sustainable way to enlarge people's options and opportunities and so promote human development. When the benefits of economic growth are widely shared, that growth is liberating. It expands opportunities for a better life.

But initial conditions and development policies have a large impact on whether economic growth exerts a liberating effect. When land is equitably distributed and government policies promote rapid increases in agricultural productivity, growth tends to be more equitable and poverty reducing. Alternatively, if land ownership is concentrated, or if policies discriminate against the bulk of the population that is earning its income from agriculture, growth will be more inequitable and have less impact on poverty. If macroeconomic, trade, and industrial policies promote labor-intensive development, growth will be more equitable and poverty reducing. But if those policies foster a capital-using, labor-saving development strategy, the benefits of economic growth will be less widely shared.

But this is not the complete story. For growth to be liberating, people must be able to take advantage of the economic opportunities created by economic growth. To do this, they must be educated and healthy. In this chapter, we assess the impact of education policies in East Asia. We also examine how social-sector policies must change in sub-Saharan Africa if growth is to take place and if that growth is to be equitable.

Thinking about Education[1]

In Western Europe and, to a lesser degree, in the United States, access to primary and secondary education (and to basic preventive health care;

see Chapter 10) is viewed as a fundamental human right. As a result, government policies have been designed to give citizens access to these services regardless of their ability to pay. Why have policies evolved this way? There are several answers.

First, the definition of fundamental human rights has been expanding. Education has come to be seen as an end in itself. It is not only a means to higher economic growth rates but also something to which everyone is entitled. To be illiterate in a literate world is to be severely disadvantaged. One's employment opportunities are severely restricted, and one is denied access to the written record of one's culture. Becoming literate is a powerfully liberating experience.

Second, basic education is different from most other goods and services that people consume in that it is a quasi-public good. This means that the benefits associated with consuming education accrue both to the educated individuals and to society at large. There are large **spillover effects** associated with an educated populace. Educated people are more productive than uneducated people; they are less likely to be unemployed, less likely to need public funds to help support their children, and less likely to commit violent crimes. For this reason, industrialized countries finance, provide, and even compel citizens to take advantage of free primary and secondary education.

■ **spillover effects** *benefits to society that result from providing goods or services to individuals*

But financing or providing these services is not without cost. Consideration of the spillover effects of public financial support for quasi-public goods like education is one way to determine the appropriate role of government. But this, by itself, does not answer the question: How much should government spend on education? One simple decision rule is that government should pay for such services at least up to the point where the marginal social benefits of paying for them are equal to the marginal social costs.

How can this simple decision rule be used to assess what governments should and should not do in education? First, the rule suggests that public monies and public policy should focus on those services with the largest social benefits or spillover effects. This means that public efforts should focus on primary education and basic literacy and numeracy rather than university education. University education is expensive, and most of the benefits go to the individuals involved and their households rather than to society at large. This decision rule also suggests that those with the ability to do so should pay for some or all of the private benefits they receive from government financing of education. This justifies, for example, charging tuition to cover part of the costs for university education. Second, the rule suggests that when public spillover effects are large, as they are for primary education, access should not be limited by the ability to pay.

Although these simple rules provide guidance on which activities to finance, which individuals should get access to them, and when to charge for the provision of quasi-public goods, they do not tell governments how to provide these services in cost-effective ways. Unless these quasi-public goods are provided efficiently, their cost can become prohibitive, reducing the public's access to these services and their willingness as taxpayers to finance them.

Education and Development in East Asia

How have these rules been used in East Asia? The easiest way to answer this question is to examine one example, the evolution of educational policy in Taiwan. As with the other East Asian newly industrializing countries (NICs), Taiwan had highly favorable initial conditions.[2] After Japan annexed Taiwan in 1905, it created the basis for a modern educational system. As a result of investments and policy changes, literacy increased from 1 percent in 1905 to 27 percent by 1940. By 1944, the primary enrollment rate was 71 percent—61 percent for girls and 81 percent for boys. The gross primary enrollment rate reached 80 percent by 1950.

Following the end of World War II and the migration of over 1.5 million refugees from mainland China between 1946 and 1950, the Taiwanese government continued investing heavily in education. In 1950, six years of primary school were free and compulsory. By 1970, Taiwan achieved universal primary education. In 1968, junior high school became free and compulsory. By 1980, the secondary enrollment rate was 80 percent. By 1985, the tertiary—college and university level—enrollment rate was 12 percent for girls and 14 percent for boys.

This rapid expansion of the educational system required an enormous increase in government expenditures.[3] In 1955–56, public expenditures on education equaled 2.1 percent of gross national product (GNP) and nearly 12 percent of government expenditures. Both of these steadily increased, reaching 5.55 percent of GNP and over 20 percent of total public expenditures in 1985–86.[4]

This kind of public-sector educational effort has occurred in all the

East Asian NICs. It dwarfs the efforts elsewhere in the developing world. As a result, each of these countries achieved universal primary education in the early 1960s, and they all had high and rising secondary and tertiary enrollment ratios.[5]

Because expansion of the educational system was expensive, great care was taken in sequencing and timing its development. In each of the East Asian NICs, the earliest emphasis was on expanding primary enrollment. This was followed with timed expansion of the secondary and then the tertiary systems. Expansion was cost-effective. Promotion from one level depended on the students successfully passing rigorous nationwide examinations. The number of student spaces created in the tertiary system was tied to employment needs.[6] Because per-student costs were so high in public universities, particularly in the sciences, the government restricted the expansion of this system while permitting the development of a private system of higher education. This limited the financial burden on the national budget and shifted some of the costs to families, who were willing to pay private university tuition in order to reap the gains from this investment in education.[7] However, many developing countries still refuse to allow private universities to exist.

A wide range of empirical evidence suggests that the social benefits of appropriate investments in education are quite large.[8] Aggregate growth studies suggest that investments in education account for between 3 and 25 percent of the overall economic growth rate.[9] In Taiwan, they accounted for 5.2 to 6.5 percent of the overall growth rate between 1963 and 1972.[10] Studies suggest that no country since 1850 has achieved self-sustaining growth without first achieving universal primary education.

The social rates of return on investments in primary education are among the highest that any country can make.[11] In Taiwan, the social rate of return on investments in primary schooling was 27 percent in 1972.[12] Other studies have documented that even low levels of education—four years—for farm men and women can significantly increase farmers' productivity by making them more receptive to new technology. Education also contributes to lower fertility rates. Even a few years of education for women has been found to exert a positive influence on child health, child nutritional status, and child mortality.

A large number of studies have demonstrated that the distribution of access to education has a large impact on the distribution of income. None of these findings should be surprising. We have known for some time that human resources are the most important resource in determining the pace and pattern of growth. People manage an economy, make scientific discoveries, and turn those discoveries into productive innovations. Unless people are literate, well educated, and healthy, development will not occur. Unless *most* people are literate, well educated, and healthy, development will not be broad based and liberating.

The Educational Challenge in Sub-Saharan Africa

The NICs in East Asia all began their post-1960 development miracles with several advantages. Land was relatively equitably distributed; agriculture was more productive than elsewhere in the developing world; and the educational system, particularly that for primary education, was well developed. In each instance, governments adopted policies that capitalized on these advantages. The result was broad-based growth that financed further human resource development.

But what should countries or regions with less favorable initial conditions, particularly in education, do? Can they catch up? Can they achieve equitable growth that promotes human development? We attempt to answer these questions by examining the educational challenge facing countries in one of the poorest regions of the developing world, sub-Saharan Africa.

These countries began their postindependence development with great disadvantages. Compared with the rest of the developing world, countries in sub-Saharan Africa were severely handicapped by a late start in education.[13] Unlike the Japanese colonialists, who invested heavily in education in their colonies (especially in South Korea and Taiwan), the Western colonial powers did not make significant educational investments in Africa. This is particularly true in French West Africa, where the French educated a tiny elite and ignored primary education. As a result of these practices, the gross primary enrollment rate in all of sub-Saharan Africa was about 35 percent in 1960, when some countries succeeded in ousting the colonialists.[14] This is less than half of the primary enrollment rate in East Asia in 1960.

In some countries—Mali, Burkina Faso, Niger, Mauritania, and those in the eastern horn of Africa such as Somalia—gross primary enrollment rates were less than 10 percent, gross secondary enrollment rates hovered near 1 percent, and university enrollment was virtually nonexistent.[15] A significant number of countries in this region began independence without any college-educated people. Many started without any native doctors, lawyers, or other highly trained specialists.

Independence in Africa was followed by a massive expansion of educational systems. Between 1960 and 1983, gross primary enrollments increased nearly fivefold, and the secondary school system expanded more than elevenfold. Tertiary enrollment grew from approximately 21,000 students in 1960, less than two-tenths of 1 percent of the college-age population, to 437,000 students, or 1.4 percent of the college-age population, in 1983.[16]

This dramatic expansion in the educational system was enormously expensive. To finance it, educational expenditures rose from $3.7 billion, or a little more than 4 percent of national income, in 1970 to nearly $10 billion, or nearly 5.55 percent of national income, in 1980.[17] The number of primary schools nearly tripled, and the number of primary school teachers more than tripled. The number of secondary school teachers increased eightfold, and the number of tertiary institutions more than tripled.

These investments paid off in several ways. First, literacy rates increased from 9 percent of the population in 1960 to 42 percent in 1983. Second, numerous studies have shown that these investments in education yielded high rates of return.[18] Recent studies have shown that higher primary school enrollment rates are positively correlated with higher rates of economic growth in sub-Saharan Africa.[19]

Despite this enormous effort, in 1990, most countries in the region still lagged behind the educational performance that the East Asian NICs had achieved by 1960. By 1980, it became clear that African educational systems were in deep crisis. In country after country, Ministries of Education were trapped by budget squeezes, enormous demographic challenges, and efficiency and quality problems.

Between 1970 and 1980, the population of sub-Saharan Africa grew by 2.8 percent per year.[20] This increased to 3.1 percent between 1980 and 1991.[21] Because Africa's population is relatively young, rapid population expansion severely taxed the capacity of governments to provide education.[22] If population is growing by 3 percent per year, countries must double the number of schools and teachers every twenty-four years just to maintain present enrollment rates. This alone is a Herculean task and allows for no increase in enrollment rates.

Countries in the region will have a hard time sustaining, let alone increasing, gross enrollment rates. In fact, without significant reform of educational systems, a revival of economic growth, and a slowing of population growth rates, gross enrollment rates will probably fall. If this happens, it will be difficult, if not impossible, to move toward broad-based development.

The demographic problem is exacerbated by the region's economic crisis. Per capita income peaked in 1977 and has been falling ever since. Per capita income in 1990 was no higher than it was in 1965. This economic stagnation has enormous consequences for governments' ability to finance the maintenance, let alone the expansion, of educational systems. Thus, as the economic crisis of the 1980s and 1990s drags on, public expenditures on education decline.[23] Not surprisingly, the decline in public expenditures is followed by declining gross enrollment ratios. The gross primary enrollment ratio fell from 75 percent in 1983 to 68 percent in 1990, and the gross secondary enrollment ratio fell from 20 percent in 1983 to 17 percent in 1990.[24]

A third major problem concerns the quality of the education offered. African students routinely score significantly lower on internationally standardized tests than their counterparts in the rest of the developing world. In large measure, the quality problem is the mirror image of the budget and demographic squeeze. Despite a huge educational effort, per-pupil expenditures are very low. Prior to the onset of the economic crisis, expenditures per pupil in primary school were about $50. This was about 60 percent of per-pupil expenditures in all of Asia and approximately 3 percent of per-pupil expenditures in the United States This low level of expenditures means that teachers often teach without textbooks or other school supplies such as chalk, pencils, and tablets.

Unfortunately, the problems associated with low expenditures per student are exacerbated by a misallocation of resources. Too many educational dollars are spent on teachers' salaries and teacher training and too few are spent on educational materials. As the economic crisis worsened, this problem worsened. For example, in Zambia in 1981, 81 percent of the educational budget was spent on salaries, but by 1983, this had risen to 91 percent.

In addition, too much of the educational budget is allocated to university education at the expense of primary education. Malawi allocates 37 percent of its education budget to higher education, Madagascar 28 percent, Kenya 25 percent, and Chad 29 percent. On average, about 20 percent of the education budget goes to higher education in sub-Saharan Africa, whereas higher education receives only 10 percent in Korea, 15 percent in Malaysia, 12 percent in Thailand, and 9 percent in Indonesia.[25] This allocation violates both of the rules of good public policy for quasi-public goods described earlier in this chapter: (1) that public monies should be spent on those services with the largest social benefits or spillover effects, and (2) that access should not be denied to those goods on the basis of ability to pay. This means that public monies should focus on primary education rather than university education. It also means that subsidies for higher education should be small and limited to those who do not have the ability to pay. This is not the case in Africa.

The misallocation of educational expenditures is compounded by an enormous inefficiency problem. Students often repeat grades. Dropout rates are high, several times the rates in East and Southeast Asia.[26] The cost of these failures is high.

Given these problems, what should African governments do if they want their educational policies to promote broad-based growth? The answers to this question are easier to outline than they are to implement.

1. *Restore economic growth.* Economic growth provides additional resources to finance public-sector expansion of educational systems. This growth dividend can be used to expand access and improve quality. Without a resumption of growth in per capita income, there won't be a growth dividend, and it will be impossible to expand gross enrollment rates.

2. *Slow population growth.* The educational successes in East Asia were easier to achieve because population growth rates declined over time. This allowed new resources to be used to improve the system rather than merely expand it. Unless actions are taken to reduce high fertility rates in sub-Saharan Africa, it will be impossible to expand gross enrollment rates and improve educational quality.

3. *Use limited educational resources more efficiently.* Unless scarce educational resources are used more efficiently, a restoration of economic growth and a decline in population growth will not have much effect. Improving the efficiency in resource allocation in education requires several changes. First, relatively more resources have to be allocated to the primary level and relatively less to the tertiary level. The only way to sustain quality and access in higher education is to move to a system of user charges (tuition) for those with the ability to pay. If higher education is subsidized, subsidies should be allocated on the basis of need. Over time, subsidies for current students should be shifted from grant to loan programs. In time, repayment of loans can provide a revolving pool of subsidies for those in need. Private universities and schools—for-profit, nonprofit, and religious—that offer excellent unsubsidized education

need to be encouraged so that the wealthy can pay for their own education without taking subsidies away from those most in need.

Within each educational level, particularly the primary level, more resources need to be allocated to teaching materials and less to teacher training and teacher salaries. Curricula need to be changed to emphasize basic literacy and numeracy. The quality of educational materials, particularly textbooks, needs to be improved. The quantity and quality of instructional time must also increase and improve. Because teachers do not teach and students do not learn in a vacuum, school management needs to be improved so that teachers and students interact in a supportive learning environment. The school principal is one of the most important variables in determining the quality of the education a school provides, because the principal sets the tone and hires and motivates the teachers. Unless these things are done, learning outcomes will not improve. Finally, efforts must be undertaken to reduce repetition and dropout rates.

The countries in sub-Saharan Africa may move toward broad-based development. There is no inherent reason that they cannot. But because countries in this region had such a late start in education, broad-based development will take time. Both we and they need to recognize this and be patient.

Notes

1. The principles developed here for education can be equally applied to health care. For a discussion of this, see World Bank, *Financing Health Services in Developing Countries: An Agenda for Reform* (Washington, D.C.: World Bank, 1987).
2. Much of what follows in the rest of this and subsequent paragraphs is drawn from J. H. Woo, "Education and Economic Growth in Taiwan: A Case of Successful Planning," *World Development* 19 (August 1991): 1029–44.
3. They increased more than 200 times, from 673,263 NT$ in 1955–56 to 138,667,203 NT$ in 1985–86. Woo, "Education and Economic Growth in Taiwan," 1040.
4. Woo, "Education and Economic Growth in Taiwan," 1040.
5. For example, South Korea achieved universal primary education by 1965 and universal secondary education by 1985. Its tertiary enrollment rate rose from 4.6 percent in 1960 to 32 percent in 1985. For a discussion of this process in the other East Asian NICs, see S. Haggard, *Pathways from the Periphery* (Ithaca, N.Y.: Cornell University Press, 1990), 238–40.

6. This led to a conscious shift in policy after 1966 away from university education and toward vocational education and away from the humanities and toward natural science and engineering. Woo, "Education and Economic Growth in Taiwan," 1032–34.

7. Woo, "Education and Economic Growth in Taiwan," 1035–39.

8. The best summary can be found in G. Psacharopoulos and M. Woodhall, *Education for Development* (New York: Oxford University Press, 1985).

9. Psacharopoulos and Woodhall, *Education for Development*, 17.

10. Woo, "Education and Economic Growth in Taiwan," 1040.

11. The average social rate of return on primary education in developing countries appears to be about 27 percent. Psacharopoulos and Woodhall, *Education for Development*, 58.

12. Psacharopoulos and Woodhall, *Education for Development*, 56.

13. There were several important exceptions to this. Gross primary enrollment rates were above 90 percent in Lesotho and Mauritius in 1960. World Bank, *Education in Sub-Saharan Africa* (Washington, D.C.: World Bank, 1988), 131. Interestingly, these two countries have had high growth since 1960.

14. World Bank, *Education in Sub-Saharan Africa*, 13.

15. World Bank, *Education in Sub-Saharan Africa*, 131–33.

16. World Bank, *Education in Sub-Saharan Africa*, 13.

17. World Bank, *Education in Sub-Saharan Africa*, 13–16.

18. For example, estimates of the social rate of return on primary school education in sub-Saharan Africa varied between 24 and 35 percent. Psacharopoulos and Woodhall, *Education for Development*, 56.

19. World Bank, *Adjustment in Africa* (New York: Oxford University Press, 1994), 39.

20. For a discussion of the effects of population growth, see Chapter 11.

21. World Bank, *World Development Report 1993* (New York: Oxford University Press, 1993), 289.

22. Approximately one-third of the region's population was of primary school age in 1988. This is two times larger than the proportion in Asia.

23. They peaked in real terms in 1980. World Bank, *Education in Sub-Saharan Africa*, 16.

24. Enrollment ratios for 1983 are from World Bank, *Education in Sub-Saharan Africa*, 13. Those for 1990 are from World Bank, *World Development Report 1993*, 295.

25. World Bank, *Adjustment in Africa*, 173, 257.

26. Psacharopoulos and Woodhall, *Education for Development*, 210.

10

Health Policies

W E BELIEVE THAT ACCESS to education and health care is an
inalienable human right like the right to life and liberty. However,
it is obvious that the quantity and quality of health care that each society
can provide to its citizens are functions of its income level.

The goal of health policy is to produce healthy people. Who is the primary producer of good health? The answer is many people and institutions. Individuals and families play a large role. Other forces include toxic
pollutants in the environment, behavioral norms such as patterns of
tobacco and alcohol use, and government health policy.

A society needs many different kinds of interventions to produce
health, most of which are outside the scope of the Ministry of Health.
For instance, the most effective way to produce healthier people is to
increase their incomes. The second most effective way to increase health
is to provide education for girls. Educated women have fewer, healthier,
and better-educated children than uneducated women. Another important step is to provide infrastructure that helps prevent disease, such as
safe drinking water and sewage treatment systems. Governments also
need to prevent toxic pollutants from contaminating the air, the land, and
the water. None of these activities is within the purview of the Ministry
of Health.

How should the government's health budget be spent? The same decision rule we enunciated in Chapter 9 on education bears repeating here.
Government should pay for health services up to the point where the
marginal social benefits of paying for them are equal to the marginal
social costs. Public funds should be used for those services with the
largest social benefits or spillover effects. Those people with the ability to
do so should pay for some or all of the benefits they receive from government financing of health care. However, access to preventive health care
should not be limited by ability to pay.

What is preventing families from producing healthy people? What are
the most important health problems in developing countries today? What

policy and program options do governments have for intervening? Can governments afford these policy and program options? These are the questions we raise in this chapter.

Government Health Policy Instruments

There are four health policy instruments available to governments. The first is information. Information can be used to mobilize people to change their behavior. An example is the 1967 U.S. surgeon general's report on smoking and health. Over the years, the surgeon general has continued to issue reports on the relationship between health and smoking. Another example is the campaign to educate people about AIDS and how it is spread. Yet another example is the effort to educate pregnant women about the damage that can be done to their babies if they smoke or drink alcohol during pregnancy. In addition, information needs to be provided to the public on the performance of health care providers and on the cost-effectiveness of various health care providers and treatments.

The second instrument is regulation—laws, standards, and codes to protect health. The U.S. Food and Drug Administration (FDA) tries to ensure that new drugs are both safe and efficacious and that food is prepared under sanitary conditions. Laws can be passed to outlaw smoking in public places; to prohibit spitting in public places; to require that milk be pasteurized; salt be iodized; and water be fluoridated. The sale and use of certain drugs can be made illegal, as has the sale and use of alcohol and tobacco by children. Regulation is a powerful tool for the production of health. Generally, the result of regulation is to force producers and consumers of the regulated products to pay a higher price in return for healthier and safer products. Business is aware of this cost increase and often spends great sums of money to oppose health regulations.

The third instrument is fiscal policies, for example, taxation and subsidies. High taxes on tobacco have been used by some countries to discourage smoking. Some propose high taxes on tobacco to help defray the costs that the public bears in treating illnesses caused by smoking. Immunizations of children have been provided free or at heavily subsidized prices. Contraceptives have often been subsidized in developing countries.

The fourth instrument is direct investments to pay for services, such as building water and sewage systems. It is generally agreed that the increase in life expectancy that took place in Western Europe and the United States in the nineteenth and early twentieth centuries was because of public health expenditures on sewage treatment and safe drinking water. In fact, it was not until the discovery of sulfa drugs and antibiotics in the 1930s and 1940s that modern medicine had a large impact on mortality rates.

Problems in Producing Health

There are serious demand constraints on producing better health. In 1988 alone, there were 2.2 million deaths in the United States, 480,000 of which were caused by tobacco. This makes smoking one of the most serious health problems in the United States. The World Bank predicts that by 2010, tobacco-related deaths in developing countries will average 2 million a year. This will rise to 12 million a year by 2020.[1] Increasing taxes on tobacco is one way to reduce tobacco consumption. But is there a consensus on doing this? You know the answer.

Health production is not just a consumer good. It is an investment. Much of the debate in the United States over whether to provide health care to everyone regardless of their income revolves around the issue of cost. Some fear that the costs to individuals, private-sector firms, and the society at large are too large. Others argue that everyone should have the right to medical care, particularly preventive care. They argue that the social benefits clearly justify the social costs, that healthy people are more productive, more creative, and make a greater contribution to society than people who are sick. In addition to the personal tragedy involved in poor health, there are enormous costs to society.

The Child Survival Strategy

The first goal-oriented, internationally organized health intervention in developing countries was the child survival strategy. In 1978, the Alma-Ata conference adopted the goal of health services for all by the year 2000. The 1990 World Summit for Children set more specific goals: reducing child mortality rates to 70 per 1,000 births, reducing maternal mortality rates by half, and eliminating polio.

The designers of the child survival strategy, the United Nations Children's Fund (UNICEF) and the World Health Organization (WHO), analyzed the available data and concluded that the most serious health problem facing children in many developing countries was death from diarrheal disease, which could be eliminated at very little cost. There was an effective and inexpensive treatment called oral rehydration therapy (ORT), which involved mothers giving their dehydrated babies water with salt and sugar in it to rehydrate them. The designers of the child survival strategy used the government instruments available. To create a demand for ORT, they mounted effective public information campaigns in developing countries all over the world. They distributed free or highly subsidized supplies widely. They made a dramatic impact.

The second phase of the child survival strategy was a campaign to immunize the children of the world against childhood diseases. The same techniques were used in this campaign as were used in the ORT effort. The goal was to cover 80 percent of the population with vaccines. It worked. But this child immunization strategy was a one-time-only effort involving doctors, nurses, midwives, the army, and community leaders. In order to sustain the child survival strategy, it must be internalized in the Ministries of Health around the world. It may become easier to immunize children against childhood diseases in the next decade. Researchers at Texas A & M University are working on introducing immunizing agents into bananas, so that children will not have to be inoculated.[2]

Other interventions to save children's lives involved considerable behavior change in families: encouraging women to breast-feed their children, providing safe drinking water, and urging people to wash their hands with soap after they went to the toilet.

Reforming Health Policy

Importance of Data

One of the problems in the child survival strategy was a lack of data on birth rates, death rates, and causes of death. Without these, policymakers could not determine the underlying causes of health problems and had difficulty determining which strategies to use for which problems.

Misallocation of Resources

Ministry of Health budgets in developing countries are often misallocated. In some developing countries, 50 to 80 percent of such budgets is spent on urban hospitals. This means that most of the health budget is spent on curative treatment for the very ill instead of on the much cheaper and more successful task of preventing illness among the relatively healthy. This spending pattern is supported by doctors and nurses and by urban dwellers, rich people, and political elites. This means that there is little money left for rural health care or clinics in the countryside. This practice must be changed if health status is to improve in developing countries.

A minimal health care package should be provided to all citizens. This package would include prenatal care, child delivery, sick child care, immunizations, family planning, and treatment for highly infectious and sexually transmitted diseases. The World Bank estimates that in the very poor countries, this minimal package could be provided at a cost of about $12 per person per year.[3]

But policy reform in health care is an intensely political process. This was evident in the health care reform debate that took place in the United States in the 1990s. There are many participants in the health sector—doctors and nurses, hospitals, insurance companies, drug companies. In addition, there are lobbying groups for every known disease—cancer, heart disease, AIDS, tuberculosis, diabetes. Each group has an intense interest in what government health policy is, how it is changed, and how this change will affect the group. Rich people in developing countries, just as in the United States, resist any change that allocates more of the health budget to the poor.

The same economic principle used for allocating education budgets should also apply in health care. Health care for the prevention of infectious disease, which benefits the whole population in addition to the individual who receives the care, should be subsidized with public funds, and no one should be denied access to this type of care due to inability to pay. Expensive curative care, which benefits primarily the individual who receives it, should be provided by both public and private health systems. The public system should provide the best care possible with the funds available to the greatest number of patients. Public funds will go farther if patients are required to pay what they can toward the care.

The great benefit of having private health care providers, to those who can afford their services and to those who cannot, is that wealthy patients who are willing to pay for high-cost private health care opt out of the publicly subsidized system and relieve the public of the cost of providing these subsidies to people who do not really need them. At the other end of the health care system, informal-sector health practitioners provide traditional medical services to those whom the public sector is not yet large or broad enough to reach.

From most people's point of view, it would be best if access to all kinds of health care could be treated as a basic right available to all. But even the wealthiest societies in the world cannot afford to make unlimited free health care available to everyone. Everywhere, health care services are rationed. In the United States, access to health care is rationed by income.

Economic sustainability is key in health policy reform. If the policies are not cost-effective and affordable, no matter how desirable they are, they will not be continued. There is growing support for government financing of health care but not government provision. This could take the form of vouchers that poor people take to private providers or subsidies to clinics that provide services to the poor and are run by private voluntary organizations.

Assessing Results in Health[4]

Between 1950 and 1990, life expectancy increased more than it had in the entire span of previous human history. In developing countries, life expectancy increased from forty years in 1950 to sixty-three years in 1990. In 1950, 28 percent of all babies born would die before reaching age five; in 1990, the under-five mortality rate had dropped to 10 percent. Smallpox, which killed 5 million people in 1950, has been eradicated. In 1994, there were no cases of polio in the Western Hemisphere, and the numbers elsewhere were dropping dramatically.

Serious problems remain, however. Child mortality rates in developing countries are still ten times higher than those in industrialized countries. Eleven million children die each year in developing countries because of their poverty. Had they been born in industrialized countries, they would have lived. Most of these deaths are caused by diarrheal and respiratory illnesses made worse by malnutrition. Also, 7 million adults in developing countries die each year from easily and inexpensively preventable or curable illnesses; tuberculosis alone kills 2 million adults each year. Almost half a million women die each year from complications of pregnancy and childbirth, and the maternal mortality rates are thirty times as high in developing countries as in industrialized countries.

New threats appear daily. Countries in sub-Saharan Africa have been particularly hard hit by the AIDS epidemic. WHO estimates that countries in sub-Saharan Africa account for only 2 percent of the world's population, but they have 60 percent of the world's HIV cases. AIDS is spreading rapidly in Asia and Latin America as well. WHO estimates that AIDS will kill approximately 2 million people a year in developing countries by the year 2000, and the death rates will rise thereafter. In developing countries, treatment of AIDS patients would absorb the entire health budget, but in most such places, those with AIDS are left to their own and their families' care.

Deaths from malaria, which had been almost eliminated, are rising as increased resistance to available drugs makes treatment ineffective. WHO estimates that malaria will kill 2 million people every year by the year 2000.

Spending for health is unequal. The industrialized countries spend about $1,500 a year for health care for each citizen. Developing countries spend about $40 per person per year, less than 3 percent of what is spent in rich countries. So although much has been accomplished, the challenges are still formidable. We have a long way to go before people everywhere can live out their lives enjoying good health.

Notes

1. World Bank, *World Development Report 1993* (New York: Oxford University Press, 1993), 3.
2. Rick Weiss, "Vaccine A-Peel," *Washington Post*, April 11, 1995, Health section, 7.
3. World Bank, *World Development Report 1993*, 10.
4. The data in this section are taken from the World Bank, *World Development Report 1993*, 1–4.

11

Population Policies

THROUGHOUT MOST OF HUMAN HISTORY, population and population growth rates have been low. Natural checks—famine, disease, malnutrition, and man-made disasters, particularly wars—kept death rates high and birthrates low. During much of this period, life was, for most people, nasty, brutish, and short. As a result, it took a million years of human history for world population to reach 1 billion. It took another 120 years to reach 2 billion. As late as 1930, the world population growth rate was less than 1 percent per year. This meant that it took at least seventy years for world population to double.

All this changed dramatically after World War II. Rapid technological advances in medicine and sanitation, the spread of these advances around the world, and economic and social development led to precipitous declines in death rates.[1] This is one of humankind's greatest achievements. But it came at the cost of a population explosion. Between 1950 and 1990, world population more than doubled, from about 2.4 billion to 5.2 billion. Most of this increase in world population occurred in the developing world. Most of the projected increases in population will also occur there. In 1990, North America and Europe accounted for 15 percent of the world's population; this will decline to 10 percent by 2020, and the population share of Africa, Asia, and Latin America will increase from 79 to 85 percent.

This population explosion is unprecedented. Our purposes in this chapter are to assess the prospects for future population growth and to examine the impact of the population explosion on national and global broad-based sustainable development (BBSD). We are most interested in questions such as, how has rapid population growth in the developing world after 1950 affected the chance of achieving BBSD? Has it undermined development in poor countries, or has it contributed to post-1950 development success? How has this population explosion affected the global environment? Does it threaten human existence on spaceship earth? Before turning to these issues, we place post-1950 population growth in historical perspective and examine future population projections.

Post-1950 Population Growth in Historical Perspective

World population history can be broken down into three stages. In the first stage, prior to 1650, death rates were high, birthrates were low, and population growth was very low, almost zero.[2] In the second stage, a small group of countries in Western Europe and North America experienced the first industrial revolution. During the 200 years of that revolution (1750–1950), population growth went through two phases. In the first phase, death rates fell while birthrates stayed constant for several decades. This led to a temporary rise in the population growth rate to about 1.5 percent per year. In the second phase, as structural transformation took place—including industrialization, urbanization, modernization, and rapid economic growth—both the birthrate and the death rate fell, and the countries of Western Europe and North America returned to a low and stable rate of population growth of about 0.5 percent per year.

The third stage of world population history occurred after 1950 in the developing countries in Asia, Africa, and Latin America. In important ways, the developing countries' population experience mirrored that of the first industrializers. To begin with, death rates fell dramatically as economic growth, modern medicine, and technology spread to these countries. Because declines in birthrates lagged behind the fall in death rates, the population growth rate rose, increasing from 2 percent per year in 1955 to 2.35 percent per year in 1965. But after that, birthrates began to decline, and so did the population growth rate, which reached a low of 1.93 percent between 1990 and 1994.

Despite the similar pattern in death, birth, and population growth rates, there are several striking differences. For one, birthrates in developing countries have been and continue to be much higher than they were in the industrialized countries when they began their economic and demographic transitions. Second, mortality rates fell much faster in the developing countries than they did in Europe and North America. As a result, population growth rates have been much higher. These two differences account for the post-1950 population explosion. Third, the drop in mortality rates took place whether countries experienced economic growth or not. The fall was essentially a result of the introduction of modern medicine, including public health measures.

What are the implications of these trends for future world population? Is there any reason to believe that world population will become so great that we will be unable to feed everyone or that the earth's ecological **carrying capacity** will be exceeded? Or is population likely to stabilize at a fairly low level?

■ **carrying capacity** *the maximum sustainable level of economic activity that does not destroy the ecosystem by depleting resources or creating too much pollution*
■ **fertility rate** *the average number of children a woman bears in her lifetime*

The population growth experiences of the first industrializers (Western Europe, Japan, and North America) and the second industrializers (the developing countries of Asia, Africa, and Latin America) provide some reason for optimism. Countries in both groups have seen population growth rates first rise and then decline. Population doubling times are now rising. In both groups, the decline in growth rates occurred because of rapid declines in female fertility following the decline in death rates. In both groups, the decline in **fertility rates** has been dramatic and irreversible.

How do these declines in recorded fertility rates affect the size of the future human population? Population projections can be derived from information about mortality rates, the age structure of the population, and fertility rates.

Because of the crucial role of fertility rates in long-run population growth, it is worth examining developing countries' experiences with fertility decline. The replacement fertility rate is 2.1 children per woman of reproductive age. At this rate, population growth will stabilize at zero. Fertility rates above 2.1 cause population to increase, and rates below it ultimately cause it to decrease. In an examination of the trends in fertility rates in a large number of countries, three features stand out.[3] First, once fertility rates start to decline, they fall rapidly. For example, fertility in China fell from 6.4 children per woman of reproductive age in 1968 to 2.0 children by 1992.[4] Second, after the rapid decline, fertility rates bottom (flatten) out. In China, the total fertility rate reached 2.3 in 1982 and stayed relatively constant after that.[5] Third, for a significant number of countries—forty-four in total, covering 38 percent of the world's population—fertility flattened out below the replacement level.[6] When this happens, population growth rates turn negative, and population decline follows.

If the decline in fertility rates continues, and the worldwide fertility rate plateaus at 1.7—the current average for nearly 40 percent of the world's population—world population will peak at about 7.8 billion in 2050 and decline thereafter.[7] Both the World Bank and the United Nations adjust this low population projection upward by assuming that once fertility rates reach the replacement rate, they will level out and stay there. Neither justifies this assumption, and it is inconsistent with the historical record. If this pattern holds, however, world population would peak at 11.5 billion in 2100.[8]

Several enormously important implications follow. First, history will show that the population explosion of 1950–90 was a temporary and one-time-only phenomenon brought about by the spread of modern medicine, economic growth and development, modernization, and urbanization around the world. These forces have led and will continue to lead to lower population growth rates.

Second, slower population growth will create new problems while it alleviates old ones. For example, smaller future populations should ease some of the pressure on the environment. This could reduce or even eliminate the need to slow income growth to make global development environmentally sustainable. Slower population growth also puts us on the brink of eliminating hunger. The achievements of the last forty years brought about by technological change and infrastructure investment in agriculture have eliminated the problem of famine in most countries, including India and China. If global population peaks at between 8 and 11 billion, there is no reason that we should not be able to eliminate world hunger sometime in the next century.

But a lower total world population and zero population growth will create their own problems. Lower population growth rates in rich countries are already changing the age structure of populations: they are getting older. It is also leading to increasing dependency ratios, as the ratio of retirees to working adults rises. There is some evidence of a similar trend in several developing countries. These changes have never occurred before, and they are expected to exert significant influence on the structure of demand for goods and services. For example, housing prices in rich countries are expected to stabilize or fall, and the demand for health and residential care for the aging population is expected to rise. The first has implications for household and hence national savings, and the second will influence the future structure of employment. The rise in the dependency ratio has been cited as one reason that existing public-sector old-age income-security schemes may not be financially viable. So far, no country in the world has responded to the challenges created by rapidly aging populations.

Population: Facing Transitional Problems

Before facing these new problems, it is important to tackle several impor-

■ **population momentum**
the necessity for popula-
tion to increase for one
additional generation after
fertility rates decline to
replacement levels

tant transitional problems resulting from the end of the population explosion in the developing world. Even though population will stabilize sometime in the next century, **population momentum** will place severe strains on our capacity to achieve BBSD. Unless we take action to make family planning available to all who want it, actual declines in fertility rates may not occur as expected, and future population growth could well exceed that projected here.

Unless we invest heavily in health and education for the world's poor, we may doom several generations to a life of poverty and misery. We must reform economic policies to increase the slow growth in work opportunities for young people in developing countries. We must continue to make investments to increase agricultural productivity, or we may fail to eradicate world hunger. And unless we act now to reduce the energy and pollution intensity of production in rich and poor countries in the former socialist world as well as in the advanced market economies, we may undermine global environmental sustainability.

All over the world, women in poor households with little education, low and insecure incomes, and poor health have many more children than those in better-off households. This high female fertility in poor households translates directly into high population growth rates. Why do poor women in poor households have more children? What, if anything, can be done about it?

A growing body of research suggests that poor parents view children as valuable economic assets.[9] Children provide real services to the family and economic security to their parents in old age and sickness. These services act as incentives to have more children. Because parents in better-off households rely on public- and private-sector retirement and health insurance schemes and on consumer durables such as telephones, household labor-saving devices, and tractors for the services that children provide in poor families, they do not view children in the same way.

What implications flow from this analysis? One is that as household prosperity increases, parents, particularly mothers, often want fewer children. But unless these mothers have access to high-quality, low-cost contraceptives, they will have many unwanted births. Widespread evidence suggests that many married women in the developing world have an unmet need for contraceptives and that one in four births in the developing world is unwanted.[10] If these births could be averted, world population by the year 2100 could be as much as 2 billion less.

Another implication is that if parents could obtain elsewhere the services now provided by children, they would not feel the need to have so many children. This will happen in time as social security, consumer durables, capital goods, and services become available. However, we might be able to speed up the process by targeting programs to provide for the aged, particularly through community social security systems. The Chinese have tried this on a large scale.

A third implication is that anything that increases the cost of having children might exert a downward influence on desired fertility and hence on population growth. The most important way to increase the cost of having children is to provide women with economic alternatives. If women have the option of gaining employment outside the home, the opportunity cost of having children rises dramatically. Providing education for women, especially secondary education, which provides the best employment opportunities, reduces the demand for children and the birthrate dramatically. As a result, educated women have fewer, healthier, and better educated children than do uneducated women.

In addition to actions to reduce female fertility, it is necessary to ensure that governments invest in human development. If this does not happen, children will not be educated and healthy. Uneducated and chronically sick children grow up to be unproductive workers. When this happens, economic growth is less liberating and less equitable and exerts less impact on poverty reduction. But financing basic investments in human development for the world's children will not be easy. This is particularly clear in sub-Saharan Africa, as noted in Chapter 9.

As demonstrated in Chapter 7 on agriculture, all too frequently, governments have taxed the labor-intensive agriculture sector, have failed to provide secure titles to land, and have not made critical infrastructure investments. Consequently, less labor is productively employed in agriculture, and farmers fail to make productivity-enhancing investments. The result is low productivity and low incomes in agriculture and an increase in rural-to-urban migration.

If urban areas productively employed the rapidly rising working-age urban populations, this might not be much of a problem. Unfortunately, import-substitution industrialization policies exacerbate the neglect of agriculture by stimulating the development of a capital-intensive, labor-saving urban industrial sector. The result has been significant urban underemployment and unemployment. This has been exacerbated by an urban bias in other government policies—in health, education, food, and energy subsidies—that encourages even more migration to cities. The outcome of this package of development policies, high unemployment, significant underemployment, and a high incidence of poverty has been seen as evidence of too rapid population growth. Although there may be some truth to this, these outcomes also clearly reflect the consequences of adopting development policies that are in conflict with declines in population growth rates.

Finally, we have to find ways to reduce local and global environmental degradation. Two examples make this clear. The World Bank and the United Nations project that population will increase by over 3 billion by 2030. Developing country industrial output is expected to increase three times by 2030. If investments are not made now to break the link between environmental pollution and expected population and income growth, mortality rates could rise. The World Bank predicts that tens of millions of additional people could die each year from environmental causes.[11]

Population pressures also exert a significant impact on global warming. As we now know, emissions of carbon dioxide, the chief greenhouse gas, are a function of the energy intensity of gross domestic product (GDP), the carbon intensity of energy use, and the size of GDP.[12] The latter is a function of population and per capita income. If per capita GDP continues to increase, population continues to grow, and we are unable to reduce the energy intensity of GDP and the carbon intensity of energy use, global temperatures could rise about four degrees Celsius.

The post-1950 population explosion has led many to believe that rapid population growth is the number-one problem facing the world. Ever since Malthus, environmentalists have feared a losing race between our ability to produce food and our ability to produce people. They recurrently predict doom and catastrophe. For example, in 1970, Paul Ehrlich predicted that 4 billion people would die of famine worldwide in the "great die-off" between 1980 and 1989.[13] He and others continue to predict calamity.[14] Events have proved him and other environmentalists dead wrong.

Many economists don't fare much better in their analysis of the relationship between population growth and development. Many have argued that rapid population growth decreases economic growth by reducing savings and shifting investment from productive sectors to social sectors. There is little evidence to support this view.[15]

Does this mean that population growth is not a problem? No it does not. As we have argued in this chapter, rapid population growth makes it more difficult to meet future food needs, to provide needed public-sector investments in human development, to provide work for all, and to slow the rate of global warming. But making all these things more difficult is not the same as making them impossible.

Several things can be done to slow population growth and enhance the prospects for good growth. For one, it is important to recognize that we are at the beginning of the end of the population explosion. If we do nothing more to reduce population growth, world population will stabilize at about 11.5 billion by the year 2100. If we take actions to reduce fertility rates, to increase access to high-quality and low-cost contraception, to provide more education for girls and more income-earning opportunities for women, world population could stabilize at about 8 billion as early as 2025. Because of the impact of population growth on the environment and on world hunger, we need to take these actions now.

But reducing population growth will not be sufficient to achieve BBSD. The population momentum will continue to exert substantial influence for some time. If the world is to meet the investment needs for human development, future investments will have to be larger, more cost-effective, and more efficient. If work is to be available for all, economic policies must be reformed. If world hunger is to be eliminated, we need more irrigated land, new green revolution breakthroughs, and more agricultural inputs.

Each of these things is doable. The end of the population explosion and the implementation of right policies suggest that we are moving to an era in which population growth will no longer be among the world's fundamental development problems.

Notes

1. Crude death rates in Europe were about twenty-three per thousand in 1850; they declined to nine per thousand in 1990. Crude death rates in the developing world were about the same level in 1950 (twenty-two per thousand) as they were in Europe in 1850; by 1990, they had declined to nine per thousand. A. Kelley, "Economic Consequences of Population Change in the Third World," *Journal of Economic Literature* 26 (December 1988): 1688, and World Bank, *World Development Report 1992* (New York: Oxford University Press, 1992), 271.

2. The estimated rate of population growth from the appearance of humans until 1650 is 0.002 percent per year. M. Todaro, *Economic Development in the Third World* (New York: Longman, 1989), 191.

3. See D. Seckler and M. Rock, "World Population Growth and Food Demand to 2050," Discussion Paper No. 25, Center for Economic Policy Studies (Arlington, Va.: Winrock International, 1995).

4. World Bank, *World Tables 1989–90* (Washington, D.C.: World Bank, 1990), 182, and *World Tables 1994* (Washington, D.C.: World Bank, 1994), 206–7.

5. In China, the post-1982 fertility rate has varied between 2.0 and 2.4. World Bank, *World Tables 1989–90*, 1994.

6. D. Seckler and G. Cox, "Population Projections by the United Nations and the World Bank," Discussion Paper No. 21 (Arlington, Va.: Winrock International, 1994), annex A.

7. Seckler and Cox, "Population Projections."

8. Seckler and Cox, "Population Projections."

9. For an introductory exposition of this perspective, see Todaro, *Economic Development in the Third World*, 221–27.

10. J. Bongaarts, "Population Policy Options in the Developing World," *Science* 263 (February 1994): 772.

11. World Bank, *World Development Report 1992*, 9.

12. J. Bongaarts, "Population Growth and Global Warming," *Population and Development Review* 18 (June 1992): 299–319.

13. R. Bailey, "Seven Doomsday Myths about the Environment," *The Futurist* (January–February 1995): 14.

14. P. Ehrlich, Anne Ehrlich, and G. Daily, "Food Security, Population and Environment," *Population and Development Review* 19 (March 1993): 1–32.

15. For a review of the literature on the relationship between population growth and economic growth, see Kelley, "Economic Consequences."

Part IV

Human Freedom and Broad-Based Sustainable Development

Introduction to Part IV

ONE DISTINCTIVE CHARACTERISTIC OF THIS BOOK is its placing of individual human well-being and human freedom at the center of the definition of broad-based sustainable development (BBSD). Although we believe that good governance, sound economy-wide policies, and sector policies that promote economic participation by all citizens contribute to human well-being and freedom, unless particular attention is paid to what happens to women, to civil society, and to human rights and democratic freedoms, development will fall short of BBSD.

To begin with, for BBSD to achieve its equity goals, it must reduce gender-based inequality. Chapter 12 describes the sources of gender inequality in developed and developing countries, examines what kinds of social change have the largest impact on ending that inequality and empowering women, and describes how a BBSD-oriented development strategy can lead to these results.

Similarly, Chapter 13 argues that a rich associational life—civil society—is instrumental in development and is an important component of human well-being. In short, it is essential to BBSD. The chapter defines what civil society is; identifies its functions as provider of social capital, facilitator of market development, and harbinger of political participation; and describes what governments must do to promote it.

Chapter 14 argues that human freedom and democratic participation, as understood by Western and Northern political thought since Locke and Montesquieu, are equally important components of BBSD. The chapter defines political democracy and human freedom, analyzes what we know about the relationship between political democracy and human freedom on the one hand and economic growth on the other, and concludes from a review of historical evidence and theory that democracy is a learned practice that can be fostered by specific government policies and international organizations in any country at any level of economic development. This conclusion permits us to identify the specific policies that governments and international organizations can undertake to promote democracy and human freedom.

12

The Role of Women

FOR BROAD-BASED SUSTAINABLE DEVELOPMENT (BBSD) to achieve its equity goals, it must reduce gender-based inequality. For the other goals of BBSD to be accomplished, the perspectives, organizations, and activities of women as well as men must be fully engaged.

This chapter starts by describing the sources of gender inequality in society and defining women's empowerment. Then it looks at the economics of unpaid household work in order to understand what kinds of social change have the largest impact on ending the inequality and creating the empowerment. It describes how a BBSD-oriented development strategy can lead to these results. Finally, it analyzes the relationship between gender equity and equitable human development, democratization, and environmental sustainability.

Gender, Household Production, and Economic Development

Worldwide, the household sector of the economy has certain shared characteristics. There is a gender-based division of household labor, wherein some tasks are seen as women's work and other tasks are seen as men's work. Which work is assigned to which gender is arbitrary in the sense that any given task can be considered women's work in some cultures and men's work in others. But there is one constant. In every culture where time-use studies have been done, the tasks assigned to women are much more time-consuming than those assigned to men. Cultures worldwide have folk wisdom similar to that expressed in the old Anglo-American saying, "Menfolks work from sun to sun, but women's work is never done."

This feature of the household economy has led some to call it the *patriarchal economy,* because the subsidy built into the system results in household women providing many more of the goods and services needed by household men than vice versa. Men's time is freed up from household tasks to go out and earn income in the economy beyond the household, to formally or informally govern the public sphere of the larger community, to engage in leisure activities, or to do all three.

Because of this subsidy, because men have more authority in the larger community, and because most of the income available to the household comes to the men, who thus control the financial resources, the gender division of labor is an unequal one. It establishes and perpetuates the subordination of women to men in the society. The impact of development on the gender inequity of a society thus depends on its impact on the division of labor in the household economy. Sometimes economic development leads to greater equality for women, and sometimes it leads to greater inequality. The crucial factor in determining the outcome of economic development is what happens to the institution of the patriarchal household.

Esther Boserup, the pioneer economist who founded the field of study now known as gender and development, documented the relationship between gender and development in her classic work *Women's Role in Economic Development*.[1] She found that, in some cases, development results in even greater disempowerment of women, expanding men's control over resources and shrinking even those spheres of domestic life where women's influence was traditionally more important. Men leave their subsistence work in the farm fields of the household economy to take up education and paid employment in the state or private sectors of the modernizing economy. They leave more of their former household work to the women, and their new paid employment displaces traditional informal-sector work that used to provide some income to women. For instance, a supermarket or a government food distribution center hires male labor and displaces some of the women who used to sell food products in the traditional market. This process is perfectly if provocatively summed up by Maria Mies under the concept of "housewifization."[2]

Sometimes, however, development empowers women and increases gender equity. When this happens, there are two kinds of linkages: (1) gender-equity linkages, or what social changes lead to increased equity for women; and (2) development linkages, or what increased equity for women does to further other dimensions of BBSD.

The most common concept that describes the gender-equity goal is women's *empowerment*. This is generally defined as a woman's increased voice in the everyday decisions that shape her life, especially decisions regarding family formation and family planning; a woman's right to participate equally in the economic, civil, and political life of the community and the nation; and a woman's increased experience of the social psychological dimensions of empowerment, increased autonomy, and self-esteem, along with decreased dependence, fatalism, and passivity.

The Economics of the Household Sector

Women's subordination is rooted in **patriarchy**. It does not originate in the workplace, where sexism is only one of many forms of division and discrimination, but in the patriarchal household, where gender roles are the essence of the division of labor. To understand both the impact of gender on development and the impact of development on gender, we must have an understanding of the household economy, its role in shaping the lives of women and men, and its role in the development process.

■ **patriarchy** *male domination in domestic relations between men and women*

The household economy is the production of goods and services within the household, by members of the household, for the direct consumption of the household itself. It is the subsistence part of the household workload, the goods and services that household members produce for themselves rather than for sale or barter to earn an income. In isolated rural households, this might be almost the entire household workload. But even in urban households in which all the adults earn income from outside work, it is a significant proportion of the total work and the total consumption of the household—all the purchasing, the food preparation, the cleaning, the laundry, the maintenance of household goods and property, and especially the care for dependent household members (the very young, the sick, and the very old).

For reasons of both sexist ideology and technical economic measurement problems, none of this work or consumption is included in countries' systems of national income accounts, the gross domestic product (GDP).[3] Domestic production has been called invisible work primarily because its products are not priced and traded in the public arena. But it has remained invisible to mainstream, Marxist, and even many feminist social scientists, because of two ideologically contaminated concepts used to analyze domestic activity: production and consumption.

Production and Consumption

Economists have failed to see that both production and consumption are parts of a continuous process beginning with the extraction of the raw materials of nature and ending with their final human use and return to nature. We decide where on the continuum production ends and consumption begins only by social convention.

The convention among economists is to draw the line in the marketplace, where the product is transferred to the final consumer, who does not intend to process it further and return it to the market for another resale. This convention assumes that any further processing outside of the market and any further nonmarket transfers are not significant. Economic activity outside the household is seen as production, work, service, social contribution; all domestic activity is seen as consumption or leisure. Production outside the household provides use value to society; domestic consumption takes it away again.

If, for purposes of analysis, we must distinguish production from consumption, where should the dividing line be drawn? Perhaps an example will help. Although a chicken egg is apparently a natural food, it takes the work of many people to get the egg from the hen to its consumer. Where does this productive work end and consumption begin? When the last wage worker checked it out of the store into the hands of the domestic worker? But of what use is it there in the store? It must be transported home, an activity no different from the productive work of others who transported it along the earlier stages of its journey. It has more use value at home than it did in the store, so hauling it home is productive work. Once home, someone unpacks the groceries and stores the egg in the kitchen. Work? It was when the egg was put into storage two or three times before, so it must be work now. After all, if it adds value to the egg to transport it to where it is needed, it also adds value to preserve it until it is needed. Later someone takes the egg out of kitchen storage and makes herself an omelet. Is that production or consumption? What if a woman who doesn't even like omelets makes it for her husband? In both cases, it's still processing, still adding value, still production. Once finally readied to eat, the food must be served, whether onto plates for a meal at home or into bags for a meal at work. (Notice how natural the difference sounds: it is embedded in our culture to think that at home is not at work, and at work is not at home.) Still more value is added, more production, more work. Even when food is set on plates in front of their faces, some members of the household, infants and the infirm, need more work from someone before they can consume it.

The division between production and consumption is a matter of arbitrary convention. Different conventions serve different ideological purposes. Whoever's ideological interest is served by drawing the line between the market and the domestic economy, it is obviously not the household workers'. Why not place it where logic would seem to require? As long as an activity adds rather than subtracts utility or use value, we call that activity production.

Thus housework is production, not consumption. In fact, it has been argued that even in an advanced capitalist economy like the United States, "the household sector consumes roughly the same number of work hours as the market sector, and . . . produces an income in kind estimated somewhere between 25 percent and 50 percent of the GNP."[4]

Women's and Men's Roles

It is useful to describe the work relations within which this production takes place, to see who produces these use values and who receives them as income. The most important work relations are those between the classes of direct producers and nonproducers. In analyzing feudalism, we focus on the relations between serfs and lords; in capitalism, between workers and capitalists. Although it is evident that in domestic production the producers tend to be women and the nonproducers men, as housework surveys have shown us over and over,[5] we lack a more precise vocabulary for describing the working and leisure classes of domestic production.

Let's call those in the working class of domestic production *dependents* and those in the leisure class *heads of households*, using the terms commonly applied to these roles. In a sense, of course, the relations of dependence are actually the reverse, since leisure classes are always more dependent for their survival on producing classes than vice versa. Domestic or **patriarchal household production** is an exploitative form of production, because the labor is almost wholly produced by the female dependents within the household and because the male head of household consumes the use values produced by his dependents. He benefits from this exploitation both in the values he appropriates and in the leisure time resulting from the fact that others provide for his needs.

■ **patriarchal household production** *system of household labor in which household members (largely women) produce use values for direct consumption or accumulation within the household*

Why Women Stay Home and Do Men's Housework

A summary description of the economic base of domestic production is this: women dependents produce most of the goods and services their household heads demand, even though they receive little or nothing in return. Why? What compels them to do this? They are driven by the same forms of power that generally force subordinates to forgo their own self-interest for the benefit of their superiors: economic, legal, and ideological sanctions backed by the threat of force. Let's examine these.

The principal economic force that has compelled women to work as household dependents has been their denial of access to ownership of capital for domestic production—a physical residence outfitted with the necessary household tools and furnishings. Before the full subordination of domestic production to capitalist and statist forms of production, this denial was accomplished by legal and ideological norms that prevented all women (with the exception of some widows) from establishing themselves as independent heads of their own households. In advanced capitalist countries, these extraeconomic norms have been replaced to some extent by economic mechanisms: the denial to household dependents of access to cash or credit necessary to rent or purchase a residence for themselves. In many developing countries, however, domestic property laws still make it difficult or impossible for women to legally possess their own residences independent of their fathers or husbands.

Once women can acquire households of their own (and capitalism, combined with the women's movement, has gone far in many countries, including the United States, toward making this possible), the domestic form of production is threatened. Women, choosing poverty over patriarchy, begin to establish their own households. As laws tying women and men to their households have begun to break down worldwide, the proportion of women and children living in households without men, households usually referred to as "female headed," has risen dramatically. Sometimes, these women have chosen not to live with the fathers of their children; sometimes they have been evicted or deserted by men who can't or won't share their income to support them. Something analogous happened at the end of feudalism. Cities filled up with desperately poor former serfs—some forced out against their will when landlords fenced common lands and evicted tenant farmers, and some attracted by the promise of greater freedom and opportunity.

But if lack of legal alternatives partially explains why women live in households with men, why do they take on the role of dependents whose labor provides for the consumption needs of men, making men into nonproducing household heads? Gender-role norms, once embodied in law but now largely legitimized only by ideology, lead women to believe that the performance of this labor is a natural and inevitable aspect of their gender roles as women, of their family roles as wives and mothers, or of their roles as partners in heterosexual love relationships. These ideologies constitute the norm of what Nazzari called the *support-service marriage*,[6] and they are seriously undermined only when women enter the workforce to help support the household, something they are now doing in unprecedented numbers.

As important as the economic and ideological factors are for the extraction of this household labor from women, they should not lead us to neglect the most primitive means of compulsion—violence and the threat of violence. Feminist work in family and criminal research has helped us understand the extent of the day-to-day violence to which men subject women within the household and without. Historically, wife beating permeated most societies; until very recently, it was permitted by law in the United States (as it still is in many developing countries). For a large but not yet estimable proportion of household dependents, fear of violence is part of the bond tying women to their household heads. Generalized male violence against women, where women are victimized by men outside of their own households, lends ideological and material support to domestic production by making women unsafe unless they are protected by their own household heads.

Under these conditions, men can exchange protection for exploitation, an exchange that has formed part of the ideological justification for most precapitalist systems of class relations, especially feudalism. Simple horticultural societies, with their division of labor between warrior men and farmer-worker women, were explicitly organized on this basis worldwide. These societies were probably the original historical form of patriarchal household production. Organized male violence against women and a woman's need to live under the domain of one male household head to protect her against the random acts of violence of other men have been central to patriarchal production since its beginning.

Let us turn now from an analysis of women's subordination, the depressing reality of victimization that many men and women would rather not confront, to the more uplifting task of describing what can be done about it and already is being done by those working for truly equitable development.

Implications for Antipatriarchal Practice

Shifts in consciousness and shifts in strategy are necessary for those of us who want development to lessen discrimination against women. It is possible to hope for more than we might have dared—the demise of patriarchy, at least in advanced capitalist countries. At the same time, it is necessary to reorient our understanding of what hurts and what helps women most.

On the one hand, economically successful capitalist countries now need almost all dependents to participate in the paid labor force, and they seek to sell services in the market that the domestic economy has traditionally provided (child care, elder care, household maintenance). On the other hand, access to household utilities such as electricity and running water has so increased the productivity of domestic labor that it is possible for every wage worker to also do his or her own domestic production, as wage-earning wives and mothers already do. This is the material condition that has made possible the dramatic increase in single-adult households in societies like the United States.

Implications for Women-in-Development Theory and Practice

The central conundrum of women-in-development thinking is whether economic development helps or harms the lot of women in developing countries. There is plenty of case study evidence that sometimes it does one and sometimes the other. Development harms women when it "domesticates" them, forces them back into the household from economic roles they played outside. Development helps women when it draws them partway out of the domestic economy, providing them with incomes and economic lives independent of their household patriarchs.

To see how and why women are sometimes drawn out of and sometimes pushed back into domestic work by economic development, we must examine the different sectors of production present in most developing countries' economies. Besides the household sector, which is quite important in developing countries, there are the capitalist and state sectors contesting for dominance, and there are two smaller sectors: self-employed microenterprise and the nongovernmental nonprofits or cooperatives. The state sector refers to goods and services produced by government entities for distribution as they choose. Self-employed microenterprise involves production for the market but without paid nonfamily labor; it is more or less synonymous with the informal sector of a country's economy. Co-op socialism is production by religious-based or community nonprofit organizations or cooperatives, more or less participatorily managed.

In developing countries today, most domestic work is done by women and most microenterprises are run by women.[7] The state and nonprofit socialist sectors overwhelmingly employ men, unless conscious effort has been made to employ women, although most unpaid voluntary work in nonprofit nongovernmental organizations (NGOs) is done by women. The capitalist part of the economy has a noncompetitive, state-regulated import-substitution sector that employs males at high wages and a competitive (often export-oriented) sector that employs women at low wages. In other words, work in household and microenterprise sectors and in the competitive sector of the capitalist economy is done mostly by unpaid or low-paid women. Paid work in the state, co-op, and noncompetitive capitalist sectors is done mostly by high-paid men. This is not a coincidence.

State and Co-op Socialist Sectors

Although there is no reason that state agencies and nonprofits should not hire women, the people running them are part of the local culture based on patriarchy. Development projects that expand employment in either the state or the co-op sector may do so at the expense of informal-sector women who used to provide those goods and services.

Women-in-development projects often involve helping women develop strong self-esteem, literacy and numeracy, good health and nutrition, family planning awareness, and other human capacities necessary to shift labor time out of the domestic economy. This work is effective only insofar as it actually helps women break out of patriarchy. None of it, even basic health care and birth control information, will do as much good if it remains an end in itself. The sectors in which these programs are working are, at least so far, part of the problem, not part of the solution. Building the state sector or building a community organization has no necessary relation whatsoever to ending patriarchy. An important part of development project work must be the constant battle, within and among organizations and agencies, to neutralize their legal and ideological support for the maintenance of the patriarchal mode of production.

Self-employed Microenterprise Production

A second approach has been to go to the one sector where women predominate and where poor women obtain most of whatever cash income they do earn, microenterprise production. The idea here is to identify and eliminate the obstacles to microenterprise expansion to increase the income of female microentrepreneurs. The basic idea is sound, and the potential exists to help many women move from barely productive and poorly compensated work in this sector to more substantial and economically independent roles. Access to credit for women, as provided by the Grameen Bank in Bangladesh, has had a tremendous impact on women's ability to start and operate microenterprises. Another idea, based on deSoto's work in Peru,[8] is to help microentrepreneurs primarily by removing licensing and regulatory obstacles that prevent them from growing into larger capitalist firms.

Household Labor

One of the material preconditions for the shift of women's labor out of unpaid domestic production is a dramatic increase in the productivity of their household labor. Traditionally, this was thought to have been accomplished by two principal mechanisms: labor-saving household machinery and the export of tasks into the monetary economy (for example, the milling of grain and the weaving and sewing of clothes). But Cowan[9] showed in the United States case that labor-saving household appliances such as vacuum cleaners, washers, and driers raise household standards of cleanliness more than they reduce labor time. Cowan also showed that moving tasks outside the household into the market merely shifts labor time from household manufacturing to shopping and transport. Both tend to improve the quality of life of the household and make the household work slightly less physically demanding, but neither actually reduces labor time much or raises its productivity.

So what does raise housework productivity? Cowan points out that nothing is as important as access to utilities. No single act reduces household labor time more than the provision of water and fuel to the household. Carrying water and gathering fuel are two of the most labor-intensive and time-consuming tasks in the domestic economy. Utilities not only save this labor but also save labor in myriad other household tasks in which a more generous use of water or heat can clean or process things faster and with less work. A second factor, surprisingly, is access to vaccinations, preventive health care, and the most simple drugs such as aspirin and oral rehydration salts. Sometimes these health measures save lives, but they always greatly reduce the actual time needed to care for the dangerously ill. In poverty environments without access to basic health services, caring for the sick can take a high proportion of a household's available dependent labor.

At least as important as these productivity enhancers are improvements in household human capital. Literacy, numeracy, and access to home economics information also lead to increased labor productivity as they build self-esteem and broaden access to extrahousehold income opportunities. What the BBSD perspective adds to traditional women-in-development thought is insight into the importance of potable water, new fuels, electrification, and vaccines as crucial empowerment activities. Women cannot move out of the patriarchal economy until investments in physical and human infrastructure have increased the productivity of their domestic labor.

The Capitalist Sector

The possibilities for ending patriarchy in developing countries can grow only with a long-term expansion of capitalist employment and production. But women's pay and working conditions in the world's clothing, electronic assembly, and agribusiness factories are awful by any civilized standard. So why do we propose the expansion of these kinds of factories and this kind of work?

The standard needed to assess women's work in these plants is not any civilized standard but one that the women themselves apply: comparison to paid and unpaid domestic work.[10] Fortunately for women, capitalism prefers hardworking, productively disciplined workers. And in the developing world, the patriarchal household sector is a much more reliable source of this kind of worker than any economic sector in which men have been engaged. Competitive-sector capitalist firms hire women preferentially without feminists making the argument for them to do so and without regard for the damage done to local, patriarchy-supporting cultural traditions. Let these firms do their historical work. Their employees see working there as a step up, not a step down.

BBSD and Women's Empowerment

What does the literature have to say about women's empowerment and development? Empowerment of women has been shown to be directly affected by increases in educational attainment and increases in independent sources of income such as employment or self-employment. The empowerment impact of income is greatest for women with the lowest incomes, but the social psychological increases in empowerment for each

■ **cultural pluralization** *exposure to gender roles and norms of cultures other than one's own*

additional unit of income are important throughout the income range. Four other variables have been shown to have an impact on women's empowerment, but their impact is greatly increased when combined with increased income, education, or both. These are (1) legal reforms resulting in human rights equality for women under the laws of the country; (2) women's self-organization, or the formation of women-oriented membership and self-help groups in civil society; (3) **cultural pluralization**; and (4) increased productivity of women's domestic work.

Since women's empowerment is a difficult term for applied social scientists to handle methodologically and politically, studies of the impact of women's empowerment on development have usually been defined as studies of the impact of women's increased education and income on development. These developmental linkages, from women's empowerment to BBSD for the whole society, are extraordinary in their variety. Every year, new studies emerge documenting new linkages.

Women's Empowerment and Human Resource Development

The most documented and by now traditional linkages are those regarding health, nutrition, and population. For twenty years, studies have demonstrated that increased income and education for women result in improved health and nutritional status for themselves, their children, and other members of their families. Studies have also shown that increased educational attainment, especially at the secondary level and beyond, and increased income opportunities both result in lower fertility. Women with more education and income want to have fewer children and have the increased means and status to translate that desire into lower lifetime fertility.

Women's increased education and income (a portion of which becomes available for reinvestment in productive activities) have also been shown to lead directly to increased productivity in women's economic activities. This has been shown to be true for women's farming and livestock management, home-based microenterprises, and small business ventures. Case studies in a variety of cultures have shown that in many circumstances women have a relatively high propensity to save and invest. This increases their productivity and at the same time makes them excellent risks for production credit programs. Worldwide, small credit programs like the Grameen Bank in Bangladesh have found that loans to groups of women enable the women to significantly increase their households' productivity and thus their standards of living at very little cost to development agencies, since the loans have such a high rate of repayment.

Women's Empowerment and Democratization

As interest has grown in the civil society and democratization aspects of BBSD, women's role in furthering these goals has come under study. First, women are much more likely to participate in the organizational life of civil society and democratic politics if they have enough education to achieve literacy and enough income security to escape the day-to-day desperation of the lowest levels of poverty. Second, suggestive case studies in Latin America, South Asia, and the Middle East show that women are more likely than men to engage in political activity with modest and pragmatic goals and less likely to accept totalistic goals of revolutionary or fundamentalist societal transformation. To the extent that this is true in a particular society and culture, the greater the participation of women in political life, the more democratic pluralism is furthered in its political culture. This has been shown to be the case in Latin America, where outstanding examples include women's organizations such as the Madres and Consciencia in Argentina and the communal kitchen movement in Peru.[11] It also seems to be the case in Islamic societies and in western and southern Africa.

Women's Empowerment and
Environmental Sustainability

The final dimension of BBSD, environmental sustainability, may also be enhanced by the empowerment of women. In many cultures, women are charged with the day-to-day management of familial and communal natural resources. In many cultures, they have shown a greater propensity to prefer a more risk-averse and environmentally sustainable pattern of agriculture than men in the same culture, who are more easily attracted to short-term, profit-maximizing commercial monocultivation. In many cultures, women, more than men, are conscious and supportive of preserving environmental assets, such as the air we breathe and the water we drink, and amenities for their children's generation.

For whatever reason, all over the developing world where there are grassroots organizations with environmental and sustainable development goals, women play a relatively more important leadership and membership role than they do in many other political movements. The best possible example of this is the Chipko movement in northern India in the 1970s, the original source of the term *tree-huggers*. This was a movement of indigenous women who saved their communal woodlots from devastating commercial logging by rising every day before the male loggers came to work and hugging the trees, one women per tree, to prevent the men from getting at them with their bulldozers and chain saws. Because of women's environmental sensitivities, concerns, and concrete activism, the literature suggests that women's empowerment will also further environmental sustainability.

Notes

Earlier versions of some of these ideas appeared in Ken Kusterer, "The Imminent Demise of Patriarchy," in *Persistent Inequalities: Women and World Development*, ed. Irene Tinker (New York: Oxford University Press, 1990).

1. Esther Boserup, *Women's Role in Economic Development* (New York: St. Martin's Press, 1970).
2. Maria Mies, *Patriarchy and Accumulation on a World Scale: Women in the International Division of Labor* (London: Zed Press, 1986).
3. See Marilyn Waring, *If Women Counted* (New York: Harper and Row, 1988).

4. Luisella Goldschmidt-Clermont, *Unpaid Work in the Household* (Geneva: International Labor Organization, 1982), 109.
5. Richard A. Berk and Sarah Fenstermaker Berk, "A Simultaneous Equation Model for the Division of Household Labor," *Sociological Methods and Research* 6 (1979): 431–66.
6. Muriel Nazzari, "The Significance of Present Day Changes in the Institution of Marriage," *Review of Radical Political Economics* 12 (1980): 63–75.
7. Carl Liedholm and Donald Meed, *Small Scale Industries in Developing Countries*, Michigan State University International Paper No. 9 (East Lansing: Michigan State University, 1987).
8. Hernando deSoto, *The Other Path* (New York: Harper and Row, 1989).
9. Ruth Schwartz Cowan, *More Work for Mother: The Ironies of Household Technology from the Open Hearth to the Microwave* (New York: Basic Books, 1983).
10. Ken Kusterer, Josefina Xuya Cuxil, and Estrada de Batres, *The Social Impact of Agribusiness: The Case of ALCOSA in Guatemala*, Special Study 4 (Washington, D.C.: Agency for International Development, 1981).
11. Ken Kusterer, "Women-Oriented NGOs in Latin America: Democracy's Decisive Wave," in *Women at the Center*, ed. Gay Young, Vidya Samarasinghe, and Ken Kusterer (West Hartford, Conn.: Kumarian Press, 1993).

13

The Role of Civil Society

ALL CONTEMPORARY ECONOMIES CONTAIN at least five different forms of organization for the production of goods and service: private enterprises, government or state agencies and departments, households engaged in subsistence work, nonprofit institutions, and self-employed microenterprises. This chapter is about the role of the nonprofit sector in broad-based sustainable development (BBSD) and about policies that foster the growth of **civil society**.

■ civil society *nonprofit, nongovernmental organizations*

BBSD as Organizational Development and the Growth of Social Capital

Achieving BBSD means encouraging firms, individual entrepreneurs, and organizations to expand in size and in productivity, to fulfill more of the population's unmet needs for goods and services, to provide more people with higher paying and more skilled and interesting work, and to increase and diversify the society's stock of social and human capital and organizational capacity. In essence, this chapter looks at the emergence, growth, and development of the nonprofit sector as organizational development. The term *organizational development* usually refers to the increase in capacity of a single organization. As used here, however, organizational development adds the idea that societal development is partially the sum of the increased capacities of all the organizations in the society. It is possible and useful to develop organizational capacity one organization at a time, but societal development requires changes in the institutional and policy environment to allow or encourage the expansion of the capacities of many organizations all at once.

All societies are characterized by social organization. Every society normally (that is, except when disrupted by the dislocations resulting from prolonged war or civil conflict) has a network of social roles and social relations sufficient to carry out the economic, political, and cultural functions necessary for that society's survival.

How should we think about organizational development, particularly organizational development of the nonprofit sector? Today, social network theory is the most powerful tool for analyzing organizational development.[1] Network theory is based on the concept of **social capital**. Capital is the total productive assets that an individual, a group or organization, or a society possesses. Capital in its original sense is **material capital**, but there is another kind of productive asset called human capital. The more material and human capital an individual or a society has, the greater its potential productive capacity.

- **social capital** *social connections or relations that have been established and can be drawn on*
- **material capital** *value of physical wealth—physical plant, tools, equipment, technology, raw materials—available*

Social capital is a third kind of productive asset. These social connections or social relations are not as free and easy as they might appear, however. Significant social investments—networking initiatives that must be taken and personal time and energy that must be expended—are needed to establish new ones. Once established, these relations must be constantly maintained with continuing investments of time and energy or they will fade away and disappear.[2] Economists use a similar concept, *transaction costs*, to refer to the time and effort needed to create or maintain economic transactions. The stock of these already established social connections is the social capital that any individual, organization, or society has available.

Because of its extreme individualism, because of the informality with which it encourages the establishment of new social relations, and probably also because of its relegation of the duty of maintaining relationships to females, American culture tends to undervalue the importance of social capital as a social asset contributing to BBSD. Firms in the United States specifically count their material capital and carefully monitor its growth. They less precisely, but no less carefully, monitor the growth of their human capital. Only in the 1980s did they begin to equally value their social capital. This new emphasis was manifest in the glut of books on Japanese management styles and techniques, in the faddish fascination with networking as a means for business expansion and career enhancement, and in the booming sales of "personal contact manager" software for personal computers. Other cultures—perhaps because social norms make the establishment of new relations of trust or exchange more difficult—have always better appreciated the value of social network connections as productive assets.

Network theory states that organizational development requires, among other things, investment and increase in social capital, strengthening the social connections and social relations within and among organizations. Ordinarily, this takes the form of formalizing, or institutionalizing, informal connections that already exist. When this happens, relations between different positions and different organizations persist, even if the individuals in those positions or organizations should change. Two individuals might have shared goals and a good relationship, and thus their two organizations can work together, but unless the relationship between the organizations is formalized, the connection will not survive when one of the individuals moves on to another position or another organization.

Formalization to strengthen the durability of existing personal connections—when it occurs in the arenas of community improvement, political advocacy, or civic action—results in the building of civil society, the network of nongovernmental, nonprofit organizations. When it occurs in the economic arena of producing goods and services for sale on the local market, it results in the transformation of informal microenterprises into formally organized successful businesses.

Civil Society

Various terms have been used to describe the organizations that make up the social network that constitutes civil society. The most common term used today is nongovernmental organization, or NGO. The traditional sociological terms that have been used for generations are secondary associations or voluntary associations. Primary associations are kinship, church, and citizenship—you are born into your family, church, and state and cannot change that fact. Secondary or voluntary organizations are ones that you choose to join. The term *voluntary* also emphasizes that you aren't paid to join; you are not an employee of the organization. Another way of thinking of these organizations is as mediating organizations that lie between primary associations on the one hand and the state on the other.

Let's look at some specific examples—the Self-Employed Women's Association (SEWA) of India and the Grameen Bank of Bangladesh. Both are organizations of poor women microentrepreneurs organized to help one another with credit, training, support, and political activism.

These organizations have small paid professional staffs, but the actual services provided to the membership are provided primarily by other members, acting as volunteers. These volunteer members are not paid anything, and all the program resources come from donations of time, money, or both. Even though some resources are used to pay the staff, very little of the money that SEWA and the Grameen Bank get comes from selling their services on the market, and very little of the revenue they get comes from government allocations. They are each a perfect prototype of an NGO.

Charities, youth groups, service clubs, church groups, trade unions, amateur soccer leagues, hobby groups, advocacy groups, community organizations, grassroots community groups, community improvement and betterment groups, self-help groups, Alcoholics Anonymous, and all other kindred organizations are part of civil society. These organizations serve three kinds of functions that have been studied by three different disciplines as if they were not studying the same set of organizations.

Sociocultural Functions of Civil Society

The sociological literature talks about the sociocultural functions of these organizations, such as social cohesion or social solidarity. The founder of French sociology Emile Durkheim, in his classic work *Suicide*,[3] demonstrated statistically that people who belong to organizations like this were less likely to commit suicide, were less likely to feel isolated, alienated, and cut off from the rest of society. It is necessary to individual personal and psychological health to be affiliated, to be part of a network. And as the primary groups broke down in the process of modernization, the church and the family no longer had the total influence they once had. It became more important for people to find alternatives that tied them to society in a freer and more voluntary way.

The sociocultural functions of civil society groups are to promote social cohesion; combat isolation, alienation, and anomie; train future leaders; develop organizational skills; and raise the self-confidence and self-esteem of members. Some groups, called affinity groups, don't have any great purpose beyond the enjoyment of their members; these include amateur athletic teams (soccer, bowling), hobby clubs (gardening, card playing), or social clubs of any sort. They still accomplish the basic sociocultural functions and thus benefit their communities as well as their members.

Economic Functions of Civil Society

Some NGOs intend to contribute to their members or communities in a tangible way. As voluntary organizations, they must add meaning and enjoyment to their members' lives to keep the members active and participating, but they also organize to meet the needs of their members or their communities. Examples include service clubs (Lions, Rotary, Junior League), community development organizations, unions, professional associations, self-help groups (Alcoholics Anonymous, Parents without Partners), youth service groups (Boy and Girl Scouts, 4-H), charitable organizations, community performing arts groups (music, dance, theater), and educational organizations of all sorts and levels. What this diverse group of NGOs has in common is that each sets its members to work to produce a good or service that adds value to the lives of either the members themselves or their communities.

These NGOs serve economic functions. They produce services, solve social problems, mobilize local resources to meet local needs, provide competitive alternatives to state agencies, and increase local self-sufficiency and decrease dependency. NGOs that do these things are often grouped under the category of *civic associations*. When a civic association becomes large enough to have a substantial paid staff in addition to its base of members and volunteers, it is classified as a nonprofit agency, such as the Red Cross, the Environmental Defense Fund, or any number of community- or church-based hospitals and universities. All nonprofits, although they have paid staffs and are thus not purely voluntary organizations, are nevertheless NGOs and part of civil society.

Nonprofits are not only conceptually different from for-profits, they actually behave differently most of the time. Most nonprofits make the services they produce available to people on some basis other than willingness to pay. For example, the admissions criteria of nonprofit private universities are not based on how much money each applicant is willing to bid for a place in the entering class. In a private, for-profit market operation, universities would choose the entering class by admitting those who were willing to pay the most. But universities decide, according to their own criteria, who the most deserving applicants are, and that is who they admit. If it turns out that some of them don't have any money, the university says, "Come anyway, we'll find you a scholarship." Imagine that you go into a for-profit store and say, "I really like that TV you sell. I would really like to have that TV, but unfortunately, I don't have any money." Would the salesperson say, "Well, we have a scholar-ship system. How much do you have?" Could you buy the TV for what-ever price you happened to be able to afford? Of course not, because for-profit companies don't raise donations to subsidize poor but worthy customers.

Nonprofits often have sliding fees, based on the client's ability to pay for the cost of the service. Nonprofit organizations are likely to be the only source of services for the poor besides the government. NGOs are not always designed to be charitable, and many nonprofits don't make their services available to the poor and don't even intend to. But some do, and if the poor aren't able to pay for the cost of the services, they are sub-sidized by the NGO.

Thus NGOs, especially grassroots NGOs, are a way of organizing people to volunteer time and labor to make services available that wouldn't otherwise exist. They can often make these services available at a lower price than anybody else could, because so many of their costs are donated. And because of the commitment of the people involved, it is possible to get them to extend themselves far beyond what a paid employee would be willing to do. As a consequence, NGOs are an effec-tive means of making services available in a society and making them available to people who otherwise would be served only by the state. This creates across-the-board competition to the state, competition that may make the state sector more efficient.

The nonprofit sector in the mid-1980s was the fastest growing employ-ment sector in the United States. It is a big and important part of the economy. In a basically capitalist market economy, many organizations that might have originated as NGOs mutate to become indistinguishable from capitalist firms. There are lots of examples of corporate organiza-tions that began as sort of socialistic communes—for instance, Amana, the appliance maker, and Oneida silverware. A similar process happened to many of the farm cooperatives started in the 1930s, such as Sunkist. Today, the same thing is going on with hospitals and other organizations that were established as nonprofit charitable organizations and may now be indistinguishable from the hospital across town that is run by a for-profit corporation. But just as the largest and most established NGOs become capitalist companies, if the civic culture is healthy and dynamic, new, idealistic, grassroots NGOs rise up to take their place.[4]

Political Functions of Civil Society

Let us turn now to political scientists and their analysis of civil society. Nowadays, when you hear people talk about civil society, they are hardly ever talking about either sociological or economic functions, important as they are. They are almost always talking about the political functions. NGOs can act as interest groups: to lobby, to mobilize people who otherwise don't have access to state power, and to gather them together in groups so that they can have some influence and participate in the governmental decision-making process.

The classic modern examples of NGOs that have transformed the international political environment and are growing in developing societies everywhere are women's organizations such as DAWN (Development Alternatives with Women for New Era), human rights organizations such as Human Rights Watch and Amnesty International, and environmental organizations such as Greenpeace and the Environmental Defense Fund. These organizations make educational and organizational services available to their members, but the most important service they provide is increased political effectiveness for governmental policy changes favoring their causes.

The political functions of civil society groups are to increase participation in political processes, provide voice and political empowerment to members, and force governments to be more open and more responsive.

It looks like an effectively functioning civil society is one of the prerequisites for a democratic political system. At the same time, these organizations with their competing interests make it difficult for democratic governments to make tough political and economic decisions.

Measuring Civil Society

Sociologists have measured a society's civil society on two dimensions. The first is the density of civil society, that is, the number of organizations there are per capita, or the per capita number of organization memberships. If we are talking about the number of organizations, we get an idea of the diversity in civil society. If we find out the number of memberships each organization has, we get an idea of how strong civil society is and how many people are incorporated in it. The United States is the society with the most such memberships. Americans stand out for their enthusiasm in forming and joining these associations, as de Tocqueville pointed out in the nineteenth century in *Democracy in America*.[5]

The second dimension of civil society we measure is its breadth, the percentage of society that belongs to such organizations. In the United States, a little under 20 percent of the people do not belong to any such organizations. We have no international standardized comparative surveys that provide this information cross-nationally or over time.

Policies that Promote the Growth of Civil Society

What policies are necessary to promote the development of social capital in civil society? Most important is protection for the human rights of free speech, association, and assembly. These rights protect the people who advocate starting civil society organizations, organize people to come together and form the group (association), and hold meetings and group activities (assembly). For civil society to develop, two levels of protection of these human rights are necessary. First, the government itself must not prohibit or repress these activities. The government may do this out of a belief in these human rights or because it lacks the will or ability to actively mobilize itself to carry out such repression. It is the latter condition that often allows civil society to get off to a flying start toward democratization in the waning days of dictatorships, when the government takes no positive steps to encourage such organizations yet lacks the will or resources to effectively repress them. Second, the government must protect civil society activities from repression by their nongovernmental enemies: repression of unions by employers, poor people's organizations by local elites, radical or innovative political and cultural groups by defenders of tradition and orthodoxy.

Security of the human right to organize is the single most important step in encouraging the expansion and formalization of existing informal or even underground social networks. This sounds simple in principle, but in actual governmental practice, it is not simple to implement. There are no governments anywhere that permit the free activity of organizations that advocate treason, the illegal overthrow of the existing government, or criminal activities such as trade in illegal narcotics. How is a government to decide whether any particular civil society organization has crossed over the bounds of illegality? In common-law legal systems, like that of England, the United States, and former British colonies, there is a presumption that all civil society organizations are legal unless the government can prove otherwise. This is akin to the principle embodied in the same legal systems that all persons accused of crimes are innocent until proved guilty. Practically, this means that organizations are free to start up and need not register with the government unless they seek some special relationship with the government, such as the right to tax exemption or the right to act as a registered lobbying organization in the legislature.

In most legal systems around the world, however, new organizations must register with the government to be legal; unregistered organizations are, by definition, illegal organizations. This is true in legal systems based on traditional Chinese law, such as in Japan, Korea, and much of Asia; those based on Roman law, which includes the legal systems of France, Spain, Portugal, and all their former colonies in Latin America, Africa, and Asia; and the legal system of the former Soviet Union. In these systems, no organization, no matter how benign or innocuous its purpose, is free to operate legally until it has filed an application with the government and the application has been approved.

In these permit-based systems of civil society regulation, permits are frequently unavailable, not necessarily due to any intent to repress human rights (although such an intent may be present), but simply because the system of governance has broken down. The regulatory agency doesn't have the resources or the system in place to routinely process and approve applications, and there is a backlog, which may mean that they are never approved. In this situation, few organizations bother to legalize themselves, which leaves them vulnerable in times of political conflict. The only organizations that do seek and receive legal status are those connected with and partially funded by foreign aid programs, in which case the government must issue the permit to receive the foreign aid, or those organizations established by people who are well connected with the governmental elite.

Paradoxically, the NGOs of civil society can expand their capacity only if the government expands its own governance capacity to regulate and enforce human rights protection. This is true in permit-based systems simply to legalize and formalize the NGOs. But it is equally true in common-law, no-permit systems, when it comes to enforcing and guaranteeing the human rights of civil society participants. All over the world, since the reinvigoration of grassroots NGO development efforts in the 1970s, there have been thousands of examples of "nonpolitical" NGO development efforts to help poor people leading to the deaths of innocent activists at the hands of threatened interests, with the government being unable to provide any effective protection. Literacy in their own language, expanded job opportunities or increased family incomes, family planning information, preservation of community environmental resources, even preservation of minority cultures—all these goals of NGO activities have been seen as threatening to powerful interests at certain times and in certain countries. Everywhere—the Philippines, Myanmar, Malaysia, Pakistan, Kenya, Nigeria, the West Bank, Sicily, Guatemala, Brazil, Peru—NGO leaders have been killed and their followers intimidated because their governments were unable or unwilling to prevent this kind of repressive violence.[6]

For all these reasons, nothing is so important to the growth of civil society as the human rights policies of governments and their capacity to enforce their own policies and protect their own citizens. These policies range from the level of general principle—a commitment to human rights and to effective governance—to the level of technical specifics—one-stop permit applications, clear and minimal grounds for permit denial, prompt and bribe-free processing of permit applications.

Beyond government, there are cultural changes that help create the conditions for rapid expansion of civil society. These cultural changes result from increased successful participation in civil society itself, which is one of the reasons that civil society often displays a "takeoff" pattern of initial slow growth, followed by rapid expansion once some critical mass of the population has gained the experience of participation. Most important of these is a "do-it-yourself" approach to the resolution of social problems rather than a total reliance on the intervention of some larger governmental or foreign assistance program.

This cultural attribute is what so struck de Tocqueville in his tour of the United States in the early days of the independent republic.[7] It requires a sense of personal and communal efficacy, and this sense can be fostered by increased social and self-esteem. In lower social strata of poor and previously oppressed peoples, this sense of efficacy can result from a number of different sources: participation in a successful movement of political liberation (de Tocqueville's American case); participation in small-scale but successful community development campaigns or organizations; participation in religious movements with a this-worldly, here-and-now orientation; increased education, both the new knowledge itself and the social recognition of the accomplishment; increased earned income; and work transition from traditional, little-respected occupations (housekeeping, sharecropping, seasonal farm labor) to other occupations with more open-ended opportunities.

Other cultural conditions that foster the development of civil society include a tradition of extrafamilial charitable responsibility, a tradition of volunteer work in service to the community, and a tradition of organized women's communal activities outside the confines of their individual households. Civil society can build these traditions independently where they don't already exist, but civil society expands faster in cultures where these traditions are already available for civil society to draw upon. Several notable developing country leaders, from Kenyatta in Kenya to Nyerere in Tanzania to Mao in China, have sought to push development with government-sponsored public-relations campaigns emphasizing these particular cultural conditions. In all these cases, the emphasis was on increasing participation in party-affiliated or government-connected organizations rather than in truly independent NGOs; nevertheless, the increased participation sought was generally achieved. In the states of the former Soviet system, political scientists have been astounded by how much the organizational skills and even the organizations themselves have been able to make the transition from a party-dominated to a truly independent civil society. As a result, societies like Poland and Russia were able to make an overnight transition from a situation of no legal independent civil society to one of broad participation in a dense civil society network.

Religion and Civil Society

In every society, the first civil society organizations to take root are those affiliated with the traditional religion of the society. This was true in early modern Europe; it was true in Latin America, the region of the developing world with the oldest and most developed civil society; and it is no less true in the Middle East today. There are three reasons for this: the church or mosque is the only formal nonkin, nonstate social connection that many rural individuals have; it is able to protect its activists from state repression better than any independent civil actors can be protected; and the content of the religion encourages some followers to take active responsibility for the moral and social conditions of their communities. So widespread is the extent of religious involvement in pioneer civil society organizations that the sociological study of voluntary organizations has always made a distinction between "traditional" organizations, meaning those with religious affiliations, and "modern" organizations, meaning those that are secular.

There is an important difference in the social consequences of the growth of religiously affiliated versus secular civil society. Civil society based on religion reinforces and solidifies existing social cleavages based on religious differences—between Christians and Jews or Muslims in early modern Europe, between Protestants and Catholics, Muslims and Hindus, Shiite and Sunni. The result is a greater probability of religious strife and civil conflict. Civil society based on nonreligious and nonethnic interests, in contrast, creates a social network that binds and overcomes previous cleavages. People who belong to a multiplicity of organizations, each with a different overlapping membership, have pluralist connections to their society and pluralist interests to defend. Secular civil society thus lessens the risk of religious strife and civil conflict. But a religious social network is always the first to develop. There is no perfect solution to this dilemma, but clearly the transition to pluralist civil society is speeded by the same governmental commitment to human rights and free association that we advocated earlier.

Notes

1. Barry Wellman, "Network Analysis: Some Basic Principles," in *Sociological Theory 1983*, ed. R. Collins (San Francisco: Jossey Bass, 1983), 155–200.
2. Larissa Lomnitz, *Chile's Middle Class* (Boulder, Colo.: Lynne Rienner Press, 1991); *A Mexican Elite Family, 1820–1980* (Princeton, N.J.: Princeton University Press, 1987); *Networks and Marginality: Life in a Mexican Shantytown* (New York: Academic Press, 1977).
3. Emile Durkheim, *Suicide* [1890] (New York: Free Press, 1966).
4. In a widely cited piece, Putnam worries that the United States is losing its civic culture with the expansion of capitalism and the market. Robert Putnam, "Bowling Alone," *Journal of Democracy* 6 (January 1995): 152ff.
5. Alexis de Tocqueville, *Democracy in America* [1838] (New York: Knopf, 1993).
6. Larry Diamond, *The Democratic Revolution: Struggles for Freedom and Democracy in the Developing World* (New York: Freedom House, 1992).
7. de Tocqueville, *Democracy in America*.

14

Freedom to Develop:
Human Rights and
Democratic Participation

EUROPEAN AND NORTH AMERICAN political thought since
Locke and Montesquieu has concentrated on questions of human
rights and democracy, their definitions, their dimensions, and their societal source and effects. There is a theoretical richness and density to this
tradition that might well inform democratization discussions in other
regions of the world.

This tradition draws heavily on the political experience of the
presently industrialized countries of the Northern Hemisphere and uses a
Northern frame of reference even when referring to democratization
processes in other parts of the world. This cultural bias means that
Northern concepts of democracy and human rights cannot be uncriti-
cally applied in other cultural contexts.

But no other tradition of discourse has focused for so long and with
such intensity on the questions of democracy. Democracy discussions
anywhere will be enriched, even if only by the addition of a comparative
context, by an examination of contemporary schools of Northern
thought about democratization and of the assumptions upon which these
schools are based.

This chapter undertakes such an analysis. It begins with definitions of
freedom and democracy, then moves on to describe three modern schools
of thought about democratization, their assumptions about the democratization process, and their prescriptions for a democratizing strategy.

Freedom and Democracy:
Clarifying the Concepts

Are the terms *freedom* and *democracy* interchangeable, merely overlapping, or representative of meaningfully distinct ideas? The recent literature

on these topics among development-oriented thinkers has been driven as much by political and ideological requirements as by the quest for analytic rigor. As a result, Freedom House and now the United Nations Development Program (UNDP) have tended to conflate concepts that are separate: freedom and democracy. The World Bank seeks to make untenable, clear separations, especially between democracy and governance, where only subtle shades of difference exist.[1]

A discussion of democratization must begin by defining what is meant by democracy. The definition used here is centered in the mainstream of political thought from Locke and the Enlightenment to Schumpeter, Dahl, and modern political science. A democracy is a political system characterized by (1) leadership selected on the basis of a competition for greatest public support, (2) decision-making processes that are both publicly known and open to public influence, (3) institutions that provide channels for public participation, and (4) institutions that secure the safety of the members of the public who choose to participate. In short, a democratic system of government is one based on competitively selected leaders, public decision making, and popular participation.

None of these three characteristics of a democracy is an all-or-nothing variable. So a system of government can be more or less competitive, more or less open, more or less participatory, more or less democratic. Nevertheless, democratization is a broader process than just changing the political system along any of these dimensions. The reason that this is so should become clear after the discussion about the sources, causes, or prerequisites of democracy.

One final point about the definition of democracy needs to be made. The unit that is more or less democratic is a *political system*. This term refers to the entire social system of political decision making—not only the actual governmental agencies and institutions but all the organizations of political action, the parties, the lobbyists, the advocacy groups, the policy experts, the citizens' groups. The entire spectrum of contemporary political science is in accord on this point. The unit of analysis in discussing democracy or any other type of political system is neither the government in isolation nor the society as a whole but something in between, the organizational arena for political action, or the political system.

This last point is important in understanding the too seldom noted difference between democracy and freedom. That which is democratic is a system of government, but that which is free is an individual. An individual is free not just because the system of government is democratic but also because none of other organizations of society coercively restricts that individual. The individual is free only if all the institutions of society provide her that freedom. Slavery, serfdom, bondage, and servitude, though they cannot exist without the tolerance of government, have usually had their sources in a society's economic and family system, not in its political system. Freedom must be defined as the absence of all oppression, not only oppression by the government.

No more eloquent statement of what is meant by freedom has ever been written than that contained in the U.S. Declaration of Independence. These words have inspired revolutionaries and freedom fighters throughout the world.

> We hold these truths to be self-evident, that all men are created equal, that they are endowed by their Creator with certain unalienable Rights, that among these are Life, Liberty and the pursuit of Happiness.
>
> That to secure these rights, Governments are instituted among Men, deriving their just powers from the consent of the governed,
>
> That whenever any Form of Government becomes destructive of these ends, it is the Right of the People to alter or abolish it, and to institute new Government.

In the classic Northern tradition of political thought, freedom has been specified in terms of a list of three kinds of inalienable human rights of individuals. These include rights of personal security, or the guarantee that, without due process of law, an individual will always be free from torture, death, imprisonment, exile, seizure, or even search of person or property. They also include rights of personal expression, or the freedom to communicate (both to speak or transmit and to listen or receive), to peacefully assemble, to associate (to organize and to join organizations), to practice one's religion, to practice one's culture, to speak one's language, and to travel or reside wherever one chooses. Finally, they include rights of political participation, in essence, the right to live in a democratic political system: to vote, to run for office, to support candidates, to petition the government. To this list of rights has been added in the past hundred years economic rights: the right of access to work or income; the right to food, shelter, health care, education; the right to a safe and healthy place of work and residence. These rights are more controversial, especially in the United States, which continues in its popular culture to regard these as personal responsibilities of individuals for themselves rather than as societal obligations to individuals.[2] But they are accepted in all the other industrialized countries, and they are accepted in the documents and treaties of the United Nations.

The human rights perspective on freedom thus calls an individual free if she is secure in her ability to pursue any and all of these rights free of fear or intimidation. Societies are referred to as free if the population of that society is free. Societies distribute freedom differentially among their populations. Majority ethnic groups may be free, minorities less so; men may be free, women less so; the affluent may be free, the indigent less so; citizens may be free, immigrants less so. A determination of how free a society is, therefore, involves two dimensions: how many rights the freer sectors of the population enjoy, and what proportion of the total population belongs to the freer sectors and enjoys those rights.

The progress of freedom, so celebrated in Northern culture and ideology, has been understood as the extension of human rights to categories of people previously excluded from the inner circles of freedom. In Europe and North America in the last 300 years, the entitlement to inalienable human rights has spread from aristocrats, to free men of property, to all male citizens, to males who were formerly slaves, and then finally to women. The only substantial group whose human rights are still in question in the core Northern free societies are indigenous people and undocumented immigrant noncitizens recently arrived from the developing world. Ironically, Northern governments that push developing country governments to respect the natural human rights of their citizens sometimes deny the rights of those same people when they migrate North.

Assumptions about the Causes and Sources of Democracy

There have been three schools of thought about democratization. The dominant perspective from the 1950s and early 1960s spoke explicitly about societal prerequisites for democracy.

From the late 1960s until the 1980s, explicit attention shifted away from democratization toward economic development and meeting basic human needs. Although they were seldom made explicit, the operative assumptions were based on the idea of a Maslow-like hierarchy of needs, which said that democratization and freedom represented higher-order human needs that could not be achieved until after the satisfaction of more basic economic and security needs.

In the late 1980s and 1990s, the assumptions shifted again. A just-do-it school has emerged based on assumptions about democracy as a learned practice. People can learn how to create democracy, and outsiders can provide useful technical assistance. The role of ideology and ideas is seen as much more important than it was before. Poor countries can practice democracy even if they haven't achieved high levels of economic development.

Each of these ways of thinking about democratization involves different ideas about the sources of democratization, the path of democratization, and the relative priority given to different efforts and interventions. It is useful to summarize these perspectives, because the assumptions involved are not necessarily mutually exclusive, each has much to offer, and the broader perspective of such an overview can help move democratization thinking forward.

Prerequisites for Democratization

Political scientists such as Almond and Dahl[3] developed a view of democracy in the 1950s and early 1960s that emphasized a dependence on the existence of key societal institutions. Some of these institutions were governmental agencies, but most were not. Without these institutions, the thinking went, democracy was impossible. The list of these prerequisites for democracy generally included:

1. An effective system of justice and law enforcement to protect individuals from violence and intimidation.
2. A minimum level of education that provided for nearly universal literacy.
3. A substantial middle class.
4. An independent media providing the population with information from competing perspectives.
5. In civil society, (a) a number of organizations serving the interests of different segments of the population, especially professional associations, trade and business associations, and unions; and (b) a higher level of national organizations, usually political parties, capable of bringing different specific interests and organizations together to engage in dialogue, discussion, and coalition formation.

Democratization as a Higher Human Need

The 1960s saw the popular acceptance of the work of humanist psychologist Abraham Maslow[4] in a whole spectrum of applied social sciences, especially business management, marketing, and public administration. This acceptance was based less on any strong evidence for his theory than on the way his assumptions about human nature reflected the assumptions of American popular culture. Maslow theorized that there is a hierarchy of human needs—from top to bottom:

1. Self-actualization
2. Self-esteem
3. Social esteem
4. Social belonging
5. Physical and economic security
6. Physiological needs: air, water, food, shelter, sex

His theory stated that people are motivated to satisfy these needs, but that a need is perceived and becomes a motivator only as the needs below it on the hierarchy are nearly satisfied.

The assumptions about human nature represented in this needs hierarchy resonated with the development ideology of the late 1960s and 1970s that nothing is so important for the poorest of the poor as meeting their basic human needs. The needs of citizens that might be met by a democratic system of government are all higher-order needs. The application of Maslow's ideas to development issues implied two things about democratization: that economic development and military security must precede democratization, and that economic development plus military security would lead to democratization as citizens sought to satisfy higher-order needs.

This perspective relied on a number of observations and common sense to back up these assumptions. For example, it was observed that democracies were strongest in more economically developed countries. A converse observation focused on the fragility of democracy in countries experiencing periods of severe economic depression or prolonged economic decline.

Also influential were beliefs focusing on the importance of a middle class as a base for democracy. The hypothesis was that democracy could flourish only after the middle class had reached a certain size, either an absolute size (the critical-mass perspective) or a relative size proportional to the population as a whole.

The democracy-as-higher-human-need perspective also pointed to peace, order, and military security as foundations of democracy. The evidence for this was the difficulty of establishing or even maintaining a democratic system of government in the face of serious military threats from neighboring states, civil war, extreme polarization (ethnic, religious, regional, or political), or civil strife and disorder. Americans of the 1970s took this lesson from their country's experiences in Asia over the previous generation, in China and Taiwan, in Korea, and especially in Vietnam.

Democratization as a Learned Practice

The third perspective sees democracy as a social practice, as a bundle of behaviors, skills, and values. Like all practices, democracy must be learned. If democracy is to work, individuals and organizations must learn their roles, develop their skills, and practice democracy. Democracy involves a complex array of specialized bodies of knowledge and specialized activities, from managing campaigns to administering elections to crafting legislation, and no democratic system of government can be successful unless and until this knowledge has been acquired and these activities have been practiced.[5]

This perspective implies that democracy can indeed be exported, that democracy spreads primarily through cultural contact with democratic systems. Skeptics characterize this process as another example of American political and cultural hegemony. Democracy advocates see it as technical assistance in the political sector, no different in concept from technical assistance in health, education, or agriculture. Many argue that it works, that democracy is spread primarily by contact between democratic and nondemocratic systems. From this perspective, the only prerequisite for democracy that really matters is a widespread desire to create a democratic political system. If the will for democracy is present, other missing elements of knowledge or experience can be learned or acquired.

Initial democratization efforts in any system are prone to error and misunderstanding. The democratic practices that result are fragile. Early democratization is marked by inflated expectations but very tentative performance, so that the democratization process is often set back or interrupted. As learning proceeds, democratization efforts become more confident and less subject to political misjudgments that lead to temporary reversals. Democratic actors grow more sophisticated, the democratization process accelerates, and the democratic system of government becomes more stable and secure.

A corollary of this idea is the hypothesis that the success of a democratization effort is best predicted by a system's previous experiences and experiments with democracy. For example, this perspective predicts that the probability of permanent democracy is higher in Poland than in Russia, because of Poland's experience before World War II, and higher in Sri Lanka than in Indonesia, because of Sri Lanka's greater experience with democracy since independence.

Strategic Implications

Since these perspectives differ on the sources of democracy and the processes of democratization, it follows that they differ as well in their prescriptions. An examination reveals differences in their prescriptions for two different sets of democratization actors: pro-democracy activists within the country on the one hand, and democracy specialists in international technical assistance agencies on the other.

Prerequisites for Democracy

The shortest and surest path to democracy is to foster the growth of its prerequisite institutions. In a predemocratic system, democratization efforts must take the form of capacity building, or institutional development work, in these key areas: law enforcement, education, the media, and organized civil society. In the absence of this prior institutional development, more direct democratizing reforms of the system of government are unlikely to succeed in the first place or to sustain themselves even if they are initially successful.

Democratic activists would do best to build the interest-representing organizations of civil society, such as trade unions or professional associations, or to create an independent media. In both roles there is a long tradition of heroic activity by democrats working for change in nondemocratic systems. International technical assistance can build capacity in nongovernmental organizations (NGOs) and in the media, but it must also work to increase the effectiveness of educational systems and the administration of justice.

Democracy as a Higher-Order Need

The shortest and surest route to democracy starts with peacemaking, conflict resolution, and economic development. If mass popular democracy can come into being only after a majority of the population has a secure income to meet basic needs, then broad-based economic development must come first. Likewise, if the need for physical security takes precedence over the need for democracy, then peace and an end to internal civil disorder are fundamental.

From this perspective, democratic activists must turn their attention toward economic development by whatever development strategy they think best. There is room for mediation work in resolving ethnic or other conflicts, but most activists would find themselves in economic development work designed to bring the benefits of development to all members of the society. This perspective looks to international agencies to do basically the things they have always done. Diplomats should resolve regional conflicts and tensions, and development agencies should assist countries in bringing about economic development.

Democracy as a Learned Practice

Just do it. Nothing leads to democracy faster than direct experimentation and experience with democracy. If at first you don't succeed, try and try again. The lessons of experience accumulate—even the lessons of unsuccessful experience—and nothing is more important than getting on with the task of learning those lessons.

Democratic activists should focus directly on the politics of democracy. Where repressive political systems make direct political advocacy of democracy impossible, there are alternatives. Local traditions of self-governance, civil society organizations, and self-employment decision making all may be training grounds for individual democrats.

In some sense, national political democracy is creating these same kinds of institutions on a larger scale. The lesson of democratization around the world, however, is that these local and small-scale experiences do not translate directly into success at national-level political democracy.

Whenever possible, activist democrats should work in the larger arena of national democratic politics.

This perspective argues that the best democratization interventions by international agencies are those that are the most direct: training and assistance in the formal processes of democracy, such as citizenship education, election administration, legislative effectiveness, and the administration of justice. Work with NGOs should concentrate specifically on building their capacities as actors in democracy: policy analysis, policy advocacy, interest-group mobilization, and voter education. Such direct involvement in the political system of a country by an international agency is too touchy unless the existing regime is actively seeking help in democratization. The logic of this perspective therefore calls for international agencies to concentrate their democratization assistance, providing it only to countries that genuinely seek their aid.

All Three Perspectives

From any of these perspectives, the primacy of human rights, particularly personal security, is clear. The tragedy of people trying to create civil society before the protection of human rights becomes established is a worldwide human political experience. Public-spirited and altruistic people, seeking only to provide information to a media audience or to organize a self-help group in a community, are viewed as threats to a repressive political order and are exiled, imprisoned, or killed. The pro-democracy consequences of their actions are known and feared by powerful antidemocrats, who respond with repression. The result is that antidemocratic political repression often arises in a political system even before there is any widespread effort to democratize.

All three perspectives, each with a different logic, agree that the path to democracy begins with the protection of human rights. Tismaneau, in his widely acclaimed book on democratization in Eastern Europe,[6] puts forward the thesis that the democratization process there began to be successful only after the Soviet Union signed the Helsinki Accord guaranteeing human rights in 1975.

Therefore, the most common strategy to support democratization in countries where the process has not yet really begun—international pressure on governments to guarantee human rights, as happened in South Africa and is now happening in China—is absolutely appropriate. The next international move in this direction is to make respect for human rights, especially workers' rights, an internationally recognized condition for participation in the World Trade Organization (WTO) and the world trading system or in regional free-trade agreements such as the North American Free Trade Agreement (NAFTA). This will be more effective than anything in getting the democratization process started in countries whose governments have so far been successful in resisting international human rights pressures.

Since its beginning, right after the defeat of Nazism and in the era of Stalinism, the General Agreement on Tariffs and Trade (GATT) has allowed member countries to exclude from their markets imported products made under conditions of forced, slave, or prison labor. The precedent is in place for countries to exclude the products of workers who have no human rights and thus have no voice or organization to improve the conditions under which they live and work. This is exactly the logic that lay behind the international boycott of South African products. In the near future, the principle will come to be applied more broadly. As this begins to happen, it will become necessary to be able to measure a nation's human rights and democratization performance fairly, objectively, and with enough accuracy to detect small changes from year to year.

Democracy is a characteristic of a system of government, but democratization is a much wider process of social change and institutional development. Democratization progress cannot be measured by mere observation of the system of government itself.

Democracy and freedom, though correlated, are not identical. There have been societies, such as Hong Kong, with little democracy and much freedom; in societies such as Israel and South Africa, there have been well-established institutions of democracy for some, but little freedom for the ethnically disenfranchised groups within their borders. Democracy requires basic human rights to sustain itself, but democratic majorities regularly endanger the human rights of minorities and thereby undermine their own democracies.

A credible, objective international human rights measuring and monitoring institution is necessary for fostering increased freedom and democracy. Even without any enforcement power, such an institution will affect public opinion within countries and internationally and strengthen the cause of human dignity and freedom. Such human rights monitoring, coupled with the implicit threat of loss of access to international trade and finance resulting from worker rights and environmental protection guarantees in the world trade regime, will make it possible to tighten the connection worldwide between economic expansion and the growth of freedom and democracy.

Notes

1. R. Bruce McColm et al., *Freedom in the World* (New York: Freedom House, 1991); United Nations Development Program, *Human Development Report* (Oxford: Oxford University Press, 1992); World Bank, *Managing Development: The Governance Dimension* (Washington, D.C.: World Bank, 1991).
2. Actual practice, however, has been to provide for the basic human needs of people "deserving" of such assistance, that is, of people who are thought to lack the capacity to provide for themselves.
3. Gabriel A. Almond and G. Bingham Powell Jr., *Comparative Politics: A Developmental Approach* (Boston: Little Brown, 1966); Robert A. Dahl, *Polyarchy: Participation and Opposition* (New Haven, Conn.: Yale University Press, 1971).
4. Abraham H. Maslow, *Motivation and Personality* (New York: Harper, 1954).
5. The influential author whose work best reflects this perspective is Larry Diamond, editor of the new *Journal of Democracy*. See his "Three Paradoxes of Democracy" in the summer 1990 issue of that journal.
6. Vladimir Tismaneau, *Reinventing Politics: Eastern Europe from Stalin to Havel* (New York: Free Press, 1992).

Part V

Environmental Sustainability

Introduction to Part V

U NTIL RECENTLY, DEVELOPMENT STRATEGIES have ignored the effect of worldwide economic activity on global resources and on the capacity of ecosystems to safely dispose of the wastes generated by economic activity. As long as world population was small and development was limited to a small portion of that population, economic activity did not strain the natural resource base enough to make this oversight a problem. But economic development now encompasses all of humankind, and most of the global growth in the next fifty years will take place in developing countries, where three-quarters of humankind lives. Because of this, we are concerned about the sustainability of development and about finding ways for development to use fewer resources and create less pollution.

Chapter 15 assesses the sustainability debate. The chapter defines the term *sustainable development*, reviews the arguments of environmental pessimists and environmental optimists regarding sustainability, and concludes that there is sufficient reason for some optimism regarding our ability to meet development aspirations without overwhelming the earth's carrying capacity.

Chapter 16 extends the discussion by identifying the chief environmental problems in poor countries, demonstrating that rich countries have been able to delink economic growth from environmental degradation, and identifying the policy actions that developing country governments can take to ensure that their development will be more sustainable. We point out that this will require environmental legislation and a public-sector environmental regulatory agency that will come at some cost to economic growth. That being said, we conclude that it is one thing to achieve national environmental sustainability and quite another to achieve global sustainability. Because of concern for the latter, we also identify a need to create a new global environmental institution that will speed the transition to sustainable global development.

15

Optimistic and Pessimistic Assessments of Environmental Sustainability

HISTORICALLY, ALL MODELS AND STRATEGIES of development ignored the effect of economic activity on the environment. This neglect was embedded in the way several generations of students have been taught. In the standard model of an economy, households are assumed to be owners of labor, capital, and natural resources, which they offer for sale to producers (firms) in markets for these factors of production. Firms combine these factors of production with plant, equipment, and technological and entrepreneurial skills to produce an output for sale in the goods market to households. Although this model implicitly recognizes that production generates pollution and uses part of the stock of natural capital, it assumes that neither places any limits on economic growth. Development consists of an ever-expanding virtuous circle in which profit-maximizing owners of firms reinvest profits in new capital and technology, which increases labor productivity. This increase then contributes to an increase in household incomes, which provides the basis for an expanding demand for the goods and services produced by firms. This encourages firms to invest even more, renewing the ever-expanding circle. Subsequent amendments to this closed economy model have ultimately resulted in the extension of this national model to the global economy.

Over the last four decades, this circle has expanded rapidly to embrace virtually all of humanity. This historically unprecedented global economic growth has resulted in equally unprecedented improvements in living standards, life expectancy, education, and the quality of life for billions of people. However, it has also been associated with serious environmental problems. Global climate change, acid rain, depletion of the ozone layer, rapid rates of deforestation, and significant increases in the rate of species loss suggest that the costs of global development are rising rapidly. At the national level, deteriorating air and water quality, scarce water and fuel, soil erosion, and deforestation are also exacting a high price.

It is now clear that the basic model needs to be amended to account for the impact of large-scale global economic activity on the environment. This can be accomplished by placing it within an ecosystem that interacts with the scale of economic activity in two ways. First, the ecosystem is a source of raw materials such as air, water, fossil fuels, metals, and forests that are used to produce marketable goods and services. Second, all economic activity generates waste (pollution). Because this waste cannot escape the ecosystem, the ecosystem acts as a sink to absorb and reprocess pollution.

We are only beginning to consider the implications of this revised model in relation to development. Reorienting our thinking forces us to ask several unsettling questions:

1. Does the revised model mean that there is an unresolvable conflict between attaining global development and safeguarding the life-giving ecosystems in which the world's human population lives?
2. If so, does this mean that there are global or national limits to economic growth? If there are, what are the consequences of these limits for developing countries, developed countries, and the international economy?
3. Is sustainable development possible? If it is, how does it differ from development as conventionally defined? What must we do to attain it?

Our purpose in this chapter is to examine these questions in some detail. We start by defining the term *sustainable development* and then move on to review the current debate over sustainability.

Sustainable Development: What Is It?

Historically, the term *sustainability* was applied to the harvesting of specific renewable species, such as a particular species of fish in a fishery or a particular type of tree in a forest. Applied to individual species, the concept is fairly easy to grasp. In fisheries, for example, if the harvesting rate (the catch rate) of Northwest coho salmon exceeds the growth rate of the stock of salmon, eventually the salmon will be fished into extinction.

Sustainable yield occurs when the catch rate of salmon in a particular fishery equals the rate of growth of the salmon in that fishery. Maximum sustainable yield occurs when the catch rate equals the maximum rate of growth of the stock.

Subsequent to this usage, ecologists adopted the term to refer to the status and function of ecological systems, such as the Amazon rain forest. Although this move from a sustainable harvesting rate for a single species to the functioning of an ecological system is intuitively appealing, it is quite problematic. There is no real equivalent for the sustainable yield of an ecosystem. In its place, we refer to ecosystem carrying capacity—the ability of an ecosystem to absorb and process the waste dumped into it. This concept of carrying capacity can best be portrayed by an example of a simple ecosystem (a fish pond) developed by Paul Hawken:

> Ordinarily, as fish create wastes and die, detritivores decompose the waste into inorganic products that feed the algae population and invertebrates, that become in turn food for the stable fish population.[1]

As long as this stable, closed system is not disturbed, a self-purifying ecological cycle is at work. Wastes from one stage in the cycle become necessary raw material for the next stage in the cycle. But what development does is disturb this steady state. For example, when chemical fertilizers drain into the pond:

> the influx causes the algae to bloom faster than it can be consumed by the slower breeding fish. As the algae dies, the decomposition uses up much of the available oxygen, causing a die-off in the oxygen deprived fish. The dead fish are more waste, creating more algae, since the fish are not consuming it. The increased levels of decomposition lower the oxygen levels even further and what was once a carefully constructed and balanced closed system collapses under the burden of rapid and accelerating growth. Today we face similar prospects on a global level. Because of potential interactions and feedback loops within the global climate system, a global warming cycle, once begun, may well progress on its own, regardless of whether we continue to combust fossil fuels.[2]

What happens when ecological carrying capacity is exceeded? The answer that worries environmentalists is that the ecosystem and the life support it provides suddenly collapse. Because we know so little about the operation and functioning of individual ecosystems, including that of planet earth, there is widespread ambiguity about both ecosystem carrying capacity and the response of individual ecosystems when that capacity is exceeded.

The idea of carrying capacity is critical to definitions of sustainable development because the term refers to some intergenerational idea of human well-being. This is exemplified by the Brundtland Commission definition of sustainable development as "development that meets the needs of the present generation without compromising the ability of future generations to meet their own needs."[3]

Pessimists versus Optimists

Because there is so much ambiguity regarding ecosystem carrying capacity and the response of individual ecosystems when that carrying capacity is exceeded, there is enormous variation in assessments of the prospects for sustainable development. Both the Brundtland Commission and the World Bank's *World Development Report 1992* argue that sustainable development can be promoted simply by better resources management.[4] Others, such as the Ehrlichs and Herman Daly, believe that the pressure exerted on natural systems already exceeds global ecological carrying capacity.[5] They cannot see how already overstressed ecological systems can tolerate the wastes discharged from further expansion in world population and global output. The differences in these outlooks can be captured by a simple example.[6] Damage to ecosystems from economic growth can be analyzed in two ways—the size of the damage and the degree of reversibility of the damage. Environmental pessimists fear that most of what we are now observing has high damage costs and that it is irreversible, whereas environmental optimists believe that damages are relatively small and reversible.

As pessimists look around the world, they see natural systems in rapid rates of decline. They see forests and agricultural land being degraded at the highest rates in history.[7] They see declining productivity of agricultural land alongside an exponential increase in insect resistance to pesticides.[8] They fear that acceleration of these trends could threaten global food supplies. They view with increasing alarm the potentially large-scale and irreversible effects of expected global population and income growth between 1990 and 2030.[9] They view products such as organochlorines with the greatest alarm. These compounds of chlorine and hydrocarbons do not appear in nature but were created by human beings. They do not break down easily; they are persistent and long lasting—perhaps for hundreds or even thousands of years. Hundreds of millions of pounds of these compounds are released into the environment annually as solvents, fungicides, pesticides, and refrigerants. They are building up in the environment and accumulating in our food, our water, and our bodies.[10] Radioactive wastes are even more alarming. They have a half-life of hundreds of thousands of years. They are stored in underground tanks around the country, some of which are leaking.[11] Environmental pessimists argue that physical laws severely limit the extent to which these kinds of pollutants can be delinked from future global economic growth, that the degradation we are now experiencing may be irreversible and cumulative, that it may cause ecological collapse, and that there may be hidden human health risks. Because of this, they support draconian action now.

Pessimists also tend to believe that in the absence of vigorous action by organized environmental grassroots groups in civil society—organizations of small farmers, fishers, and laborers who see their soil being eroded, their fish being killed by pollution, their forests being cut down by big logging companies—governments will not take action now. Everywhere in the world, politics and economics are shaped by the exploitation of natural resources by large vested interests. In most developing countries, particularly, those vested interests control both the resources and the government. But even in rich countries such as the United States, vested interests reap huge profits from the profligate use of resources. They do not want to change, and they will spend billions to keep from changing. Businesses everywhere in the world oppose environmental regulations, and they have successfully watered down those that have passed.

Environmental optimists do not disagree with pessimists about the environmental and ecological consequences of a linear expansion of global growth. But they do see greater possibilities for delinking growth from pollution and resource degradation. They believe that natural capital, physical capital (plant and equipment), and human capital (educated people) are relatively substitutable. Because of this substitutability, they view most damages to the ecosystem, including potentially large-scale damages such as global warming, as easily reversible at relatively low cost, or at least easy to mitigate. As long as investments in human capital, physical capital, and technological change can fully compensate for the large-scale loss of natural capital, global sustainable development is possible.

These different assessments of the potential ecological damage from global growth are reflected in radically different policy prescriptions. If global economic actions, such as the current attempt to extend development to the rest of world, result in high and irreversible damage to life-supporting ecosystems, nothing short of a fundamental rethinking of what we are now doing is required. We must act now to prevent the system from overshooting its carrying capacity. Herman Daly argues that acting now requires doing three things.[12]

1. Achieving zero population growth. One way to do this would be to give everyone on the globe an equal right to bear one child. This is just enough to make sure that there is no net population growth. These rights could be bought and sold in markets. There must be mechanisms to make sure that people do not have children beyond their entitlement to do so.

2. Limiting further physical economic growth. Growth must approach a steady state—zero economic growth. Although moving in this direction requires stopping physical economic growth—growth that uses resources—it does not mean that we cannot have qualitative improvements. But limits must be set on what is taken from the earth as a source and what is dumped back into the global sink. This requires setting limits on the use of scarce natural capital. This could be achieved by setting depletion quotas for each resource and selling these quotas in markets. Limits on dumping into the global sink could also be established, and the rights to dump could be sold.

3. Redistributing income. Because of high levels of global poverty and income inequality, effective action to protect global life-giving ecosystems requires international income redistribution. The present system of inequality is legitimated as being a necessary incentive for economic growth. But if growth is stopped, the poor will no longer accept their poverty. So there must be a mechanism for the international redistribution of income, and there must be minimum and maximum income limits.

Because optimists view most of the environmental damages we observe in ecosystems—such as the buildup of greenhouse gases in the atmosphere—as reversible at relatively low cost, they see these recommendations as destructive of human freedom and virtually impossible to implement. They also believe that human and physical capital can be substituted for natural capital. The historical path of economic growth has resulted in economic transitions from dependence on the primary sector (farming, logging, mining—resource extraction) to the secondary sector (manufacturing, processing of physical products) to the tertiary sector (producing nonmaterial services such as information, finance, and entertainment). In other words, the economic development trajectory is away from resource- and pollution-intensive activities and toward knowledge-intensive activities. The environmental protection task is not to prevent economic development but to speed and augment its natural trajectory.

Because of this perspective, technological optimists are more likely to apply standards of economic efficiency to the sustainability problem. This is accomplished by treating the environment as an economic asset that yields a stream of services. Looked at this way, the task facing managers of sustainable development is to make sure that the extra benefits from the use of environmental assets is at least as high as the extra costs of using those assets.

Most environmental assets are not treated this way because of government policy failure and market failure. Policy failures occur when government policies encourage economic inefficiency and environmental degradation. This happens when governments subsidize the use of polluting products, such as energy and pesticides, without forcing users to pay for the pollution they cause. It also happens when government policies encourage uneconomic and excessive use of scarce commodities such as clean water, or when those policies promote excessive and economically inefficient logging and cattle ranching in tropical rain forests. Policy failures can also occur when governments fail to make public environmental investments with high social rates of return, such as investments in water and sanitation, soil conservation, family planning, and the education of women.

Market failure occurs because of the lack of clear property rights in most environmental assets. This is the case for the air we breathe, the water we drink, the forests we cut. If the costs as well as the benefits of using environmental assets do not accrue to clear owners, if property rights are not transferable, or if they are not secure from encroachment by others, these assets will be misused and environmental degradation will occur. Some environmental assets, such as air, are not clearly owned by anyone. As a result, the costs of polluting the air are generally not borne by either owners of polluting factories or users of fossil fuels. For other environmental assets, such as water, property rights are either not transferable or not easily transferable.[13] For many environmental assets, such as fisheries, property rights are not secure from encroachment by others.

When property rights for environmental assets are unclear, markets fail to allocate use of those assets efficiently. Most typically, environmental assets are underpriced and overused. When this happens, environmental degradation occurs. In such instances, governments need to implement policies and make investments to correct market failures. Those policies include imposing taxes on emissions and wastes, regulating the disposal of hazardous wastes, and placing fees on the extraction of renewable resources such as timber and fisheries.

But these are not the only things that can be done. Policies can also be designed to significantly reduce, if not eliminate, the use of material wastes in production and consumption. This can be done by adopting pollution prevention and waste minimization programs. Recent work by the World Environment Center in Eastern Europe and the former Soviet Union suggests that waste minimization programs have the potential to significantly reduce the pollution intensity of production. In addition, we are beginning to see that consumer durables such as cars and refrigerators could be made truly durable and totally recyclable. One way to achieve this is to lease these items from suppliers rather than buy them. When they are no longer useful, the consumer takes them back to the supplier. The supplier would then have an incentive to make these items from recyclable materials. Paul Hawken suggests how this can be accomplished. It requires an incentive system that sends signals to producers to design goods using less material per unit of output, including carbon-based fuels.[14]

Optimists believe that sustainable development can be achieved by government policies that correct policy failures; reduce market failures; provide incentives for producers to reduce, if not eliminate, pollution in production and consumption; and undertake sufficient public and private investments in human capital, physical capital, and technology so that those assets can quickly substitute for overdependence on environmental capital.

Which view is right? Unfortunately, these issues are hotly debated, and neither theory nor evidence gives a clear answer. This is one reason that the current debate about sustainability is so heated. Nevertheless, we come down on the side of the optimists. Why? The policies recommended by the pessimists are just not going to happen, and if the human race can be saved in no other way, then the universe will just have to evolve without us.

Moreover, there are a number of reasons for optimism. First, policies and practices put in place in the developed countries since the 1970s have shown that it is possible to delink economic growth from both pollution and natural resource use. We have come far in a short time, but we still have a long way to go. Extending what we have learned to the developing countries offers substantial opportunities to break the link between global growth and global pollution.

Second, the developed countries are rapidly moving from simple environmental regulations to reduce pollution to much more environmentally sustainable pollution prevention and waste minimization programs. Several examples of this are quite exciting. In Germany, automobile manufacturers are required to reprocess material from old cars into new cars. This is an important step toward sustainable industrial production, using old wastes rather than natural resources for inputs and eliminating the dumping of used-up products back into the environment. Similarly, large multinationals such as Nike have learned how to reprocess waste from shoe production into material that can be used to make additional shoes. Nike recently extended this process to its manufacturing facilities in Asia. These moves toward pollution prevention are being incorporated in new international production standards in Western Europe. Those standards will require producers in Europe and exporters to Western Europe to demonstrate that their production facilities are equipped with pollution prevention technologies. There is even some evidence that United States multinationals are requiring their suppliers to demonstrate that they are using pollution prevention technologies.

Third, rapid growth in the developing world, particularly in Asia, will lead to a replacement of virtually all the electricity generating capacity and all the industrial plant and equipment in one generation. This provides a historically unique opportunity to make electricity generation and industrial facilities substantially cleaner.

Fourth, the information and communication revolutions are speeding the transition in the most developed countries toward dematerialized growth. New products and technologies embody more value in less material products (microchips replace electronic products that required many pounds of rare and precious metals; communication technologies send more information over thinner cables).

Fifth, production and consumption of services rather than goods use fewer materials and pollute less.

If these trends accelerate, it may be possible to break the global link between economic growth and pollution and resource degradation. But this will not be automatic. Experience in the industrialized West shows that the private sector fights environmental regulations. But that experience also shows that growing environmental problems, income growth, and vigorous environmental NGOs can lead to new laws and regulations to reduce and eliminate pollution and environmental degradation. The spread of this experience to the entire globe provides an opportunity for green global growth.

Notes

1. Paul Hawken, *The Ecology of Commerce* (New York: Harper Business, 1993), 30.
2. Hawken, *Ecology of Commerce,* 30.
3. World Commission on Environment and Development (Brundtland Commission), *Our Common Future* (Oxford: Oxford University Press, 1987), 43.
4. World Bank, *World Development Report 1992* (New York: Oxford University Press, 1992).
5. Herman Daly and R. Cobb, *For the Common Good* (Boston: Beacon Press, 1989); and Paul Ehrlich and Anne Ehrlich, *Healing the Planet* (Reading, Mass.: Addison Wesley, 1991).
6. Much of what follows is drawn from M. Toman, "The Difficulty in Defining Sustainability," *Resources* 106 (Winter 1992): 3–6.
7. Hawken, *Ecology of Commerce,* 21–22.
8. Lester Brown et al., *Vital Signs: 1994* (New York: W. W. Norton, 1994), 41, 92.
9. The World Bank predicts that population and income growth could lead to a 3.5-fold increase in industrial production; unless action is taken, the emission of pollutants could rise with production, and "tens of millions more people would become sick or die each year of environmental causes." World Bank, *World Development Report 1992,* 9.
10. Hawken, *Ecology of Commerce,* 40–41.
11. Hawken, *Ecology of Commerce,* 46.
12. Herman Daly, *Steady-State Economics* (San Francisco: W. H. Freeman, 1977).
13. For a discussion of trades in water rights between urban and rural users of water, see Sandra Pastel, *The Last Oasis* (Washington, D.C.: WorldWatch Institute, 1992), 170–76.
14. Hawken, *Ecology of Commerce,* 64.

16

Environmental Policies to Achieve Broad-Based Sustainable Development

M OST OF THE GLOBAL GROWTH that will take place in the next forty years will occur in the developing world, where three-quarters of humankind lives. Because of this, achieving sustainable development will depend on finding ways to make development in the developing world less polluting and less resource-intensive. How might this be accomplished? Before addressing this question, this chapter analyzes the particular environmental problems facing developing countries. Following that, we identify those government policies necessary to achieve environmentally sustainable broad-based growth.

The Environmental Situation in Developing Countries

Analyzing environmental problems in the developing world is an exceedingly difficult task. Good environmental data for developing countries are scarce. Time-series data sufficient to identify trends are even scarcer. Although there is an increasing quantity of biophysical data for more and more countries that indicate deterioration in the environment in developing countries, it is not always clear what these data mean. For example, developing country forests are being lost at about 1 percent per year, and species loss is approximately one mammal and one bird each year.[1] Both losses are higher than previous historical trends, but exactly how serious these losses are is not clear.

Despite these problems, both data collection and analysis are getting better. The World Resources Institute, the United Nations Environment Program's (UNEP) Global Environmental Monitoring System (GEMS), and the World Bank are developing better data on environmental indicators.[2]

What do these data and analyses tell us about the state of the environment in developing countries? It is important to realize that different environmental problems have very different impacts. Some, such as urban air quality, affect the health of urban residents today. Others, such as greenhouse gas emissions or deforestation of tropical rain forests, affect global climate change. The impact of this change on ecosystems and on human health is much harder to assess. Moreover, these impacts are more likely to be global rather than local. Still others, such as the clouding over of the Grand Canyon because of smog, may have no impact on human health or the globe, but they destroy the view. These differences require us to make hard choices about what is important. We have decided to do this by focusing the discussion of the environmental problems in poor countries on those that affect human health. There are other environmental problems that are no doubt just as important, but there is no agreement about what they are. When environmental problems threaten human health, their importance is no longer subject to doubt.

Using the human health criterion, what are the most serious environmental problems in the developing world? Recently, the World Bank analyzed this problem. Although the World Bank's poor environmental record is good reason to doubt the perspective of this study, it is the best empirical overview we have. The study ranked developing country environmental problems in the following order of importance: (1) poor water quality, scarce clean water, and inadequate sanitation; (2) increasing air pollution (both indoor and in urban areas); (3) declining agricultural productivity; and (4) loss of biodiversity.[3]

Poor water quality and lack of access to safe drinking water exact a high human health toll in the developing world. More than 3 million deaths per year are directly related to waterborne diseases.[4] Although the dominant source of contamination of drinking water is untreated human waste, both industry and agriculture have polluted rivers and seas with toxic chemicals and carcinogenic heavy metals. Scattered data suggest that this is an increasingly important problem. For example, data from Jakarta Bay in Indonesia show that large percentages of shellfish exceed the World Health Organization (WHO) safe level for lead, mercury, or cadmium.[5]

Poor urban and indoor air quality also exacts a large human health toll. By World Bank estimates, 65 percent of the urban population in the developing world—roughly 1.3 billion people—live in areas where total suspended particulates (smoke and dust in the air) exceed WHO safe standards.[6] The amount of smoke and dust in the air in urban areas in the poorest developing countries is roughly five times measured levels in rich countries, and these levels of pollution are rising.[7] Urban populations in developing countries also suffer from high concentrations of chemicals such as sulfur dioxide and lead in the air.[8] Because rural poor people in most developing countries rely on fuelwood and animal dung for cooking and heating, they are exposed to poor indoor air quality. Several studies show that indoor air concentrations of smoke and dust are large multiples of safe standards.[9] As the World Bank argues, most of those who are continuously exposed to high kitchen smoke and dust levels are women and children.[10]

The health impacts of indoor and urban air pollution on the billions of people in developing countries are not well understood. The World Bank suggests that if smoke and dust levels in developing country cities were brought down to safe levels, between 300,000 and 700,000 deaths could be averted annually.[11]

Because agriculture is the dominant source of livelihood for developing country populations, the productivity and fertility of land are very important. There is reasonably good data on agricultural productivity (or yields) of agricultural land. But reliable estimates of changes in soil fertility or of agricultural land lost to desertification, soil erosion, waterlogging, or salinization are not available. At least one recent study of land degradation cited by the World Bank suggests that "almost 11 percent of the earth's vegetated surface have undergone moderate or worse soil degradation."[12] Unfortunately, at this time we are unable to assess the impact of this kind of degradation on human health, agricultural productivity, or global environmental problems.

There are enormous differences in the environmental problems facing particular developing countries and regions. Most of the large industrial cities in rapidly developing Asia face severe urban air pollution. Most of Asia, particularly higher-income East Asia, also suffers from the environmental consequences of chemical-intensive agriculture. Both of these problems are less severe in sub-Saharan Africa. In that region, rapid population growth and low-productivity agriculture have contributed to declining soil fertility and a rapid expansion of area cultivated.[13] This expansion of low-productivity agriculture has contributed to deforestation and to biodiversity and species loss due to destruction of habitat. Countries in Eastern Europe and the former Soviet Union face yet a different problem, what to do with large stockpiles of industrial and nuclear hazardous waste.

Policies for Sustainable Development

The starting point for identifying policies for sustainable development is to learn from the experience of the industrialized countries. Since the 1970s, when the rich countries began to tackle their environmental problems, they have made much progress in breaking the link between environmental degradation and economic growth.[14] They have done this by altering policies that reduced economic efficiency and economic growth and degraded the environment. They also carried out public-sector investments with high social rates of return that enhanced environmental quality, such as new waste-treatment facilities. They created environmental regulatory structures, analyzed environmental problems, established environmental priorities, set environmental standards, monitored performance relative to standards, and enforced standards by penalizing violators. Most recently, they have changed incentives to reward those in agriculture and industry who reduce the pollution intensity per unit of output produced.

Actions in each of these areas provide opportunities for most developing countries to reduce resource use and the wastes created per dollar of gross domestic product (GDP). But achieving similar gains will not be easy and will require government action. Large public-sector investments are required to ensure clean drinking water, adequate sanitation, and environmentally sound municipal waste disposal. Because these investments yield large social rates of return, they are good economic and good environmental investments. Developing countries also need to create cost-effective environmental regulatory agencies that provide incentives for reducing the resource intensity and pollution (waste) intensity of GDP. When the rich countries did this in the early 1970s, it contributed to substantial improvements in environmental quality. As the World Bank states, "particulate emissions have declined by 60 percent and sulfur oxides by 38 percent. Lead emissions have fallen by 85 percent in North America and by 50 percent in most European cities."[15]

In some instances, the costs of complying with environmental standards have led to the discovery of new technologies that are more economically efficient and less polluting.[16] Some firms in the United States are experimenting with pollution prevention and waste minimization models of production.[17] The purpose of pollution prevention technologies is to reuse virtually all the wastes created in one production process in other production processes. The purpose of waste minimization programs is to reduce the pollution per dollar of output produced; limited evidence suggests that it is also economically efficient to significantly reduce pollution per unit of output. Some developing countries have taken advantage of these cleaner technologies, but others have not.[18] More developing countries should actively consider adopting these cleaner technologies. They also need to agree on environmental standards that ease negotiations with multinational investors.[19]

Developing countries can reap significant improvements in environmental quality and economic efficiency if they correct government policies that are not good for growth or for the environment. Chief among these are government subsidies for energy use. When rich countries allowed energy prices to rise following the first oil price shock in 1973, this rise in prices led to a delinking of energy use from GDP growth.[20]

Government subsidies on energy, particularly coal in Eastern Europe and the former Soviet Union, are large. They have a big impact on local urban air pollution and greenhouse gas emissions. The World Bank suggests that removal of all subsidies on the use of energy in these countries could lead to a 50 percent reduction in urban air pollution and up to a 10 percent reduction in global carbon emissions.[21]

Other subsidies that are economically inefficient and hard on the environment include those for cattle ranchers, who destroy tropical forests or use fragile pasturelands; for fertilizer and pesticides; for the use of irrigation water; and for logging. Several studies of large-scale cattle ranching in the Brazilian rain forest have documented how a wide range of government subsidies encouraged the development of economically inefficient cattle ranching, which contributed to significant deforestation.[22] Government subsidies for fertilizer and pesticides are large in some countries and encourage inefficient application rates that contribute to groundwater pollution and residues on crops.[23] Inefficient pricing polices for logging operations have been associated with deforestation.

Building on the win-win opportunities to achieve economic efficiency and environmental protection also requires government action to clarify and improve property rights. When people have open access to forests or fishing grounds, they tend to overuse them. Overuse undermines the sustainability of the environment by contributing to deforestation, soil erosion, and declines in fisheries stocks. Because species and biodiversity loss results from habitat destruction, the degradation of forests, soils, and water can contribute to losses of these important environmental assets.

These results—the delinking of pollution (waste generation) and resource use from economic growth following concerted public action—

are consistent with cross-country data that show that some environmental problems, particularly air and water quality, initially tend to worsen as per capita income rises but then improve as incomes continue to rise.

Much more remains to be done. Policies need to be designed to speed the transition to dematerialization of production and consumption in industrialized and developing countries.

Other proposals being tried in rich countries include taxes on pollution and pollution permits that are bought and sold in markets. Both the United States and Europe have achieved good results with these tradeable permits. In the United States, pollution permits have been used since 1990 to deal with sulfur dioxide emissions. Originally, industry estimated that it would cost $1,500 per metric ton to reduce pollution. The U.S. Environmental Protection Agency estimated that it would cost $600 a ton. In 1993, it actually cost about $150 a ton.

The problem with taxes and pollution permits is that they permit pollution. The goal should be to eliminate pollution. This can be approached by reducing the number of permits allowed each year until there is no pollution and there are no more wastes—all products of the production process are recycled and used by other industries or other species. Hawken describes an example of this in a complex of industries at Kalundborg, Denmark. A coal-fired power plant, an oil refinery, a pharmaceutical company, a sheetrock plant, concrete producers, a producer of sulfuric acid, the municipal heating authority, a fish farm, some greenhouses, local farms, and other enterprises work cooperatively to use one another's by-products as raw materials in their operations.[24]

Another way of dealing with toxic wastes relies on parking lots. Cities and states establish parking lots to store toxic wastes, and manufacturers pay fees for the right to store these wastes forever. This shifts the cost of disposing of these products onto manufacturers rather than on cities and states, as is now the case.[25]

Policies for Broad-Based Growth: Their Impact on Environmental Sustainability

Many of the suggestions made here for promoting sustainable development, especially those regarding correcting government policy and market failures, are consistent with the economic policies for broad-based growth outlined in various chapters in this book. Does this mean that the policies for broad-based growth are consistent with policies to promote sustainable development? Although research in this area is limited and indicative rather than definitive, there are some reasons to suspect that there is less conflict than most people think between the economic policies for broad-based growth and policies to promote sustainable development. But this does not mean that there is no conflict.

For instance, what do we know about the impact of moving to export-oriented trade policies on the environment? Existing evidence on the relationship between trade policy and the environment is mixed. Some of the early research suggested that open trade policies are more environmentally friendly than the most widely practiced alternative (import substitution industrialization, or ISI).[26]

But not all the evidence supports an all-good-things-go-together hypothesis. The growth rate of dirty industries in developing countries appears to be faster than that in clean industries. Developing countries also appear to be gaining comparative advantage in dirty industries faster than they are gaining it in clean industries.[27] Even more worrisome is the evidence from East Asia, where trade regimes generally promote exports, which suggests that a wide range of pollutants are growing faster than real GDP and that, as a result, toxic releases per unit of output are increasing.[28] Some empirical research also demonstrates that developing countries with export-oriented trade policies had higher pollution per dollar of GDP than countries practicing ISI.[29]

Trade policy might also affect industrial location patterns by encouraging "pollution-haven" effects;[30] that is, dirty industries in rich countries with more stringent environmental standards move to poor countries with less stringent standards. There is little empirical evidence that this has happened, however.[31] This absence of pollution-haven effects has been attributed to relatively low pollution control and abatement costs, even for the dirtiest industries; the importance of other factors—wage rates, exchange rates, and political risks—in the industrial location decisions of firms; and the emergence of a corporate environmental ethos.[32]

What can we conclude from these results? There appear to be some instances (Eastern Europe and the former Soviet Union) in which a shift to export-oriented trade policies might lead to a reduction in pollution per dollar of GDP. But empirical research also indicates that these results may not hold for most of the developing world.

This suggests that it would be a mistake to count on development policies alone to bring about environmental improvement. But this should not be surprising. Experience in the developed countries shows that attaining improvements in environmental quality requires more than getting growth policies right. It requires environmental legislation and a public-sector environmental regulatory structure that comes at some cost.[33] Recent evidence from Thailand and much of the rest of East Asia suggests that this lesson applies equally to developing countries pursuing export-oriented growth policies.[34]

The Future of Growth, Development, and the Environment

Nothing said so far addresses the issue of long-term global environmental sustainability. It is one thing to argue that attaining improvements in environmental quality requires environmental legislation and a public-sector environmental regulatory structure. But it is quite another to argue that this leads to sustainable development. If national environmental laws and environmental regulation get us only partway to sustainability, as seems likely, it will be necessary to build a global environmental institution to ensure global sustainability.

The most important charge of this new global environmental institution will be to speed the dematerialization of global industrial production. We have already gone far in this direction in agriculture. In the United States, 3 percent of the population feeds the nation, and much of the rest of the world as well, through their farming activities. They do this using only about half the land, and hardly more fixed capital, than was once devoted to agriculture. In the nineteenth century, when most of the people in the United States were farmers, such an outcome of economic development would have been inconceivable. In the next generation, a similar transition in manufacturing, already under way, will be complete. A tiny fraction of the population will produce all the industrially processed goods we need, using a small percentage of the raw materials and emitting a small percentage of the industrial pollutants that we once thought were inevitable by products of economic development. Most of the nation's GDP, and most of its workforce, will be in the service sector, producing no things and thus little waste and pollution, but providing us with information, investment, and entertainment services that we can only imagine today but that our children will take for granted.

In the process of this transition, new technologies have been created, and many more will be created, that developing countries can use to reduce the time, cost, and environmental consequences of their own developmental transitions. We need environmentally sustainable development policies to speed these transitions, not policies that slow them down in the name of preserving familiar lifestyles such as cotton farming, cattle ranching, and steelmaking that were not beneficial for either the world's environment or workers' lives.

Notes

1. World Bank, *World Development Report 1992* (New York: Oxford University Press, 1992), 58.
2. World Bank, *World Development Report 1992*, 192–205; and World Resources Institute, *World Resources: 1992–93* (New York: Oxford University Press, 1992).
3. World Bank, *World Development Report 1992*, 4–6.
4. World Bank, *World Development Report 1992*, 5.
5. World Bank, *World Development Report 1992*, 46.
6. World Bank, *World Development Report 1992*, 51–52.
7. World Bank, *World Development Report 1992*, 51.
8. World Bank, *World Development Report 1992*, 53.
9. K. Smith, "Air Pollution: Assessing Total Exposure in Developing Countries," *Environment* 30 (1988): 16–35.
10. World Bank, *World Development Report 1992*, 5.
11. World Bank, *World Development Report 1992*, 52.
12. L. R. Oldeman et al., *World Map of the Status of Human-Induced Soil Degradation: An Explanatory Note*, rev. 2nd ed. (Wageningen, the Netherlands: International Soil Reference and Information Centre, 1990), as cited in World Bank, *World Development Report 1992*, 55.
13. K. Cleaver and G. Schreiber, *The Population, Agriculture and Environment Nexus in Sub-Saharan Africa* (Washington, D.C.: World Bank, Africa Region Technical Department, 1992).
14. World Bank, *World Development Report 1992*, 40.
15. World Bank, *World Development Report 1992*, 40.
16. D. Wheeler and P. Martin, "Prices, Policies and the International Diffusion of Clean Technology: The Case of Wood Pulp Production," in *International Trade and the Environment*, ed. P. Low (Washington, D.C.: World Bank, 1992), 197–224.
17. For example, 3M developed a pollution prevention program that significantly reduced waste from production. Over fifteen years, 3M reduced its air pollution by 120,000 tons, its wastewater by 1 billion gallons, and its solid waste by 410,000 tons. Paul Hawken, *The Ecology of Commerce* (New York: Harper Business, 1993), 61.

18. Wheeler and Martin, "Prices, Policies and International Diffusion," discuss the international diffusion of a less polluting technology for pulp and paper making.

19. See H. S. Brown, J. J. Himmelberger, and A. L. White, "Development-Environment Interactions in the Export of Hazardous Technologies," *Technological Forecasting and Social Change* 43 (1993): 125–55.

20. Between 1973 and 1985, real GDP in the United States increased by 40 percent, but the absolute amount of energy consumed did not change. For the industrialized countries as a whole, the rise in energy prices after 1973 led to a 15 percent reduction in the energy intensity of gross national product. T. Tietenberg, *Environmental and Natural Resources Economics* (New York: HarperCollins, 1992), 608.

21. World Bank, *World Development Report 1992*, 11–12.

22. D. Mahar, "Deforestation in Brazil's Amazon Region: Magnitude, Rate, and Causes," in *Environmental Management and Economic Development*, ed. G. Schramm and J. Warford (Baltimore: Johns Hopkins University Press, 1989), 87–116.

23. R. Repetto, "Economic Incentives for Sustainable Production," in *Environmental Management and Economic Development*, 69–86.

24. Hawken, *Ecology of Commerce*, 62.

25. Hawken, *Ecology of Commerce*, 70.

26. N. Birdsall and D. Wheeler, "Trade Policy and Industrial Pollution in Latin America: Where are the Pollution Havens?" in *International Trade and the Environment*, 159–68.

27. On the former, see C. Brandon and R. Ramankutty, *Toward an Environmental Strategy for Asia*, World Bank Discussion Paper No. 224 (Washington, D.C.: World Bank, 1993), 182, and P. Low, "Trade Measures and Environmental Quality: The Implications for Mexico's Exports," in *International Trade and the Environment*, 105–20. On the growth in comparative advantage in "dirty" as opposed to "clean" industries, see P. Low and A. Yeats, "Do 'Dirty' Industries Migrate?" in *International Trade and the Environment*, 89–103.

28. Brandon and Ramankutty, *Toward an Environmental Strategy for Asia*.

29. Michael T. Rock, "Pollution Intensity of GDP and Trade Policy: Can the World Bank be Wrong?" Discussion Paper No. 23, Center for Economic Policy Studies (Arlington, Va.: Winrock International, 1995) and *World Development*, forthcoming.

30. W. Baumol and W. Oates, *The Theory of Environmental Policy* (New York: Cambridge University Press, 1988), 265–66.

31. H. Jeffrey Leonard, *Pollution and the Struggle for the World Product* (New York: Cambridge University Press, 1988); J. Tobey, "The Effects of Domestic Environmental Policies on Patterns of World Trade: An Empirical Test," *Kyklos* 43 (1990): 191–209; and Low and Yeats, "Do 'Dirty' Industries Migrate?"; Low, "Trade Measures and Environmental Quality"; R. Lucas, D. Wheeler, and H. Hettige, "Economic Development, Environmental Regulation and the International Migration of Toxic Industrial Pollution: 1966–1988," in *International Trade and the Environment*, 67–86; and

Birdsall and Wheeler, "Trade Policy and Industrial Pollution in Latin America."

32. Low, "Trade Measures and Environmental Quality." For discussion of the emergence of an environmental ethos in multinational corporations, see Brown, Himmelberger, and White, "Development-Environment Interactions."

33. D. Jorgenson and P. Wilcoxen, "Environmental Regulation and U.S. Economic Growth," *Rand Journal of Economics* 21 (Summer 1990): 314–40; G. Christiansen and R. Haveman, "The Contribution of Environmental Regulations to the Slowdown in Productivity Growth," *Journal of Environmental Economics and Management* 8 (December 1981): 381–90.

34. See World Bank, *Thailand: Mitigating Pollution and Congestion in a High Growth Economy* (Washington, D.C.: World Bank, 1994), 4–6, 19–38; and Brandon and Ramankutty, *Toward an Environmental Strategy for Asia.*

Part VI

Reforming the International Order

Introduction to Part VI

WE CLOSE THE BOOK BY EXAMINING the impact of alternative international economic orders on developing country development performance and by identifying what reforms are needed in the post–Cold War Bretton Woods economic order if we are to move closer to global broad-based sustainable development (BBSD). We do this because we are only too keenly aware that international economic orders matter. As Chapter 17 demonstrates, the classic gold standard forced countries to subordinate domestic economic objectives to the balance of payments, requiring them to sacrifice too much autonomy. In the end, countries responded to this by constructing barriers to trade and capital flows. The interwar Versailles economic order was even more protectionist and contributed to the collapse of world trade, the global depression, and the rise of fascism in Germany and Japan. The Bretton Woods economic order contributed to unprecedented global economic expansion. So international orders matter, particularly if we are to move toward BBSD at a global level.

Chapter 17 suggests the kinds of reforms that should be considered in the global economic order—Group of Seven, the International Monetary Fund, the World Bank, and the new World Trade Organization—if we are to approach BBSD. It also argues for the creation of a new World Environment Organization. Without reforms in these areas, movement toward BBSD will be difficult.

17

International Economic Orders and Broad-Based Sustainable Development

MOST OF THIS BOOK HAS FOCUSED ON what governments in developing countries must do if they want to promote broad-based sustainable development (BBSD). As we have made clear, part of what they must do is structure their participation in the international economy in ways that enhance the prospects for BBSD. Some of this depends on their own doing—on their own policies with respect to trade, foreign investment, foreign aid, and macroeconomic management. But a large part of it also depends on the international rules of the game governing economic interaction between countries. In this closing chapter, we examine how the economic rules governing trade, investment, aid, and balance-of-payments adjustment affect development prospects in developing countries and identify reforms needed to create a more broad-based and sustainable world economy.

In analyzing the impact of international rules on developing country development performance, it is important to ask three questions: What functions must an international political-economic order perform? How have previous orders, including the Bretton Woods system, met these obligations? What reforms are needed in the current order to promote national and global BBSD?

Experience over the past 200 years has demonstrated that a viable international economic order must perform four important functions. First, it must make it possible for every country to gain from international trade. If the gains from trade and investment are not large enough, countries will forgo participation in the international economy. Moreover, the gains from trade and investment must be equitably distributed between rich and poor countries. Second, the order must provide opportunities for shifting capital from capital-rich and balance-of-payments-surplus countries to capital-poor and balance-of-payments-deficit countries. Because poor countries are also capital poor and tend to run balance-of-payments deficits, the recycling of surpluses accumulated in rich countries is vital to the well-being of poor countries. It also entices them to participate in the world economy. Third, it must provide stability in exchange rates so that firms, countries, and individuals can trade and invest. If exchange rates are too unstable, trade and investment break down. When this happens, everyone loses. Finally, the international economic order must make it possible for all countries to achieve balance-of-payments equilibrium without having to sacrifice too much control over domestic economic policy and domestic economic objectives. If the domestic costs of balance-of-payments adjustment are too high, countries will try to reduce those costs by reducing their participation in the world economy.

Laissez-Passer: Free Trade and the Gold Standard

The first capitalist international economic order, which lasted from 1815 to 1914, stressed free trade, free movement of capital and labor, and a pure gold standard. Under this system, there were limited controls on trade, and balance-of-payments equilibrium was restored through the working of the gold standard. Under the gold standard, gold functioned as the international currency. Each country denominated its currency in gold and established a fixed exchange rate in terms of gold.[1] Each nation kept gold reserves to back its currency and changed its domestic money supply in response to changes in its gold reserves.

Countries experiencing balance-of-payments deficits paid for the deficit by exporting gold and reducing the domestic money supply. This led to a fall in incomes, imports, and domestic prices and therefore an increase in exports. Countries with a balance-of-payments surplus received gold inflows, increased their money supply, and thus stimulated the domestic economy, which caused prices to go up, discouraging exports and increasing imports. In both cases, balance-of-payments equilibrium was achieved.

There were several important positive results of this international economic order. The greatest accomplishment was that there were no world wars for 100 years. There were substantial increases in the standard of living for many people in the industrializing countries. There was rapid economic growth worldwide and an equally rapid expansion of international trade. The century was also characterized by relatively stable prices and large capital movements from Europe to North and South America, Africa, and Asia.

But the negative results of the order were impressive. The international economy was highly unstable. There were great fluctuations in economic activity. Depressions were transmitted from country to country as the result of gold movements necessary to equilibrate the balance of payments. Governments could do nothing to offset economic depression at home under the rules of the gold standard. Free trade led to great dislocations of people and communities.

In the end, the system required too much subordination of domestic economic objectives to the need to sustain balance-of-payments equilibrium. Because countries came to see this as unacceptable, protectionism grew as governments relied on tariffs to protect infant industries, regions, and people from the great instability accompanying free trade. Governments also established central banks to regulate the domestic money supply. This broke the link between domestic monetary policy and movements in a country's supply of gold reserves. This meant that equilibration of the balance of payments was no longer automatic. With the end of World War I, the system broke down.

League of Nations–Versailles Order

The countries that won World War I created a new international economic order— the Versailles economic order. How did the Versailles order differ from the previous order? To begin with, free trade was replaced by a system of regional trading blocs organized by the imperialist powers. The British sustained a pound bloc, the French a franc bloc, the United States a dollar bloc, and the Japanese a yen bloc. Within each bloc, trade was controlled by the dominant power, and there was protectionism against trade between blocs. Second, there was limited international finance during this period, and capital did not flow easily from surplus countries to capital-deficit countries. Finally, there was no clear system for maintaining exchange rate stability or for restoring equilibrium in a country's balance of payments.

The Versailles order was short-lived. A worldwide depression began in the late 1920s and lasted until the outbreak of World War II. Countries responded to depression at home by currency devaluation, to make their exports cheaper and thus to expand exports and jobs. They also imposed high tariffs to keep imports out and stimulate the production of import substitutes. Because individual countries resorted to competitive devaluations and ever-rising tariffs, international trade was reduced to a trickle. This spread the depression to almost every country in the world. The depression led to fascism in Germany, Italy, Japan, and several other European countries. Germany restored prosperity through an arms buildup and territorial expansion. Italy and Japan followed suit, leading to the outbreak of World War II.

The experience of this period convinced many that the international rules of the game mattered. As a result, the designers of the next international economic order, the Bretton Woods order, sought to create an order that made it possible for countries to reap the gains from trade and investment without having to sacrifice too much national autonomy. They also sought to provide for more stability of exchange rates and for free but managed trade.

Bretton Woods Order

After World War II, the United States became the hegemonic power, and it made and enforced the economic rules of the game. It fostered the creation of several new international financial institutions—the International Monetary Fund (IMF), the International Bank for Reconstruction and Development (IBRD), and the General Agreement on Tariffs and Trade (GATT). These institutions led to a system of management of the international economy. How did the new system operate? How did it affect BBSD? What reforms are necessary in this system if we are to move toward a broad-based sustainable world?

Three principles governed the new system. First, loans the United States made to its Allies during World War II were to be canceled or written down dramatically. Second, the creators of the Bretton Woods system wanted there to be liberal international finance, so they created the IMF. The IBRD, or the World Bank, was created to overcome the imperfections in the international capital markets in the period after World War II and make loans for the reconstruction of Europe and the development of developing countries. Finally, the trading blocs of the previous order were to be replaced by an open global trading system as the imperialist powers lost their colonies. This led to creation of GATT.

International Monetary Fund

The IMF began operations in Washington, D.C., in 1946 with a membership limited to capitalist countries. The Articles of Agreement spelled out the following purposes: (1) promoting international monetary cooperation through a permanent institution that provides for consultation and collaboration on international monetary problems, (2) promoting exchange rate stability and avoiding competitive exchange rate depreciation, (3) giving confidence to members by making the general resources of the fund temporarily available for the purpose of correcting maladjustments in their balance of payments, and (4) shortening the duration and lessening the degree of disequilibrium in the international balances of payments of its members.[2]

Members agreed (up to 1971) to:

1. Establish and maintain an agreed-upon fixed exchange rate system for their currencies, in which the value of all countries' currencies was fixed with respect to the U.S. dollar and the U.S. dollar was fixed with respect to gold.

2. Change the foreign exchange rate only after consultation with the IMF and only if the member had a fundamental disequilibrium in the balance of payments that could not be ended without devaluing the currency. This imparted some flexibility to exchange rates.

3. Move to abolish all restrictions on the conversion of local currency into foreign currency; that is, each country agreed to move toward having a convertible currency.

4. Create a revolving pool of credit that member countries could draw on to adjust temporary balance-of-payments deficits.

This revolving pool of credit was created by each member's contributing a sum of money, called a quota subscription. Countries' quotas were determined by the size of the country's economy and its share of world trade. Larger and richer countries had the largest quotas; smaller and poorer countries had the smallest quotas. By 1994, the 178 members of the IMF had paid in about 144.9 billion special drawing rights (SDRs) in quotas. This was roughly equivalent to $200 billion.

The IMF is governed by a board of governors, but day-to-day operation of the fund is carried out by its twenty-two executive directors. Although the IMF tries to reach consensus regarding individual loans, if a vote needs to be taken, vote shares are granted in proportion to a country's quota.

The larger a country's quota, the larger its share of votes in IMF decisions. Currently, the United States has the largest quota; it controls about 20 percent of the votes and has virtual veto power over major changes in policy. Five countries—the United States, the United Kingdom, Germany, France, and Japan—controlled more than 40 percent of the votes in 1994. The IMF is clearly run by and in the interest of the rich countries.

The IMF provides loans, called stand-by arrangements, to member countries with payment problems. Under a *tranche*, or share arrangement, the IMF's loans are made available to member countries in five equal tranches of 20 percent of a country's quota. Drawings from the first tranche are automatic. Drawings on the remaining tranches are conditioned on the IMF's satisfaction with the borrowing country's economic policies.

International Bank for Reconstruction and Development

The IBRD, or World Bank, began operations in 1946 in Washington, D.C. The initial task facing the bank was to make loans for the reconstruction of Europe, and the bank's early operations were limited to a small number of European countries. It became apparent very early that the bank did not have and could not obtain the resources necessary for this task. So the United States initiated a massive aid flow, called the Marshall Plan, and the bank was reduced to irrelevance in Europe.

It then turned its attention to the "development of productive facilities and resources"[3] in the Third World. The Articles of Agreement stated that one of the purposes of the World Bank was "to promote foreign investment by guarantees or participations in loans or other investment made by private investors" and, when necessary, to supplement private investment with its own loans and to arrange these loans so that "the more useful and urgent projects, large and small alike will be dealt with first."[4] It was also to promote the long-range balanced growth of international trade and the maintenance of equilibrium in the balance of payments of member countries by encouraging private direct foreign investment and "thereby assisting in raising productivity, the standard of living and conditions of labor."[5]

Today the World Bank group consists of five distinct entities: the IBRD, the International Development Association (IDA), the International Finance Corporation (IFC), the International Center for Settlement of Investment Disputes (ICSID), and the Multilateral Investment Guarantee Agency (MIGA). Each of these entities has different responsibilities.

The IBRD borrows money in private capital markets all over the world and then loans it to developing countries at virtually commercial rates of interest.

In 1960, the IDA was created with funds contributed by the rich countries, led by the United States, in an effort to offset a proposed foreign aid organization at the United Nations. Unlike the IBRD, the IDA's loans are restricted to developing countries with the lowest incomes. Borrowers are granted a ten-year grace period and a 50-year repayment period with a service charge of less than 1 percent per year.

The IBRD and IDA have traditionally made loans to governments or to entities with government guarantees for specific projects, particularly for infrastructure such as roads, ports, and electrical generating stations. In the 1960s, agriculture was added, and in the 1970s, projects in the social sectors, such as health, education, and population, were added. In the 1980s, the bank moved to nonproject loans, or structural adjustment loans (SALs), to help countries adjust their economies so that they could service their debts to the commercial banks in the rich countries. In the 1990s, it continued making SALs and has moved to adjust the structures of the countries in Eastern Europe and the new industrial states in their transition to market economies. In the 1990s, the environment was finally added as a concern, after being ignored for the first forty-five years of lending.

The World Bank has several entities that promote private-sector development and direct foreign investment. The IFC was created to provide loans to privately owned firms, not governments. The IFC also provides guarantees against risks and buys shares in some private enterprises.

In 1965, the ICSID, which deals with disputes between member countries and foreign firms, was created. In 1988, the MIGA was created to encourage the flow of private investment to developing countries. It does this by providing investment guarantees against noncommercial risks (wars, civil strife, nationalization). It works closely with the IFC, and they have created a joint facility, the Foreign Investment Advisory Service (FIAS), to provide technical assistance to developing countries that want to attract direct foreign investment.

The bank attempts to provide intellectual leadership and impose its ideology on other aid donors and on developing countries: planning and import-substitution industrialization in the 1960s, basic needs and growth with equity in the 1970s, structural adjustment in the 1980s and 1990s.

Commercial banks and governments providing foreign aid often refuse to lend to countries unless they have the seal of approval of both the IMF and the World Bank. Thus, the reach of these institutions extends well beyond the amount of money they make available. In fact, by 1991, the World Bank group had been reduced to virtual irrelevance in terms of the quantity of lending to developing countries, lending about 9 percent ($7.5 billion) of the developed world's foreign aid[6] to developing countries ($81.95 billion).

General Agreement on Tariffs and Trade

Unlike the other Bretton Woods institutions, which have grown quite large and powerful, GATT operated with a small secretariat and lacked any power to enforce its rules. GATT's principal weapon was moral suasion. It could jawbone and cajole, but it had no enforcement powers. Its main tasks were to oversee settlements of trade disputes, monitor compliance with GATT regulations, and provide a structured forum for managing reductions in trade barriers.

Management of reductions in trade barriers under GATT were governed by three principles. Nondiscrimination, or the most-favored-nation principle, states that countries should not grant one member or group of members preferential trade treatment over others. If one nation is given preferential treatment for its exports, all nations must be given the same treatment. The intent of this rule is to get each member country to treat others the same as the most favored country. The reciprocity principle meant that an action by one country to open its market was seen as a concession, and concessions from other countries were required in turn. The transparency principle required countries to replace nontariff barriers, such as quotas, with tariffs and then to "bind" tariffs (promise not to raise them again).

As a result of GATT's efforts, there has been a significant reduction in tariff barriers. However, nontariff barriers, voluntary export quotas such as the United States imposes on Japanese cars, trading blocs, common markets, and free-trade areas have been moves away from an open global trading system.

Assessment of the Bretton Woods Economic Order

The post–World War II economic order had positive results. Economic growth was more widespread and rapid than ever. The world economy grew almost fourfold, and world trade increased almost twelvefold between 1950 and 1980.

This global growth was accompanied by improvements in human well-being. Surpluses of food were produced in Australia, Canada, Europe, and the United States. These surpluses plus the increasing output of the green revolution in developing countries led to world prices of grains falling dramatically since 1950.

Expansion of food output almost eliminated famines. The exceptions are those that are brought on by bad government policies such as in Mao's China and in communist Ethiopia, where there was no free press to publicize what was happening nor a democratic government that had to respond to popular pressure to do something.[7]

Between 1950 and 1971, the original Bretton Woods system worked well. The United States acted as the hegemonic power and global stimulator for growth in the global economy by running balance-of-payments deficits and providing dollars to finance increased international trade and investment. The United States was the leading capital exporter, first through the Marshall Plan and foreign aid flows, and then through private capital movements. But by the late 1960s, it was clear that the United States could no longer play its role successfully. This was because of a basic contradiction in the system.

Because the world came to depend on the U.S. dollar as the international currency, increasing global liquidity depended on the United States running balance-of-payments deficits. Under the Bretton Woods rules, the United States agreed to redeem dollars for gold at $35 per ounce. As long as the United States held a large stock of gold and the number of dollars outstanding was relatively small, this was not a problem. But by the 1960s, it was clear that the United States could not continue to redeem dollars for gold at $35 per ounce. As more and more U.S. dollars were accumulated by others, the less confident the rest of the world became in the United States' ability to meet its obligation to redeem the dollars for gold at $35 per ounce.

In August 1971, President Nixon broke the link between the dollar and gold and announced that the United States would no longer redeem dollars for gold at $35 an ounce. Immediately, the dollar fell in value against other currencies. Countries holding dollars lost value. In response, the major industrial countries shifted to a system of floating or flexible exchange rates, in which the international price of a nation's currency is determined by the forces of demand and supply in the foreign exchange market. This effectively ended the Bretton Woods system as it was initially designed.

Alternative International Economic Orders

With the breakdown of the Bretton Woods system in 1971, it became clear that it was time once again to reform the international economic rules of the game. How might they be reformed to promote a broad-based sustainable world?

Expanding the Group of Seven

Reform of the international economic order should begin by increasing the number of actors involved in global economic decision making. At the present time, an informal group that was not and is not an official part of the Bretton Woods system, the Group of 7 (G-7), makes and enforces the economic rules. This group comprises Canada, France, Germany, Italy, Japan, the United Kingdom, and the United States. The president of Russia has been allowed to sit in on the last few annual meetings of the heads of state of the G-7.

The population of the G-7 countries is approximately 654 million, or less than 9 percent of the world's population. Yet this tiny group makes the economic policies for the whole world. At the very least, the membership might be broadened to include the secretary-general of the United Nations, China (which has a larger gross domestic product, measured at purchasing power parity, than five of the countries in the G-7), India, and representatives elected by and from the other countries of Asia, the countries of Latin America, North Africa and the Middle East, and sub-Saharan Africa.

Reforming and Re-creating International Economic Organizations

Decision making in the Bretton Woods institutions has to be broadened to give users, particularly developing countries, a larger role in making fundamental decisions. Currently, a small group of rich countries dominates the process and makes decisions that benefit themselves.

Developing countries should also have a larger role in fundamental decision making in the IMF, the World Bank, and the World Trade

Organization (WTO). Users' councils should be established in these organizations, representing developing countries. These councils would make recommendations on policy and on the operation of these institutions, and the executive directors would have to respond to these councils, explaining why they did or did not follow their recommendations.

Reforming the IMF

Because rich countries provide most of the currency for the fund's revolving pool of credit, it is unlikely that they will be willing to relinquish much control over IMF decision making to developing countries. Thus, we propose a users' council as an intermediary between individual developing country borrowers and executive directors who control IMF decisions in the interest of the rich country members. The purposes of this users' council would be to assess the need for more liquidity and review individual IMF loans to developing countries. Membership on this council would be limited to developing country users, and a majority vote on all issues would be sent to the executive directors for review and action. If the executive directors voted not to accept the recommendations of the council, they would have to publicly communicate their reasons.

Another reform would give the IMF power to tax balance-of-payments-surplus countries on their surpluses, as the British proposed in 1944. At present, the IMF has power only over countries running a balance-of-payments deficit. These countries come to the fund to borrow money, and the fund can impose conditions on them—force them to change their economic policies if they want to get loans. No such power exists over the surplus countries. Germany and Japan can continue to run balance-of-payments surpluses for years, and there is no effective way to get them to open their economies and import more. An IMF tax on surpluses would give these countries an incentive to open their economies and reduce their surpluses. This would, of course, help the deficit countries adjust, because it would make it easier for them to export. This symmetry of adjustment would reduce burdens on deficit countries and shift more of the responsibility to surplus countries. The United States resisted this proposal in 1944, because it was virtually the only country with a balance-of-payments surplus at the time. Now the Germans and Japanese would resist such a move. But if developing countries and progressive governments in industrialized countries could unite on this proposal, it stands a chance of adoption.

A shift must be made from the U.S. dollar as the international reserve currency to the SDRs issued by the IMF. Again, such a system was proposed by the British in 1944 but was not accepted by the United States. It is clearly needed now. There is an obvious contradiction in the present system whereby the United States creates international liquidity by running balance-of-payments deficits, which causes a loss of confidence in the dollar. The wild fluctuations in exchange rates pose problems for long-term investors. We are moving very rapidly toward a highly integrated global economy. We can no longer rely on one national currency to facilitate trade and payments. Because the volume of dollars outstanding is so large, a long-term plan would have to be developed so that nations holding dollars as reserves could redeem them for SDRs. Of course, the United States can veto major changes in the IMF and might still fight this move. But more and more people are becoming convinced that the present system is not in the long-term interest of the United States.

Privatizing the World Bank

We can see no clear reason for the existence of an institution such as the World Bank, which makes commercial loans to developing countries, because there is no clear market failure in the international capital market to justify public-sector intervention in this area. We propose privatizing the World Bank or its hard-loan window.

It would be highly useful to give careful scrutiny to the International Development Association, the World Bank's agency for dispensing foreign aid contributed by member governments. Could it operate on the profits that have been made by the commercial loans of the IBRD and on the loan money being repaid? If so, and if it can be demonstrated that the IDA produces more benefits than costs to developing countries, we see no reason to end the IDA. But the bank's record of disregard for environmental concerns, its top-down, know-it-all approach to development, its commitment to ideology in the face of dramatic contradictory evidence, the arrogance of its staff, its unwillingness to involve those affected by its projects in planning and designing, and its commitment to only one goal—to lend more money—have convinced many people that both the bank and the IDA should be closed. "Fifty years is enough" is a slogan that resonates around the world.

If the IDA is continued, a users' council should be established. This body would try to ensure that policies and practices toward any one country were not overwhelmingly influenced by the foreign policy considerations of any member country, that the organization did not become overly ideological in its conception and approach to development, and that all assistance to member countries could be shown to contribute to BBSD.

Empowering the World Trade Organization

We need a new international trade organization that has the power to enforce trade agreements. The new international trade organization created by the Uruguay round of GATT negotiations in the 1990s, the WTO, should have the power to impose fines and even trade embargoes against countries that egregiously violate the international rules of the game. It should also have the capacity to help finance trade adjustment assistance when liberalization leads to significant loss of employment.

This new trade organization will need to operate in ways that are more hospitable to poor countries. For far too long, reductions in trade barriers have disproportionately benefited rich countries. As a result, protectionism in agriculture and in manufacturing in the industrialized countries discriminates against the exports of those goods in which developing countries have a comparative advantage.

In addition, there should be a Trade Adjustment Assistance Council (TAAC) within the new WTO. The purpose of the TAAC would be to make recommendations to the governing body of the WTO on the allocation of adjustment assistance to countries where trade liberalization imposes real hardships on workers. In some industrialized countries, previous trade agreements have recognized the effects on employment and have provided for trade adjustment assistance to those who lose their jobs. This idea needs to be revived, expanded, and multilateralized.

The WTO should have the power to exercise influence over domestic policies, such as producing exports with prison or child labor or without regard to workers' occupational safety and health. There should also be minimal standards to prevent countries from exporting products that destroy the environment.

Obviously, the standards that apply in countries just beginning the industrialization process will be different from those that apply in already industrialized countries. But over time, the standards need to be raised so that firms have no advantage in moving to poor countries simply because of lax safety, health, or environmental standards.

Establishing an International Bankruptcy Court

Another necessary reform is the establishment of an international bankruptcy court. This court would allow nations to declare bankruptcy, to pay what they can on their debts, and to resume borrowing. The court would have to have the power to impose sanctions on countries that did not keep the binding legal commitments they make in court proceedings.

Bankruptcy courts have been a feature of industrialized economies for decades and are a necessary addition to the international economic system. This change will be politically difficult to bring about, but if the developing countries can get organized to push for it and can recruit allies among progressive governments in industrialized countries, it has a chance of succeeding. Capitalist firms in the United States resisted bankruptcy courts too, but they were established.

Regulating Multinational Corporations and Multinational Banks

There is a pressing need for an international institution to regulate multinational corporations and multinational banks. At present, a nation-state can control economic activity only within its own borders. But multinational organizations operate worldwide. They can frustrate the national economic policy of one country by moving to another country. They can avoid taxes by shifting profits to low-tax countries. They can evade minimum-wage laws, child labor laws, and health and safety standards of rich countries by moving to countries with weaker standards.

This unlimited freedom of movement of international capital undermines the social welfare state in industrialized countries and pits workers in rich countries against their brothers and sisters in poor countries. Unless regulation occurs, workers in rich countries will turn against workers in poor countries, as they already have in some cases. This can only lead to further protectionism and further breakdown in international economic interaction.

The lack of regulation of multinational banks leads to debt crises and to unscrupulous banking practices. The agreement of the industrialized countries, working through the Bank for International Settlements (BIS) in Basel, Switzerland, to impose common capital and reserve requirements on multinational banks was a first step toward international regulation. More steps in this direction are necessary.

Creating a World Environment Organization

We need to replace the United Nations Environmental Program (UNEP) with a new World Environment Organization (WEO) that would be concerned with (1) identifying global and regional transboundary environmental problems, such as depletion of the ozone layer; the accumulation of greenhouse gases, radioactive wastes, and organochlorines; the pollution and overfishing of the oceans; and the allocation of watershed water rights; (2) researching cost-effective solutions to those problems; and (3) implementing those solutions. The new WEO will need to establish international environmental standards, monitor performance relative to standards, and devise tax and fine systems to ensure compliance.

Currently, multinational firms can evade tough environmental regulations in one country by relocating in countries with laxer standards. At present, those nations that do control their corporations' polluting activities increase their corporations' costs and make them less internationally competitive.

All industrialized nations need to agree on the same environmental standards. Some work on this has already begun through the International Standards Organization (ISO) in Geneva, Switzerland. Those standards are based on the idea of pollution prevention, on recycling everything so as not to create wastes to dump in the environment. The WTO and the WEO must play a role in pressing the international community of nations to adopt clean technology standards.

What Are the Prospects for Reform?

We think that the prospects for reform are good. With the increased globalization of economic activity, it is clear that the nation-state can no longer provide many absolutely necessary functions. The nation-state can no longer provide for national security in the age of intercontinental ballistic missiles and nuclear weapons. The nation-state can no longer provide a healthy global environment. Nation-states can no longer set rules and enforce them on the global economy. Markets are not coterminous with nation-states' boundaries. Capital markets now transfer funds instantaneously on a global basis.

Technological change is continuing apace and making it increasingly difficult for any one nation to regulate economic activity. Eventually it will become clear to all that economic activity cannot take place without international organizations to make the rules and enforce them. Businesses themselves will become advocates of greater international coordination and regulation.

Achieving BBSD: A Basis for Hope

For the last two centuries, markets and capitalism have been extending their reach around the globe. The collapse of communism, rapid technological change, and the internationalization of capital, production, and consumption are creating the possibilities for BBSD on a worldwide scale.

Markets are wonderful institutions; they can function with great efficiency and have played an important role in benefiting humankind. But unregulated markets do not lead to social justice or a good society. Unfortunately, there appears to be no alternative to capitalism in the world today. But capitalism is surely not the final product of human imagination and creativity; someday it will be replaced by a more just, more participatory, and more sustainable system. Unfortunately, not even the outlines of this new system are visible yet. This should not be surprising.

People do not design political-economic systems in the abstract. No one designed the market economy. When Adam Smith wrote *The Wealth of Nations* in 1776, he was the first person to put it all together and understand how a market economy operated. But he was reporting on what was happening, not designing it.

No one can design the system that will succeed capitalism. We can only study and make recommendations about how to move toward a different and better system. The two distinctive economic institutions of capitalism—private ownership of the means of production and markets as the mechanism to allocate most resources—will no doubt continue in the new system. But the new system must transcend the present system in which consumers and producers pay only the private costs of their activities and dump the social costs, such as pollution, onto the society. Social costs must be paid by the people producing those costs. We must move to a system of production in which fewer and ultimately no wastes are created, in which everything is recycled. We are beginning to do that as we move toward a dematerialization of production and consumption. We must ensure that the benefits of growth are made available to all people.

What is needed today is a new burst of social creativity like that which occurred after World War II. Many of us have been the beneficiaries of the present international political and economic order. Now it is time for us to create a new one that will serve our descendants equally well.

Notes

1. For example, one ounce of gold was equal to US$20, or each dollar was worth one-twentieth of an ounce of gold.
2. International Monetary Fund (IMF), *Articles of Agreement of the International Monetary Fund* [1944] (Washington, D.C.: IMF, 1992).
3. International Bank for Reconstruction and Development (IBRD), *Articles of Agreement: As Amended February 16, 1989* (Washington, D.C.: World Bank, 1989), 1–2.
4. IBRD, *Articles of Agreement*, 1–2.
5. IBRD, *Articles of Agreement*, 1–2.
6. Total receipts net, including total (net) official development assistance (ODA) loans and grants and total (net) other official flows (OOF) and private loans and grants. Organization for Economic Cooperation and Development (OECD), *Geographical Distribution of Financial Flows to Developing Countries 1988/91* (Paris: OECD, 1993), 314.
7. Amartya K. Sen, *Poverty and Famines: An Essay on Entitlement and Deprivation* (New York: Oxford University Press, 1981).

Index

Note: For brevity, the abbreviation BBSD refers to broad-based sustainable development.

About the Authors

JAMES H. WEAVER is professor emeritus of economics at The American University. He served as senior economist of USAID's Development Studies Program until 1992. Among his books is *Economic Development: Competing Paradigms*. He received his M.Div. from Wesley Theological Seminary in 1996.

MICHAEL T. ROCK is senior economist for the Winrock International Institute for Agricultural Development. He held the position of associate director for the Winrock Center for Economic Policy Studies from 1992 to 1994. He has published numerous articles on economics and the environment. Previously, he was dean of faculty at Bennington College where he taught economics and international political economy.

KENNETH KUSTERER is chairperson of the department of sociology at The American University. He coedited *Women at the Center: Development Issues and Practices for the 1990s* with Gay Young and Vidyamali Samarasinghe published by Kumarian Press.